INTRODUCTION TO ANALYTICAL JURISPRUDENCE

INTRODUCTION TO ANALYTICAL JURISPRUDENCE

Dr. Anne Wade

SOCIETY Publishing

www.societypublishing.com

Introduction to Analytical Jurisprudence

Dr. Anne Wade

Society Publishing
224 Shoreacres Road
Burlington, ON L7L 2H2
Canada
www.societypublishing.com
Email: orders@arclereducation.com

ISBN: 978-1-77469-852-5 (Hardcover)

ABOUT THE AUTHOR

Dr. Anne Wad has been a researcher and a professor in the Criminal Justice field for over 30 years. She currently holds a position as a Provost/CAO in a University, and Director of Research at another university. She holds an Ed.D. in Educational Leadership and a Ph.D. in Public Safety Leadership/Criminal Justice. Her research interests are in Criminology, Victimology, and the Human Services. She is married to Wesley Wade. She is an artist, writer, researcher, professor, and university administrator.

TABLE OF CONTENTS

LIST OF FIGURES

LIST OF ABBREVIATIONS

ADR	Alternative Dispute Resolution
CEPEJ	European Commission for the Efficiency of Justice
CHH	Carbon Dioxide is Heavier Than Hydrogen
ECHR	European Convention on Human Rights
HLC	Hydrogen is Lighter Than Carbon Dioxide
JP	Joint Programs
NJRS	National Judicial Reform Strategy
TEJSU	Transparency and Efficiency of the Judicial System of Ukraine
UCL	University College London
VC	Voluntary Contributions

PREFACE

The legal maxim *"Ubi civitas ibi lex"* [where there is State, there will not be anarchy] is central to our understanding of the analytical school of jurisprudence. The maxim signifies the fact that the state has an interest in maintaining law and order. Implicit is the assumption that stateless people are likely to be disorderly and lawless. Moreover, this maxim creates a justification for the state machinery to design, monitor, and enforce laws. The analytical school is noted for its preference for dealing with the law as it already is rather than creating new laws.

According to the analytical school, it is pertinent to merely deal with the law as it exists and that the law is the direction of the sovereign or leader in that context. Therefore, the analytical school has sometimes been known as the imperative school. The heyday of the analytical school was in the 19th century. One of its assertions is that morals are not objective in their conceptualization and operationalization. However, the law must be objective in its conceptualization and operationalization. This already suggests a tension between morality and law. The tension means that a moralistic law is no longer objective and is therefore not acceptable. It is not surprising in these circumstances that the analytical school adopted a positivist perspective on societal legal issues.

The main concern of the positivists is whether the law is found (positum). They therefore reject the notion of the ideal law. To them, the ideal law is the one which is perfect for the circumstances in a society. That is a different proposition from the law which is found. The latter concerns the welfare thinking that is involved during the legislative process. Hence, the found law is logical. The most important sources of found law include customs, precedent, and legislation. England was a notable space for analytical schools. Hence, this perspective established the fundamental elements and fabric of the law.

Examples of the applications of the analytical school include the notion of state sovereignty. This is a heavily contested issue in the era of globalization and the insidious use of sanctions to punish those that fail to comply with the prevailing world order. The analytical school is also largely responsible for the emergence and development of several niches including the administration of justice. Relying on proponents such as Salmond, Austin, Holland, and Bentham; this book seeks to explore the conceptualization of the analytical school and its relevance to jurisprudence.

Therefore, this book reflects on the essential aspects of analytical jurisprudence. The book deliberately adopts an international approach in highlighting the diversity of interpretations and practical applications of this approach to this school. Above all, the book emphasizes the possibility that the law becomes an instrumentality of human development rather than merely seeking to control or even oppress the citizenry.

Overall, this book is aimed at undergraduates of law in all its forms. Hence, the book will be relevant to those studying administration, government, social welfare, criminal justice, commercial law, and the constitution. The book may also appeal to members of the public that are trying to untangle the workings of the law. I hope you enjoy reading this book and series.

CHAPTER 1

Introduction to the Analytical School of Jurisprudence

Contents

The opening chapter of this book provides an outline of the analytical school of jurisprudence. First, the chapter explores how the philosophical underpinnings of the analytical school emerged. It then details and distinguishes the various philosophical approaches that have since been adopted. The chapter untangles the analytical philosophy as a distinct category, but which has since been incorporated into jurisprudence. The works of two luminaries of the analytical jurisprudence school (Herbert Lionel Adolphus Hart and Jeremy Bentham) are used as closing case studies. The overall goal of this chapter is to introduce the reader to the analytical school of jurisprudence as a preamble to the critical analysis that will continue throughout the book. A good starting point for this introduction is the development of the philosophy underpinning this school.

1.1. DEVELOPING A PHILOSOPHY OF ANALYTICAL JURISPRUDENCE

The underlying philosophical positioning that birthed analytical jurisprudence is positivism in the law (Sheldon & Wilkinson, 1997, 1998; Shepherd, 1995; Shevory, 1990; Shewmon, 1997). This was a movement that commenced at the turn of the 19th century as described by the likes of Dias. The movement was seen as a reaction to a priori thought. That thought had turned away from the reality of the law to uncover the universal validity principle. That principle was located within reason or nature.

The ideas that emerged from the movement had been used to condemn, critique, or explain existing or conceived legislation (Fluss & Zeegers, 1990; Fortin, 1991; Gelman, 1994; Glass & Speyer-Ofenberg, 1996; Glick, 1992; Gormally, 2002). According to analysts such as Hart, positivism was imbued with a wide range of connotations that were not always well understood. For example, there was an interpretation that laws were orders. Austin and Bentham, who founded British positivism, acknowledged this idea. Under this thinking, it is argued that judges do not make law and any laws that they create should be rejected as morally and practically indefensible.

Auguste Comte was a French philosopher who has been credited with initially using the term positivism. However, this term has been applied in a range of disciplines, especially with regards to developing and defending research paradigms (Shewmon, 1997; Shultz, 1990; Singleton Jr, 1989; Skene & Parker, 2002; Somerville, 1989; Spurr, 1993; Stacy, 1994). Positivist philosophy and legal positivism shared an antipathy to metaphysical inquiry. Similarly, they shared the same approach in the quest for ultimate principles.

In this instance, metaphysics refers to studies that are not accessible through objective studies of material reality.

Examples of metaphysical studies that have been rejected by positivism include ontology and cosmology (Okin, 1990; Oster, 2021; Paliwala, 2016; Paris & Poorman, 1995; Pellegrino & Sharpe, 1989; Ploughman, 1995). The positivists rejected the notion that lawyers and other practitioners in the legal profession could detect and define a concept of the law that transcended the factual basis of existing legal systems. Hence, jurisprudence would no longer concern itself with value judgments. Instead, the discipline would focus on the investigation and dissection of positive legal orders. Figure 1.1 summarizes the basic implications of this position.

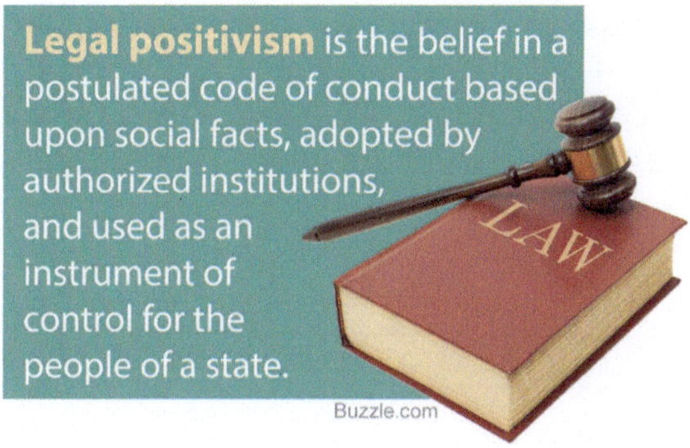

Figure 1.1. Conceptualization of legal positivism.

Source: Opinion Front via Buzzle.

There is an assumption that only positive law comprises the law (Sharpe & Pellegrino, 1997; Sheldon & Wilkinson, 1997, 1998; Shepherd, 1995; Shevory, 1990). Indeed, positive law comprises of nothing more than the legal standards that have been created by the supreme power in a state. One of the most important contexts for legal positivism is analytical jurisprudence. That is why some literature refers to analytical jurisprudence as analytical positivism. The starting point for the law under this paradigm is a given legal order. Thereafter, there is a distillation of certain concepts, notions, and distinctions.

The way in which analytical positivism is conceived and operationalized distinguishes it from a predominantly inductive method (Stauch, 2000; Stein, 1998; Steinbock & McClamrock, 1994; Strauss, 1992; Stroud, 1996; Sullivan & Goldzwig, 1995; Sulmasy, 1989). Nevertheless, it is expected that there will be some level of comparative analysis. This analysis is designed to find areas of commonality as well as identifying the features that distinguish analytical positivism from the inductive method. The various names that have been attached to analytical jurisprudence give credence to some of its key characteristics.

A case in point is the reference to the positive school of law as an alternative term for the analytical school (Sheldon & Wilkinson, 1997, 1998; Shepherd, 1995; Shevory, 1990; Shewmon, 1997). This is because the positive school is not concerned about the future or history of the law. Rather, their focus is on the law as it currently exists. Because of its dominance in England, the analytical school has also been referred to as the English school. Others speak of the Austinian school in reference to John Austin who was credited with founding this philosophical perspective.

One of the features of the analytical school is the tendency to take the legal system for granted (Fluss & Zeegers, 1990; Fortin, 1991; Gelman, 1994; Glass & Speyer-Ofenberg, 1996; Glick, 1992; Gormally, 2002). This is because of the assumption that the evolution of the legal system will have addressed any lingering doubts about its veracity and supremacy. Rather, the school logically analyzes and classifies the key principles of existing laws. One of the possible outcomes of this analysis is to demonstrate the interrelationships that exist between and among the various facets of the law.

Speaking of analytical jurisprudence suggests the methodological concerns of this school (Shewmon, 1997; Shultz, 1990; Singleton Jr, 1989; Skene & Parker, 2002; Somerville, 1989; Spurr, 1993; Stacy, 1994). Jurists that adopt this school will try to understand the structural character that underpins the legal system. In fact, these jurists reject any discussions concerning justice because they perceive them to be unnecessary and even dangerous. The danger in discussing justice according to them is that it confuses the law with personal feelings and values. Hence, the analytical positivists will not look behind the law or seek a higher purpose other than the one stated in the legislative process.

The emphasis on the mandates of the sovereign is a critical feature of the school (Okin, 1990; Oster, 2021; Paliwala, 2016; Paris & Poorman, 1995; Pellegrino & Sharpe, 1989; Ploughman, 1995). Legislation is the primary and ultimate source of the law. Indeed, the notion of the law will underpin the entire legal system as perceived by this paradigm. Rather than producing its own premises, analytical jurisprudence relies on the law to produce them. The role of jurisprudence in this paradigm is to accept the premises provided by the law and then break them down into certain atomic constituents.

Ultimately, these constituent parts of the law as it exists may be organized into a legal framework (Sharpe & Pellegrino, 1997; Sheldon & Wilkinson, 1997, 1998; Shepherd, 1995; Shevory, 1990). Critics perceive analytical jurisprudence as insular and closed since it does not fully consider the influence of values and norms when interpreting the law. An example of those perceptions is where the analytical school fails to account for the changes in societal attitudes on issues such as race, human sexuality, and family life. Rather, the analytical school merely examines the law as it is rather than as it ought to be.

Despite the criticisms levelled against analytical jurisprudence, its proponents perceive certain uses that can only be met with this approach (Stauch, 2000; Stein, 1998; Steinbock & McClamrock, 1994; Strauss, 1992; Stroud, 1996; Sullivan & Goldzwig, 1995; Sulmasy, 1989). One such purpose is to examine the foundational principles of law. This is done whilst largely disregarding the evolution, historical origins, validity, and ethical importance of the law. Salmond suggests that a book of analytical jurisprudence analyzes the conceptualization of the law. It can also explore the relationships between civil and other forms of law. Such an analysis may review the constituent ideas behind complexities of the law.

Above all, the analytical jurisprudence school will emphasize the role of the sovereign which represents the power of the state. It is this state that determines the administration of justice (O'Donovan & Gilbar, 2003; Oberman, 1992; Okin, 1990; Oster, 2021; Paliwala, 2016; Paris & Poorman, 1995; Pellegrino & Sharpe, 1989). The analytical school will provide an account of legal sources through which the law emanates and proceeds. Moreover, the school can be useful for investigating the theory of legislation. Although these functions are not the exclusive preserve of the analytical school, the perspective has been found to be particularly effective in framing them.

The analytical school is significant in jurisprudence (Kozłowski, 2021; Lane & Grodin, 1997; Mathieu, 1992; May, 1999; McConnell, 1991; McCoy, 1992; Meisel, 1992). First, it has been credited with providing clarity in legal reasoning. Additionally, this school is associated with vocabulary that is more precise and concise than other schools. Besides, this is a school which is scientific and systematic in its approaches to the law. Austin expressed a goal of making the law clearer than the other perspectives had done. For instance, the analytical school deliberately leaves out aspects which are not relevant when considering the law. Several founder advocates have been instrumental in establishing the analytical school. Examples include

Austin, Sir William Markby (1829–1914), Holland (1835–1926), Bentham (1742–1832), Salmond (1862–1924), Prof. HLA Hart (1907), and Sheldon Amons (1835–1886). Whereas the analytical school is closely associated with England, it has found fertile ground in the USA. This is due to the work of Gray and Hohfled. In Europe, the spread of analytical jurisprudence was aided by the likes of Korkunov, and Kelsen. According to Bentham, the imperative conception of law was of paramount importance. In these cases, command and sovereignty are cardinal dictates.

The writings of Bentham suggest that he accepted partial and divided sovereignty (Raymond, 1999; Resnik, 1997; Rich, 1997; Rivard, 1992; Robertson, 1996, 1999; Savulescu, 1994; Schneider, 1992). There would be a contrast between logical necessity and social desirability which would be manifested in the evolution of law. Bentham debated the legal constraints that were placed on sovereign authority. The role of sanctions is downplayed in Bentham's theory when compared to the more important role they play under the models suggested by Austin.

According to Bentham, an edict by the sovereign authority would constitute law even if they were supported by nothing more than moral or religious consequences (Hill, 1991b; Hope & Fulford, 1994; Hylton, 1990; Kadish, 1992; Kahn, 1991; Kalb, 1990; Kamisar, 1993; Kamm, 2001; Kass & Lund, 1996). However, Bentham also accepts that there is an allure of incentives and rewards in following the law. These ideas were simplified and republished by John Austin (1790–1859), an English lawyer. This philosophy of the law set the agenda for important literature on the subject during the 20th century. Bentham had criticized common law. He argued that it was the exclusive domain of judges, lawyers, and the professional elite.

Common law was critiqued under Bentham for being obscure and relying on overly technical language (Brock, 1995, 1999; Brody, 1998; Cantor, 2005; Capron, 1990, 1999; Chandler, 1990; Chervenak & McCullough, 1991). This meant that the law was permanently shrouded in mystery. From the perspective of ordinary citizens, this meant that the law was no longer as relevant to them as it ought to be. The language and discourses on common law are therefore meant to perpetuate its mythological status.

Bentham argued that lawyers are experts in artificial reasoning (Thomson, 1999; Truog et al., 1991; Turrina et al., 2021; van Delden & Laurie, 2004; Van Der Burg, 1997; Van der Burg & Brom, 2000). This is a proposition that had first been made by the likes of Coke. There is a contrast between expositorial jurisprudence (what the law is) and censorial jurisprudence (what the law ought to be). An extension of Bentham's arguments is that the law is nothing more than an assembly of affirmations, signals, and intentions that are chosen and conceived by the sovereign within a given state. It is important to note that despite acknowledging the powers and roles of sovereignty, Bentham also believed in the economically liberal idea of laissez faire.

That position may suggest that Bentham preferred a non-state dominance in private affairs (Pogge, 1991; Purdy, 1990; Quante, 1999; Rae & DeGiorgio, 1991; Ravven, 2016; Raymond, 1999; Resnik, 1997). Such a notion may not always sit comfortably with the idea of a sovereign that is the source of all laws. Although Bentham advocated for minimum government interference in economic activity, he also called for a form of utilitarianism which was imbued with the legitimate purpose of legislation. The purpose of that legislation was to create maximum pleasure for the maximum number of people.

According to Bentham, utility is the tendency or property of being able to prevent some evil or pain or better as well as pleasure. Hence, the role of legislation is to achieve these goals by providing abundance, sustenance, equality, and security (Thomson, 1999; Truog et al., 1991; Turrina et al., 2021; van Delden & Laurie, 2004; Van Der Burg, 1997; Van der Burg & Brom, 2000). Some literature has referred to this as the hedonism doctrine. Others speak of it as a doctrine of pain and pleasure. Critics argue that Bentham's model is too simplistic. For example, suffering and pleasure cannot be the final measure of the fitness of a law.

Another important figure in this philosophy was John Austin (1790–1859). A lecturer at the University of London, Austin was a proponent of analytical techniques. He suggested that the law should be rigorously evaluated and examined (Pogge, 1991; Purdy, 1990; Quante, 1999; Rae & DeGiorgio, 1991; Ravven, 2016; Raymond, 1999; Resnik, 1997). This would allow for the discovery of the principle that underpins the law. Hence, Austin limited his research to positive law. This is sometimes known as Jus positivism. Here, the law is set by political superiors and is applied to political inferiors. Figure 1.2 summarizes the contributions of John Austin.

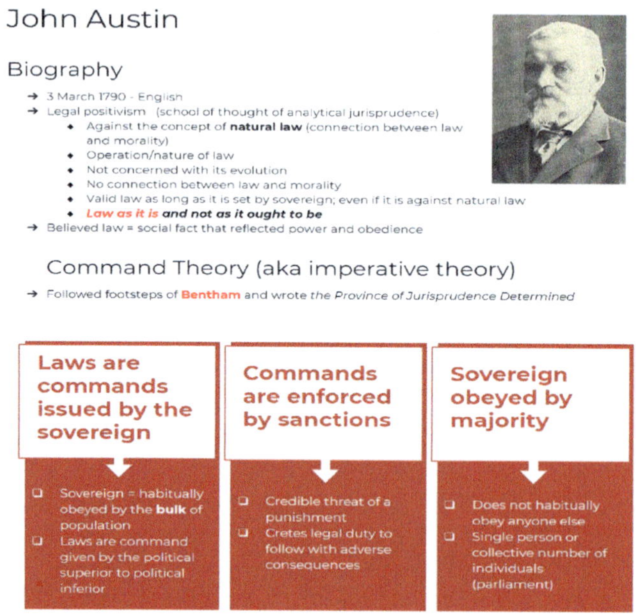

Figure 1.2. Contribution of John Austin to the law.

Source: Student Document.

The seminal work that has turned Austin into a founder of the analytical school of jurisprudence is titled "*The Province of Jurisprudence Determined*." According to Austin, the law was set down by someone with intelligence, power, and authority (Viljoen, 2012; Walters, 1991, 2012; Waymack, 1991; Weithman, 1999; Whitaker & Edwards, 1990; White, 1990). The law therefore is an expression of power and authority. Austin suggested that proper law should encompass God's law, positive laws, and human laws. There are certain improperly named laws as defined by this perspective. These include positive morality which incorporates laws that are not imposed by people such as political superiors.

The same criticism can be levelled at laws that are imposed through analogy (Gelman, 1994; Glass & Speyer-Ofenberg, 1996; Glick, 1992; Gormally, 2002; Gostin, 1995; Greenberg & Kamin, 1993). A case in point are fashion laws. Another questionable category of laws is those that are imposed in the pursuit of a right. Laws that were not sanctioned by the state were improper laws. Three elements are necessary to occur. They include the command to behave in certain ways. Another constituent ingredient as sanctions. The third, and perhaps most important element is the sovereign.

Under this paradigm, the sovereign orders their subjects to refrain from certain actions with the pain or pleasure of sanctions becoming rewards or punishments for compliance or non-compliance (Menzel, 1992; Merrick, 1990; Morreim, 1991; Munzer, 1994; Nelson, 1994; Nobles, 2012; O'Donovan & Gilbar, 2003; Oberman, 1992). The implied threat of punishment is essential for adherence to the law. In these cases, the command comprises a declaration of an individual or group wish that another person does or refrains from doing something that would result in some kind of evil. Disobedience must then elicit a sanction or punishment.

The command can be specific in terms of being directed to a single individual or group of people (Andrews, 1996; Arinta et al., 2021; Ayres et al., 1993; Bekrycht & Mańko, 2020; Bianchi, 2017; Blair & Kaserman, 1991). However, it can also be universal where it is directed to the community. Other laws inform certain classes of acts and forbearances. These are often referred to as continuous orders. Austin suggests that a specific command is effective when the subject is obedient. However, a general command is successful when most members of the political society obey it on a regular basis.

Where a definite human superior (who is not in the habit of obedience to a similar superior) gains habitual obedience from the mass of a society then the determinate superior becomes the sovereign of that society (Shultz, 1990; Singleton Jr, 1989; Skene & Parker, 2002; Somerville, 1989; Spurr, 1993; Stacy, 1994; Stauch, 2000). It is on that basis that it can be argued that sovereignty is an exercise of power and is determined by obedience. Accordingly, the powers of the sovereign are indivisible and unrestricted. Hence, under that paradigm there can be no separation of powers. The sovereign cannot be constrained by any legal restrictions of the laws that they have given to society.

The arguments advanced by Austin mean that in civilized nations, only legal systems can become legitimate subject matters of jurisprudence (Khushf, 1994; Knoppers & LeBris, 1991; Kozłowski, 2021; Lane & Grodin, 1997; Mathieu, 1992; May, 1999; McConnell, 1991). The sovereign can only execute the law with the right apparatus which may include justice systems and law enforcement agencies. Austin's definition is not concerned with concerns because they do not necessarily pertain to the apparatus that is used to enforce the commands of the sovereign. Three types of laws are acknowledged under this framework. They include declaratory or explanatory laws. Then there are the laws of repeal. Finally, there are the laws of imperfect obligations where no sanctions are attached. It then follows that constitutional law derives its force from the weight of public opinion about its morality and expediency.

There have been certain criticisms of the thesis presented by Austin (Allen, 1990, 1992; Alward, 2002; Amaraskekara & Bagaric, 2004; Anderson, 1993; Andrews, 1996; Arinta et al., 2021). For example, people may obey laws even if there is no threat of punishment or even when they are not bothered by the threat of punishment. Putting too much emphasis on punishment distorts the meaning and progress of law in a community. Moreover, the dismissals of voices that seek a law beyond manmade constructs mean that this theory is diametrically opposed to certain belief systems. Critics argue that there is an organic growth of the law which has been ignored by the likes of Austin.

For the modern mind, the law is little more than the collective will of the people (Capron, 1999; Chandler, 1990; Chervenak & McCullough, 1991; Chesterman, 1998; Clark, 2002; Clerkin, 2021; Coady, 2002). The notion of an all-powerful sovereign is increasingly and successfully being questioned in and outside jurisprudence. The existence of constitutional law and conventions means that even where a sovereign is recognized, they are under the control of those conventions and constitutions. Some of these conventions are not even enforceable under the law but they continue as a matter of custom and practice. Additionally, it is important to recognize the fact that past case law can become the law without a command from the sovereign.

Justice Holmes has critiqued the ideas presented by Austin because they create and discuss distinctions between positive law and positive morality (Chervenak & McCullough, 1991; Chesterman, 1998; Clark, 2002; Clerkin, 2021; Coady, 2002; Cohen, 1989; Coughlan, 1989). According to Holmes, these notions are designed to avoid considering virtue and badness from the law. Austin rejects ideals and justice in the law. That is a highly textual reading of the law which fails to contextualize the circumstances under which legislation is fashioned. In some cases, this might mean following laws that are distasteful to society if they are commanded by the sovereign. Clearly, such a proposition would encounter stiff opposition from modern communities that are significantly more egalitarian than the communities of the 18th or 19th century.

The analysis that is presented by Austin ignores the laws which are permissive as well as those that are designed to grant privileges (van Delden & Laurie, 2004; Van Der Burg, 1997; Van der Burg & Brom, 2000; van

Schooten, 2014; Viljoen, 2012; Walters, 1991). A case in point are the laws relating to wills or bonuses in the workplace. Others like Bryce have expressed disagreement with the notion that Austin is a major contributor to the development of the law since his views are very static and conservative. It is for this reason that some critics have argued that Austin should no longer be part of the essential curriculum.

Perhaps the biggest failing of Austin's ideas in the modern context is the failure to account for egalitarian societies that no longer unquestioningly accept the commands of sovereigns (Gormally, 2002; Gostin, 1995; Greenberg & Kamin, 1993; Grondelski, 1989; Hamblin & Somerville, 1991; Hardwig, 1991). Even the notion of sovereignty is being increasingly questioned with international sanctions, meaning that nation states are always fearful of offending the hegemonic powers who dominate what is known as the international community. This is despite the existence of dictatorial and traditional societies in which the ideas espoused by Austin might still hold sway. In any case, an examination of Austin is still pertinent when exploring the philosophical approaches to the law.

1.2. PHILOSOPHICAL APPROACHES TO THE LAW

The philosophy of the law is also known as legal philosophy (Shewmon, 1997; Shultz, 1990; Singleton Jr, 1989; Skene & Parker, 2002; Somerville, 1989; Spurr, 1993; Stacy, 1994). This category of discipline is primarily associated with exploring and providing a generalized philosophical analysis of legal institutions and the law. There are many issues that could be included in the philosophy of the law. Examples include the abstract conceptual questions that determine the nature of legal systems. It could also cover the construction and effect of legal systems.

Others may explore normative questions about the inter-relations that exist or do not exist between morality and law (Shewmon, 1997; Shultz, 1990; Singleton Jr, 1989; Skene & Parker, 2002; Somerville, 1989; Spurr, 1993; Stacy, 1994). Added to this is an exploration of the various legal institutions and the effect of their existence. The topics in legal philosophy are more abstract than related topics in other disciplines such as applied ethics and political philosophy. A case in point is how the interpretation of the US constitution is associated with democratic theory which is in turn a part of political philosophy.

The same issue is treated rather differently in legal philosophy. For instance, there may be an emphasis on legal interpretations (Coady, 2002;

Cohen, 1989; Coughlan, 1989; Crigger, 1995; Crossley, 1993; Crouch & Elliott, 1999; Daniels & Sabin, 1997). Another illustrative example of these subtle differences is the discussion concerning the morality of capital punishment. This issue is sometimes considered in applied ethics. In legal philosophy, the discussion may focus on whether punishment as an institution is justified.

Legal philosophy can be broadly re-categorized into three major items (Sharpe & Pellegrino, 1997; Sheldon & Wilkinson, 1997, 1998; Shepherd, 1995; Shevory, 1990). The first is analytic jurisprudence. The second is normative jurisprudence. The third comprises the critical theories of law. In analytical jurisprudence, one can analyze the essence of laws. This allows the analyst to understand the points of difference and intersectionality that exist between the law and systems of norms including ethics.

In normative jurisprudence, one can examine the evaluative, normative, and prescriptive issues that pertain to the law (Skene & Parker, 2002; Somerville, 1989; Spurr, 1993; Stacy, 1994; Stauch, 2000; Stein, 1998; Steinbock & McClamrock, 1994). Some of the elements that could be discussed include the obligation to obey the law, conditions under which freedom may be curtailed, and the grounds for meting out punishment. Meanwhile, the critical theories of law include feminist jurisprudence and critical legal studies that challenge the traditional forms of legal philosophy.

A holistic view of jurisprudence (*see* Figure 1.3) is called for when trying to understand the philosophy of the law (Clark, 2002; Clerkin, 2021; Coady, 2002; Cohen, 1989; Coughlan, 1989; Crigger, 1995; Crossley, 1993; Crouch & Elliott, 1999). The areas that might be covered in this holistic view include natural law theory, analytical jurisprudence, legal positivism, social fact theses, the third theory by Ronald Dworkin, the separability thesis, freedom in legitimate law, normative jurisprudence, and legal moralism. Other key areas may include obligations under the law, the offense principle, legal paternalism, punishment, critical theory, realism, and the economics of the law. There exists extensive literature that compares all these topics whilst threading their commonality and contribution to jurisprudence.

Analytic jurisprudence has emerged as one of the important research interests (Capron, 1990, 1999; Chandler, 1990; Chervenak & McCullough, 1991; Chesterman, 1998; Clark, 2002; Clerkin, 2021). The main goal of analytical jurisprudence is to distinguish the law from norms and their systems. It could therefore be argued that analytical jurisprudence seeks to provide nothing more than the necessary conditions of the law that distinguish it from non-law. There may be disagreement and even confusion about the character and value of conceptual analysis in the philosophy of law. Leiter (1998) argues that philosophy of law is one a kind in its category because it focuses on conceptual analysis. The other families of philosophy have preferred a naturalistic turn.

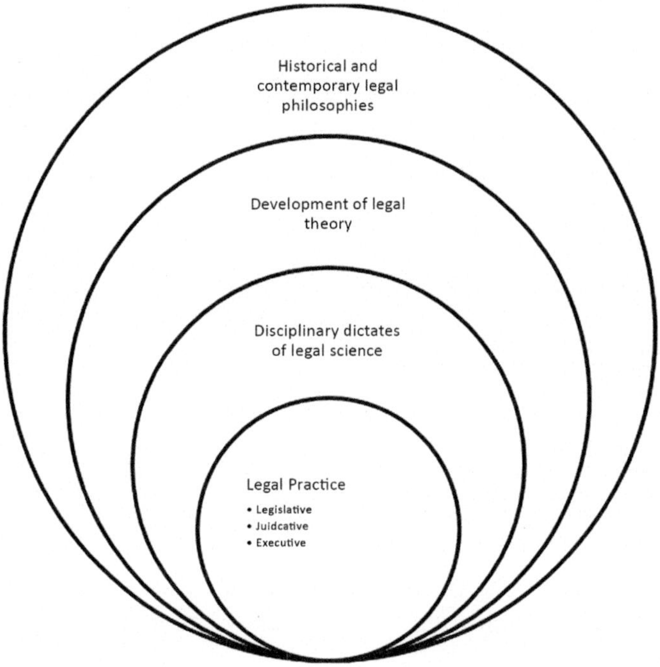

Figure 1.3. Holistic view of jurisprudence.

Source: Adapted from: Indarti (2016).

That naturalistic turn involves incorporating methods and tools of the sciences (Walters, 2012; Waymack, 1991; Weithman, 1999; Whitaker & Edwards, 1990; White, 1990; Wicclair, 1991a, b). Bix (1995) attempted to clarify the conceptual analysis of the law. Here, he distinguished several purposes that can be served through the conceptual claims that are relied on. The first purpose is to track linguistic usage. Another is to stipulate meanings. Then there is the goal of explaining what is important or essential about a class of objects. Finally, there is the goal of establishing an evaluative test for the concept-word.

The conceptual analysis that was envisaged by Bix focused mainly on class or object essentials and evaluating the concept-word (Grondelski,

1989; Hamblin & Somerville, 1991; Hardwig, 1991; Harris, 2003; Harris & Holm, 2002; Harvey & Chadwick, 1992). Although conceptual analysis of the law remains an important aspect of contemporary legal theory, it is nonetheless controversial and contested. Two principal headings have emerged in contemporary literature concerning the conceptual theories of the law. The first category relates to those that affirm a conceptual relationship between morality and law. The second category denies the existence of any such relationship.

Some literature has teased out and re-characterized the Ronald Dworkin view as a third theory (Strauss, 1992; Stroud, 1996; Sullivan & Goldzwig, 1995; Sulmasy, 1989; TÄNnsjÖ, 1992; Thomson, 1999). This approach has been adopted because Dworkin is not clear about his position on the conceptual relationships that may or may not exist between morality and the law. Therefore, his views are sometimes seen as a third way that sidesteps what has become a controversy in jurisprudence. This is especially true where the morality in question is attached to a specific denomination or belief system such as Christianity, Judaism, Islam, or Atheism.

Natural law theory is another important point of discussion in the development of jurisprudence (Wicclair, 1991b; Wildes, 1997; Wilson, 1994; Woliver, 1990; Wyld & Cappel, 1990; Yamada, 2019; Zohar, 1991; Zomerski, 2020). It has been suggested that natural law theories in all their configurations and forms will inevitably subscribe to the overlap thesis. This is a thesis which posits that there are necessary and undeniable relationships between morality and the concepts of law. To that end, it becomes impossible to fully articulate the concept of law without referring to some moral notions.

Some have argued that the overlap thesis is so ambiguous that it can be interpreted in several complex and diverse ways (Morreim, 1991; Munzer, 1994; Nelson, 1994; Nobles, 2012; O'Donovan & Gilbar, 2003; Oberman, 1992; Okin, 1990; Oster, 2021). For example, there is a very strong form of overlap thesis interpretation which is closely associated with classical naturalism. Some of the exponents of this form include William Blackstone and St. Thomas Aquinas. According to Blackstone, the law of nature is coeval as far as mankind is concerned. This is a law that is dictated by God meaning that it is superior to any other obligation and universally binding.

This type of law remains relevant to all people and all situations regardless of their context (Coady, 2002; Cohen, 1989; Coughlan, 1989; Crigger, 1995; Crossley, 1993; Crouch & Elliott, 1999; Daniels & Sabin, 1997). That means that it is not limited by human laws and conventions. Indeed, God's law under this paradigm supersedes any legislation or consideration. That means that any laws and conventions that are contrary to it are rendered invalid. Those laws that are valid then derive their authority, force, and immediacy from the originality of God's law.

When Blackstone is analyzed in detail, two claims emerge (Hope & Fulford, 1994; Hylton, 1990; Kadish, 1992; Kahn, 1991; Kalb, 1990; Kamisar, 1993; Kamm, 2001; Kass & Lund, 1996). These claims comprise the theoretical core of classical naturalism. The first claim is that there can be no legally valid standards which conflict with or contrary to the natural law. The second claim is that all the valid laws are authorized and fall under the auspices of natural law. Hence, the maxim from Augustine that an unjust law is no law at all.

Neo-naturalism is related to classical naturalism but is distinguished from it in important ways (Hill, 1990, 1991a, b; Hope & Fulford, 1994; Hylton, 1990; Kadish, 1992; Kahn, 1991; Kalb, 1990; Kamisar, 1993). A key figure in neo naturalism is John Finnis (1980) who posited that Blackstone and Aquina should not be construed as conceptual accounts of conditions that are necessary for the existence of the law. Bix (1996) and Finnish (1980) suggested that the classical naturalists were not specifically vested in providing a conceptual account of legal validity. Instead, the classical naturalists were concerned with explaining the moral force of the law.

Such explanations explore the principles of natural law as read together with the obligatory force that is attached to positive laws (Shanley, 1990; Sharpe & Pellegrino, 1997; Sheldon & Wilkinson, 1997, 1998; Shepherd, 1995; Shevory, 1990). This holds true even when reading the principles alone does not constitute the law. Finnis was of the view that the essential function of the law is to provide justification for state coercion. Such an argument does not directly support the overlap thesis. For example, an unjust law can be legally valid. However, it does not provide adequate justification for the use of state force. That means that such a law is not fully obligatory.

Another way of looking at that issue is to suggest that unjust laws fail to realize the moral ideals that are implicit in the conceptualization of the law (Van Der Burg, 1997; Van der Burg & Brom, 2000; van Schooten, 2014; Viljoen, 2012; Walters, 1991, 2012). Although legally binding in many instances, an unjust law is not fully law. However, writers like Lon Fuller (1964) reject the notion that there are any imperative moral constraints on the content of the law. Nevertheless, the law is subject to procedural morality which is expressed in a set of eight principles as follows:

- the laws or rules must be administered in a manner consistent with their wording;
- the laws or rules must be consistent with one another;
- the laws or rules must be expressed in general terms;
- the laws or rules must be expressed in understandable terms;
- the laws or rules must be prospective in effect;
- the laws or rules must be publicly promulgated;
- the laws or rules must not be changed so frequently that the subject cannot rely on them;
- the laws or rules must not require conduct beyond the powers of the affected parties.

According to Fuller, no system of rules can achieve the essential purpose of social order through rules that guide behavior unless it is consistent with the principles stated above (Stacy, 1994; Stauch, 2000; Stein, 1998; Steinbock & McClamrock, 1994; Strauss, 1992; Stroud, 1996; Sullivan & Goldzwig, 1995). For instance, a failure to adhere to these principles might mean that society is unclear about the requirements of the rules. To that end, Fuller suggests that his principles are internal to the law since they are built into the existential conditions of the law. If any one of the principles is violated, then the system of laws is necessarily bad and cannot be properly referred to as a legal system.

Legal positivism has been examined as a perspective that contributes to the development of jurisprudence (Pogge, 1991; Purdy, 1990; Quante, 1999; Rae & DeGiorgio, 1991; Ravven, 2016; Raymond, 1999; Resnik, 1997). This is a perspective that is implicitly and explicitly opposed to all forms of naturalism. There are three theoretical commitments that comprise legal positivism. The first of these is the social fact thesis. The second is known as the conventionality thesis. The third is the separability thesis. The social fact thesis is also known as the pedigree thesis. It posits that legal validity is a function of certain social facts.

The conventionality thesis emphasizes the conventionality of the law (Meisel, 1992, 1996; Menzel, 1992; Merrick, 1990; Morreim, 1991; Munzer, 1994; Nelson, 1994; Nobles, 2012). Hence, it posits that social facts lead to legal validity which is authoritative in terms of signaling the virtue of a social convention in a community. In contrast, the separability thesis simply denies any overlap between morality and law. The implication is that the law and morality operate in entirely separate spheres.

Based on the conventionality thesis, there exists a certain conceptual truth concerning the law (Paris & Poorman, 1995; Pellegrino & Sharpe, 1989; Ploughman, 1995; Pogge, 1991; Purdy, 1990; Quante, 1999; Rae & DeGiorgio, 1991). The implication is that legal validity can be explained in terms of authoritative criterion based on the virtues of certain social conventions. A case in point is how Hart (1996) posits that the criterion for legal validity emanates from recognizing rules which set the foundation for changing, creating, and adjudicating laws. Hence, recognition is authoritative when clarifying the virtue of a convention among officials.

This virtue can be in terms of the standards that govern the behavior of officials (Kaveny, 1991, 2006; Khushf, 1994; Knoppers & LeBris, 1991; Kozłowski, 2021; Lane & Grodin, 1997; Mathieu, 1992). Joseph Raz differs from this position by not recognizing the master rule of recognition which contains the criterion for validity. Nevertheless, Raz believes that the validity criterion is authoritative in the virtue of a convention among officials. These are subtle elements that might contribute to our understanding of the social fact thesis (*see* Figure 1.4 for a definition of social facts).

Figure 1.4. Overview of social facts.

Source: Sociology Group.

Based on the social fact thesis, legal validity is necessarily a function of specific social facts (Brock, 1995, 1999; Brody, 1998; Cantor, 2005; Capron, 1990, 1999; Chandler, 1990; Chervenak & McCullough, 1991). This argument borrows from the work of Bentham and Austin. It suggests that the legal system is distinguished by the presence of a sovereign authority or power. That is an entity that is habitually obeyed by the majority. However, they are not in the habit of obeying any determinate human superior. A rule only legally becomes value or a law if in a specific society that rule is commanded by the sovereign and is backed up with the threat of sanction.

Therefore, a relevant social fact will confer validity to the rule (Field, 1990, 1991; Figueira-McDonough, 1990; Finer, 1991; Fluss & Zeegers, 1990; Fortin, 1991; Gelman, 1994). This was a view that was supported by Austin in his writings. The legally valid rule is promulgated by a sovereign that is able and willing to impose sanctions if that rule is not obeyed. Critics may argue that such absolute sovereignty is no longer feasible in Western democracies. However, the role of the sovereign may be taken by institutions of that society such as the executive, judiciary, and legislature which work together for the governance of communities.

Hart has differed from the social fact thesis in believing that the Austin framework is at best an account of one typology of rules (Harvey & Chadwick, 1992; Hasnas, 1995; Hill, 1990, 1991a, b; Hope & Fulford, 1994; Hylton, 1990). Specifically, this category comprises of primary rules that are distinguished by the fact that they prohibit certain types of behavior. Hart argued that Austin had overlooked other typologies of primary rules that confer rights, responsibilities, and privileges. These may be imbued with the power to modify, create, and extinguish certain obligations and rights in other people.

A case in point are the rules governing contract law (Somerville, 1989; Spurr, 1993; Stacy, 1994; Stauch, 2000; Stein, 1998; Steinbock & McClamrock, 1994; Strauss, 1992). These may not fit easily into the restrictive framework that has been described by Austin. Indeed, the laws of contract do not restrict freedoms in the way that Austin had envisaged. Neither are they backed by the threat of a specific sanction from the sovereign in the traditional sense. Additionally, Hart posits that Austin has overlooked secondary meta-rules whose subject matter is primary rules.

These meta-rules distinguish advanced and organized legal systems from primitive systems of laws (Crossley, 1993; Crouch & Elliott, 1999; Daniels & Sabin, 1997; Den Hartogh, 1997; Downie, 1992; Downie & Randall, 1997). In any case, secondary rules differ from primary rules. This is because they are concerned with primary rules and are not primary rules in themselves. Primary rules are concerned with the actions or inactions of individuals in a society. Secondary rules ascertain and organize the ways in which primary rules can be understood, eliminated, introduced, and varied. The fact of violating primary rules can be conclusively determined by secondary rules.

There are three types of secondary rules that are identified by Hart (Gostin, 1995; Greenberg & Kamin, 1993; Grondelski, 1989; Hamblin & Somerville, 1991; Hardwig, 1991; Harris, 2003). Indeed, these categories are necessary for the transition from primitive forms of law into a full legal system. The first typology is that of recognition. This specifies some features and features of possession which emanate from a suggested rule. These are then taken as a conclusive affirmative indication that the rule is supported by the social pressure it exerts within the group to which it pertains. The second category is that relating to the rule of change. Such a typology enables society to remove, add, and modify valid rules. The third category is adjudication which creates mechanisms for determining whether a valid rule has been violated.

According to Hart, all societies with full-blown legal systems utilize the rule of recognition (Harris, 2003; Harris & Holm, 2002; Harvey & Chadwick, 1992; Hasnas, 1995; Hill, 1990, 1991a, b). This is because it articulates the criterion for determining legal validity. Moreover, such a category includes provision for changing, enacting, and adjudicating laws. Hart then posited that law comprises primary and secondary rules which are harmonized into a single framework that is greater than the sum of its parts. Although the law is a combination of primary and secondary rules, they each have distinguishing characteristics that must not be ignored in analysis.

Hart suggests that a proposition can only be legally valid in a society of it satisfied the criterion contained in the recognition category (Gelman, 1994; Glass & Speyer-Ofenberg, 1996; Glick, 1992; Gormally, 2002; Gostin, 1995; Greenberg & Kamin, 1993). This criterion must be binding in that society to have credence. Indeed, this condition is consistent with the conventionality thesis in which rule recognition is only binding if there is a social convention among officials that it is the definition of standards of behavior in that group. Hence, the Hart maxim that rules of recognition that specify criterion for legal validity as well as the rules of adjudication and change must be accepted as common public standards among officials.

The separability thesis straddles the latter two in the tripartite group (Oberman, 1992; Okin, 1990; Oster, 2021; Paliwala, 2016; Paris & Poorman, 1995; Pellegrino & Sharpe, 1989; Ploughman, 1995). Yet, the separability thesis is widely acknowledged as the foundation of legal positivism. This thesis asserts that morality and the law are conceptually distinct from each other. Several interpretations have been attached to this abstract formulation. For instance, some writers interpret it as a meta-level claim to the effect that definitions of the law must be moral-free. According to this interpretation, any moral considerations when defining the law are inconsistent with the separability thesis (Den Hartogh, 1997; Downie, 1992; Downie & Randall, 1997; Draper, 1993; Dresser, 1995, 2003; Dworkin, 1991, 1992). The same conclusions apply to legal systems and legal validity. A more common interpretation is that the separability thesis is only making an object-level claim about the existence of conditions that are necessary for legal validity. Hart suggests that this thesis is a simple contention that laws do not necessarily satisfy certain moral demands even though they often do so. The implication is a possibility of a legal system in which there are no moral considerations or constraints when assessing its validity.

Positivists generally agree that there could be legal systems without any moral constraints (Glass & Speyer-Ofenberg, 1996; Glick, 1992; Gormally, 2002; Gostin, 1995; Greenberg & Kamin, 1993; Grondelski, 1989). Nevertheless, there are differing views on whether such systems exist. Inclusive positivism or "incorporationism" or soft positivism suggests that society's rule recognition can incorporate moral constraints based on the content of the law. Those that follow this view include Hart and Jules Coleman. They maintain that the rule of recognition can incorporate criteria of legal validity conformity that includes substantive values or moral principles.

Examples of these moral judgments are found in the 16th and 19th Amendments of the US Constitution. These amendments allowed the establishment of religion as well as abridging the right to vote (Crossley, 1993; Crouch & Elliott, 1999; Daniels & Sabin, 1997; Den Hartogh, 1997; Downie, 1992; Downie & Randall, 1997). That is a position that is very different from the one that has been adopted by exclusive positivism. This is also known as hard positivism. According to this perspective, it is impossible to incorporate moral constraints when defining legal validity. Some of the notable exclusive positivists include researchers such as Raz (1979).

Those exclusive positivists may subscribe to the source thesis (Hill, 1991a, b; Hope & Fulford, 1994; Hylton, 1990; Kadish, 1992; Kahn, 1991; Kalb, 1990; Kamisar, 1993; Kamm, 2001). According to this thesis, the content and existence of the law can always be determined by referencing its sources. This means that there is no requirement to reference moral judgments. Hence, the sources of the law include the circumstances surrounding its promulgation as well as any available interpretative materials. Examples of these include court cases that have applied that law.

Ronald Dworkin developed a third theory which rejects the social fact thesis as espoused in legal positivism (Figueira-Mcdonough, 1990; Finer, 1991; Fluss & Zeegers, 1990; Fortin, 1991; Gelman, 1994; Glass & Speyer-Ofenberg, 1996; Glick, 1992; Gormally, 2002). According to the third theory, there are some legal standards whose authority cannot be explained by social facts. A case in point occurs when judges are deciding hard cases. Here, the jurists may involve moral principles which do not derive their legal authority from social criteria. Neither is their legality necessarily contained in the rule of recognition.

Because judges are bound to consider any such principles in their rulings, they must be characterized as law since they significantly impact on the outcomes of court cases (Capron, 1990, 1999; Chandler, 1990; Chervenak & McCullough, 1991; Chesterman, 1998; Clark, 2002; Clerkin, 2021). According to Dworkin, if we treat principles as law then we are necessarily rejecting the first tenant of legal positivism. That tenet is that the law of any community is distinguished from alternative societal standards which are tested by a form of a master rule.

According to Dworkin, adjudication in law should be interpretive (McCoy, 1992; Meisel, 1992, 1996; Menzel, 1992; Merrick, 1990; Morreim, 1991; Munzer, 1994; Nelson, 1994). To that end, he calls for judges to decide hard cases through interpreting the political structures that exist within their communities. That may require judges to find a special way of justifying their findings based on political moralities. A case in point is the management of private law of tort and contract cases where those political realities might be relevant.

Nevertheless, these interpretations must be successful lest they lead to absurdities or injustices (Eldridge, 2021; Elhauge, 1994; Emanuel, 1999; Feinberg, 1991; Fentiman, 1989; Field, 1990, 1991; Figueira-Mcdonough, 1990). To that end, there are two elements that comprise a successful interpretation. The first element is to interpret the law in as far as it justifies specific practices in a specific society. The interpretation must fit those practices which have been defined and conferred with validity using existing legal materials. The second element is the provision of moral justification for the selected practices. Here, the practices must be presented in their best moral light.

Dworkin therefore provides a rough template on how judges should endeavor to interpret hard cases (Meisel, 1996; Menzel, 1992; Merrick, 1990; Morreim, 1991; Munzer, 1994; Nelson, 1994; Nobles, 2012; O'Donovan

& Gilbar, 2003). The thoughtful judge must begin by establishing a rough threshold of fit. This is the entry point for any interpretation data received to be acceptable. If more than one interpretation meets this threshold, certain criteria are established for choosing substantively the best option rather than engaging in further or more precise comparisons between the different options. The substantive advantages are based on the options which are better at promoting the political ideals that the judge considers correct.

The propositions by Dworkin lead to the conclusion that the legal authority of binding principles derive from their contribution to the best moral justification of the legal practices in a society in its entirety (Sulmasy, 1989; TÄNnsjÖ, 1992; Thomson, 1999; Truog et al., 1991; Turrina et al., 2021; van Delden & Laurie, 2004; Van Der Burg, 1997). Two conditions must be met for a legal principle to maximally contribute to the best moral justification. First, the principle must cohere with existing legal materials. Secondly, the principle must be the most morally attractive standard that satisfies expectations. Hence, the correct legal principle is one that makes the law the moral best it can possibly be.

This can be perceived as a constructivist view of the law in a sense that it allows judges to make moral judgments on which they create new laws (Morreim, 1991; Munzer, 1994; Nelson, 1994; Nobles, 2012; O'Donovan & Gilbar, 2003; Oberman, 1992; Okin, 1990; Oster, 2021). Later, Dworkin expanded his views beyond adjudication and included legal theory. However, he distinguishes artistic or creative interpretation from conversational interpretation. To that end, Dworkin likens interpreting social practice to artistic interpretation. The most common example of interpretation is during conversation. Here, people interpret marks, sounds, and a host of other clues concerning the meaning of their communication.

Yet, judicial interpretation is constrained in ways that will be familiar to artistic interpreters (Harris, 2003; Harris & Holm, 2002; Harvey & Chadwick, 1992; Hasnas, 1995; Hill, 1990, 1991a, b). Specifically, the dimensions of justification and fit are critical in interpretation. We impose purpose on a practice or object during constructive interpretation. This is done to enable create a genre or form that the item may belong to. According to Dworkin, the main purpose of general theory of law is to interpret complex and related social practices. These are created by people and communities as an entity that is distinct.

It is for these reasons that Dworkin posits that the process of development a general theory of law is constructivist in nature (Lane & Grodin, 1997;

Mathieu, 1992; May, 1999; McConnell, 1991; McCoy, 1992; Meisel, 1992, 1996; Menzel, 1992). Based on that assumption, general theories of law are necessarily abstract since they seek to interpret the structure and main point of legal practice. This is different from the notion that these interpretations are some parts of the object of their interpretation. Despite all the abstractions that are involved, they remain constructive interpretations.

These interpretations attempt to show legal practice in its best light (Meisel, 1992, 1996; Menzel, 1992; Merrick, 1990; Morreim, 1991; Munzer, 1994; Nelson, 1994; Nobles, 2012). Hence, they seek to achieve equilibrium between practice as they found it and the best justification of that practice. To that end, there is no firm line that divides adjudication from jurisprudence or any other aspect of legal practice. Dworkin perceives a very strong and tight relationship between adjudication and jurisprudence. Hence, he argues that jurisprudence is nothing more than the most general part of adjudication. To that end, the opinion of a judge is a form of legal philosophy. This ties in neatly with the notion of analytical philosophy.

1.3. INTRODUCTION TO ANALYTICAL PHILOSOPHY

The basis of analytical philosophy can be crystalized to the work of key figures in this discussion (Field, 1990, 1991; Figueira-Mcdonough, 1990; Finer, 1991; Fluss & Zeegers, 1990; Fortin, 1991; Gelman, 1994; Glass & Speyer-Ofenberg, 1996). It has emerged as a distinctive form of analysis that is essential to the development of jurisprudence. One of the key figures that contributed to this aspect of legal development is Frege. Figure 1.5 shows that relationship between Fregean and Russellian content. The latter also takes inspiration from another great voice in this debate.

One of the features of Frege's work is the enormous potential of logical analysis that it demonstrates (Abrams, 1996; Agich & Spielman, 1997; Allen, 1990, 1992; Alward, 2002; Amaraskekara & Bagaric, 2004; Anderson, 1993). Nevertheless, it is important to note that Fregean analysis is not compatible with other forms of analysis and is therefore limited to some extent. Indeed, some have argued that the foundation and justification for Fregean analysis is to prepare for other forms of analysis. This is a point that was made strongly by philosophers in the second school of analytic philosophy. A case in point is the perspective of the Cambridge school.

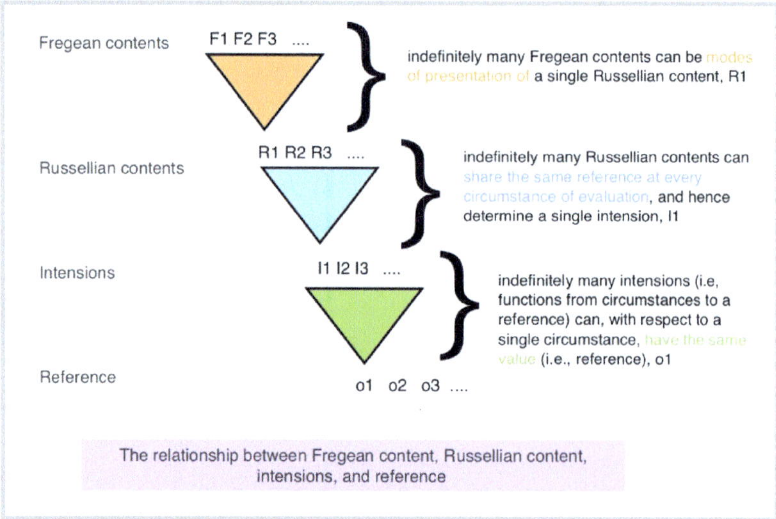

Figure 1.5. Relating Fregean and Russellian content.

Source: Stanford.

This is related to traditional "decompositional" analysis (Raymond, 1999; Resnik, 1997; Rich, 1997; Rivard, 1992; Robertson, 1996, 1999; Savulescu, 1994; Schneider, 1992). Under such a perspective, the whole is resolved into its constituent parts. Examples may include propositions, thoughts, and constituents. Existing literature has shown that decompositional analysis is part of Frege's philosophy. However, there is an even more important component in terms of the use of functional-argument analysis. This latter approach has some divergence from whole-part analysis which has been incorporated into Fregean analysis.

One of the milestones in developing Fregean logic was Frege's "*Begriffsschrift*," a seminal book which is notable for the presentation of simple but deeply meaningful and impactful statements (Den Hartogh, 1997; Downie, 1992; Downie & Randall, 1997; Draper, 1993; Dresser, 1995, 2003; Dworkin, 1991). A case in point is the statement that "*Socrates is mortal*" which is transformed away from the anticipated subject-predicate form. Instead, Frege analyzes the statement in terms of a function argument form. In this case, "*Socrates*" is the argument while the section "*is mortal*" is the function. The function yields as a value or judgeable content.

There have been some arguments about the extent and implications of the ways in which Frege understands arguments, functions, and judgeable content. However, this is superseded by his contribution to the development of jurisprudence or its analyses (White, 1990; Wicclair, 1991a, b; Wildes, 1997; Wilson, 1994; Woliver, 1990; Wyld & Cappel, 1990). Later, Frege would consider the effect of saturating a concept with an object value so that it becomes a truth-value. This later analysis and theorizing are what allowed him to develop the quantificational theory that was instrumental in exploring complex mathematical statements.

There are important philosophical implications associated with the function-argument analysis (Pogge, 1991; Purdy, 1990; Quante, 1999; Rae & DeGiorgio, 1991; Ravven, 2016; Raymond, 1999; Resnik, 1997). This is well-illustrated by an example giving in Begriffsschrift. Here, the starting point is the statement that "*(HLC) Hydrogen is lighter than carbon dioxide.*" There are two main ways in which Frege suggested analyzing this statement. These options are dependent upon whether one decides to take hydrogen as an argument whereas the fragment "*is lighter than carbon dioxide*" is the function. Another option is to consider carbon dioxide as the argument and the phrase "*is heavier than hydrogen*" becomes the function.

When respecting the subject-predicate formula, we might rephrase the statement as: "*(CHH) Carbon dioxide is heavier than hydrogen.*" According to Frege, hydrogen (HLC) and carbon dioxide (CHH) have the same content or what Frege refers to as '*Inhalt.*' Hence, hydrogen and carbon dioxide are merely different and alternative ways of analyzing the content of being heavier. Function-argument analysis allows us to acknowledge what these elements have in common whilst opening the possibilities of analyzing different functions using different arguments, albeit coming to the same result.

The critics of Frege have posited that his analyses presuppose a conclusion in which two arguments are identified with a function that has two arguments (Sullivan & Goldzwig, 1995; Sulmasy, 1989; TÄNnsjÖ, 1992; Thomson, 1999; Truog et al., 1991; Turrina et al., 2021; van Delden & Laurie, 2004). These presuppositions may not always hold true. For example, Michael Dummett (1981) posits that we distinguish decomposition from analysis. Hence, there can be alternative decompositions which are then turned into component concepts. Nevertheless, there is always a single analysis which has been divided into two unique constituents.

It is worth noting that when talking about analysis, Dummett is referring to what others call decomposition (Thomson, 1999; Truog et al., 1991; Turrina et al., 2021; van Delden & Laurie, 2004; Van Der Burg, 1997; Van der Burg & Brom, 2000). In this instance, decomposition implies a unique product which is greater than analysis. When he speaks of decomposition, Dummett is really speaking about function-argument analysis. The processes and justifications for making selections can be complex and interwoven.

There are several areas of Fregean philosophy that have been challenged (Brock, 1999; Brody, 1998; Cantor, 2005; Capron, 1990, 1999; Chandler, 1990; Chervenak & McCullough, 1991; Chesterman, 1998). For example, controversy surrounds Frege's criterion for sameness of content. Additionally, there is concern about the ways in which content can be bifurcated. Moreover, some critics question the fruitfulness of definitions. Then there are those that query the relationships between compositionality and the context principle.

Russell is an important voice in the development of the philosophy of the law in much the same way as Frege is considered (Skene & Parker, 2002; Somerville, 1989; Spurr, 1993; Stacy, 1994; Stauch, 2000; Stein, 1998; Steinbock & McClamrock, 1994). The seminal reflective work titled "*My philosophical development*" hinted that Russell had abandoned the philosophies of Kant and Hegel. Instead, he sought solutions to philosophical problems through analysis. To him, analysis was the only plausible way of dealing with philosophical problems. Nevertheless, critics have argued that Russell is vague about his definition of analysis. Others argue that his practice did not reflect this focus on analysis.

There are examples of Russell's work which reflect some of these contradictions (Walters, 2012; Waymack, 1991; Weithman, 1999; Whitaker & Edwards, 1990; White, 1990; Wicclair, 1991a, b). A case in point is the paper titled "*The regressive method of discovering the premises of mathematics*" which was published in 1907. Here, Russell talks of analysis in a regressive sense. The philosopher will work back to reach the ultimate logical premises. Hence, the assertion that the analysis in this case is an inductive rather than deductive process. Another example is the abandoned 1913 manuscript titled "*Theory of knowledge*." In that paper, Russell suggests that analysis is the discovery of constituents of the complex whole.

Decompositional analysis was a lynchpin of the philosophical ideas that had been presented by Russell (Robertson, 1999; Savulescu, 1994; Schneider, 1992; Schuck, 1994; Sevelin, 2019; Shanley, 1990; Sharpe & Pellegrino, 1997; Sheldon & Wilkinson, 1997). In some respect, Russell still references the ideas of Frege in as far as they value the possibilities of logical analysis. For example, both Frege and Russell are noted for the formalization of ordinary language statements into logical language. Indeed, the theory of descriptions which became one of the most important outputs of Russell includes logical analysis. The first example of this representation was published in a work titled "*On denoting*" which was released in 1905. Ramsey referred to this as a paradigm of philosophy which eventually contributed to the development of analytic philosophy.

One of the outcomes of the Russell approach is that the analytical problems that other philosophers encountered are decompositionally dealt with so that they disappear (Coughlan, 1989; Crigger, 1995; Crossley, 1993; Crouch & Elliott, 1999; Daniels & Sabin, 1997; Den Hartogh, 1997; Downie, 1992). For example, there is a simple statement that "the present king of France is bald." One of the problems with that statement is that there may not be a king of France. In that instance, the subject term would lack meaning. Russell resolved this problem by analyzing away the definitive description which has no meaning in itself. This is done by drawing on resources provided by the logical theory such that quantificational structures and logical constants are revealed before being clarified.

Similarly, Frege had provided a diagnosis of what is inherently wrong with the ontological argument in its traditional form (Savulescu, 1994; Schneider, 1992; Schuck, 1994; Sevelin, 2019; Shanley, 1990; Sharpe & Pellegrino, 1997; Sheldon & Wilkinson, 1997). Russell followed suit by showing the possibilities of avoiding unnecessary reification of the purported objects of discourse. During the translation of a problematic expression into logical language, some of the analytical challenges that would otherwise hinder us fade away during the process. Frege did not fully comprehend or appreciate the "eliminativist" possibilities of his philosophy. Russell saw and explored these possibilities in his own theory.

The resultant reductionist program of analysis has been influential since that time (Pellegrino & Sharpe, 1989; Ploughman, 1995; Pogge, 1991; Purdy, 1990; Quante, 1999; Rae & DeGiorgio, 1991; Ravven, 2016). Whitehead and Russell acknowledge the role that Frege played in logical analysis. For example, the preface to "*Principia Mathematica*" pays tribute to Frege for the emergence of eliminativism. The underlying outcome is that it is possible that Frege is being recognized for a contribution to philosophical analysis which he had not explicitly promoted or acknowledged himself. That does not take away from the value of the contribution itself.

Moore emerged as one of the founders of analytic philosophy, as evidenced by substantial swathes of existing literature (Kamm, 2001; Kass

& Lund, 1996; Kaveny, 1991, 2006; Khushf, 1994; Knoppers & LeBris, 1991; Kozłowski, 2021). Despite this reputation, Moore's early conception of analysis is more traditional than modern. For example, "*The nature of judgement*" (1899) suggests that analysis is a decomposition of complex concept. At the time, Moore perceived propositions to be complex concepts which had to be broken into their constituents. In fact, the complex is so much so that initially the subject of the analysis is opaque until it becomes visible following analysis.

The publication of "*Principia Ethica*" was another watershed moment in the development of Moore's philosophy. A case in point is the open question argument which has become iconic in existing literature (Kamm, 2001; Kass & Lund, 1996; Kaveny, 1991, 2006; Khushf, 1994; Knoppers & LeBris, 1991; Kozłowski, 2021). Figure 1.6 is graphical demonstration of the contributions that were made by Moore.

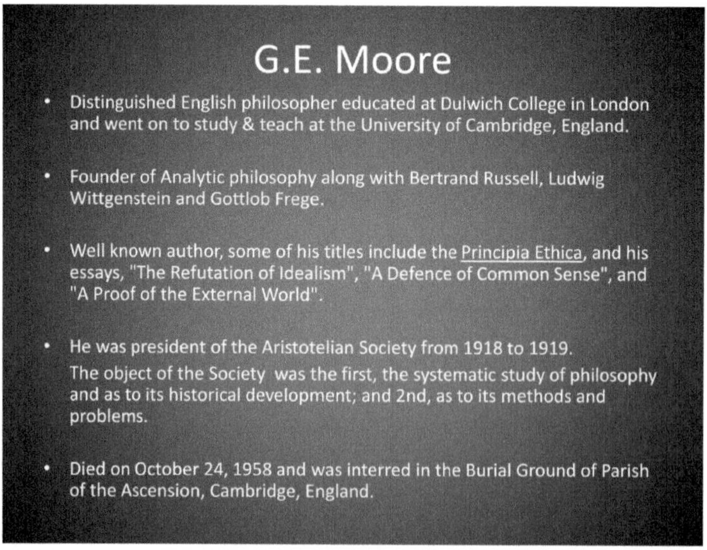

Figure 1.6. The work of GE Moore on philosophy.

Source: Opa Perez (2014) via Slide Serve.

There are specific examples of Moore's philosophies being used in practical and abstract situations (Chesterman, 1998; Clark, 2002; Clerkin, 2021; Coady, 2002; Cohen, 1989; Coughlan, 1989; Crigger, 1995; Crossley, 1993). A case in point is the initial chapter of "*The subject-matter of ethics*." Here, Moore considers the definition of good. In that sense, Moore is looking for a real (as opposed to nominal) definition. The focus is not on the meaning of the word, but rather on the nature of the object that it denotes. It is at that point that Moore concluded that the term "good" is undefinable.

The main reason for that conclusion is the assertion that the term "good" lacks constituent parts that can be decomposed, a key aspect of philosophical definitions (Harris & Holm, 2002; Harvey & Chadwick, 1992; Hasnas, 1995; Hill, 1990, 1991a, b; Hope & Fulford, 1994). Indeed, the term falls under what Moore describes as simply notions. These are notions that cannot be explained unless the person already knows them, e.g., the term "yellow." Typical and standard definitions tell us what a word is used to mean rather than what it means. Real definitions are only possible when the notion or object is complex.

A case in point is the word "horse" which has many qualities and properties which can be broken down as constituent parts. To define it well, Moore requires a concept that has qualities and properties that can be enumerated (TÄNnsjÖ, 1992; Thomson, 1999; Truog et al., 1991; Turrina et al., 2021; van Delden & Laurie, 2004; Van Der Burg, 1997). Once the enumeration process is complete and the concept has been reduced to its simplest terms then it is no longer possible to define those terms. At that point they become concepts that can be perceived and thought of. Additionally, it is impossible to communicate their nature to those who still cannot think or perceive those concepts.

Complexity, according to Moore, is the possibility of being defined in terms of component parts (Crossley, 1993; Crouch & Elliott, 1999; Daniels & Sabin, 1997; Den Hartogh, 1997; Downie, 1992; Downie & Randall, 1997). In the absence of an ad infinitum process, eventually all definitions will reach simple parts which cannot be defined. To that end, terms such as "yellow" and "good" are not a complex notion and cannot therefore be defined. One of the support mechanisms for this way of thinking is the *open question argument* that was posited by Moore.

A case in point is the exploration of the term "the good" (here denoted as "X"). It could be argued that the suggested candidates for "X" are those that either cause pleasure or are desired. Hence, "the good" has the same meaning as "X" or it does not. If indeed "the good" means the same as "X," the definition becomes trivial since it is merely analytic. However, if "the good" does not mean the same as "X" then the definition is incorrect. If there is any substitution for "X" other than "the good," then "the Good" (now denoted as "G") becomes analytic. The implication is that we can always raise an open question about whether "G" is true. Hence, "X" cannot mean the same thing as "the good," meaning that it can be offered as a definition of "good." Overall, any attempt to provide a naturalistic definition of good is bound to fail. Moore referred to the contrary view as being a "*naturalistic fallacy*."

Since that time, the argument offered by Moore has been controversial and yet influential in metaethical discussions (Fortin, 1991; Gelman, 1994; Glass & Speyer-Ofenberg, 1996; Glick, 1992; Gormally, 2002; Gostin, 1995). Some have suggested that in its general form, this argument is a paradox of analysis. Others perceive the problem as going back to the paradox of inquiry. This was formulated in "*Meno*" by Plato. The term has also been used by Frege. The first time that the term "paradox of paralysis" was used was in reference to the work of Moore (Langford, 1942).

This paradox of analysis can be demonstrated by the form "A is C." In that case, "A" is the analysandum (or what is being analyzed) while "C" is the analysans (or what is offered as the analysis). To that end, either "A" or "C" have the same meaning. If that is true, then the analysis expresses a trivial identity. If they do not (which is the alternative interpretation) then analysis is incorrect. Overall, this shows that there is no analysis that can be simultaneously correct and informative (Capron, 1999; Chandler, 1990; Chervenak & McCullough, 1991; Chesterman, 1998; Clark, 2002; Clerkin, 2021; Coady, 2002). That is the gist of the paradox of analysis.

There can be and has been significant commentary about the paradox of analysis. For example, some suggest that it calls for a distinction between two kinds of meaning (Khushf, 1994; Knoppers & LeBris, 1991; Kozłowski, 2021; Lane & Grodin, 1997; Mathieu, 1992; May, 1999; McConnell, 1991). A case in point would be the distinction between "reference" and "sense" which was highlighted in the work of Frege. Indeed, some have argued that Frege highlighted this distinction to respond to the paradox of analysis. This can be simply expressed in the notion that an analysis can be correct if the "A" and "C" in the example provided above have the same reference. It can also be informative if "C" has a different or more richly articulated sense than "A."

The paradox of analysis was put to Moore in 1942. He responded by speaking of the analysandum and analysans as the same concept when using a correct analysis. However, he also acknowledged that they had different expressions (Pellegrino & Sharpe, 1989; Ploughman, 1995; Pogge, 1991; Purdy, 1990; Quante, 1999; Rae & DeGiorgio, 1991; Ravven, 2016). Nevertheless, Moore admitted a lack of a clear solution to the problem of the paradox of analysis. Based on that admission, no definition of good is possible regardless of whether it is naturalistic or otherwise.

Despite not providing a general solution to the paradox of analysis, the work of Moore is important in unravelling this problem (Draper, 1993; Dresser, 1995, 2003; Dworkin, 1991, 1992; Dyck, 1992; Eisenstat, 1991; Eldridge, 2021). For example, Moore offers clarifications with regards to individual concepts. This is typified by his later writings which pay significant attention to the minute details and nuances of language. Indeed, Moore was a significant influence on Oxford linguistic philosophy. His work contributes significantly to certain aspects of analytical jurisprudence and Moore therefore remains an important figure in the development of the philosophy of the law.

Another of those important figures in this development is Wittgenstein (Somerville, 1989; Spurr, 1993; Stacy, 1994; Stauch, 2000; Stein, 1998; Steinbock & McClamrock, 1994; Strauss, 1992). Perhaps the starting point is the preface to "*Tractatus Logico-Philosophicus*" where Wittgenstein acknowledges the influences he received from Russell and Frege. For example, he highlights the Fregean assumption concerning the logic of language in which propositions are a function-argument form. Meanwhile, Wittgenstein credits Russell with teaching him about the significance of the theory of descriptions.

Perhaps the distinguishing feature of Wittgenstein is that he thought that ordinary language was in perfect order (Waymack, 1991; Weithman, 1999; Whitaker & Edwards, 1990; White, 1990; Wicclair, 1991a, 1991b; Wildes, 1997). This contrasted with the philosophies of Russell and Frege which critiqued ordinary language. Wittgenstein sought to demonstrate the perfect logical order of ordinary language through the construction of an ideal notation as opposed to exploring an ideal language. His work revealed that the underlying semantic structure of ordinary propositions did not necessarily suffer from being obscured by their surface syntactic forms.

Another area of difference with Frege was the argument that Wittgenstein once believed that a proposition has one complete analysis at the time of publishing Tractus (Agich & Spielman, 1997; Allen, 1990, 1992; Alward, 2002; Amaraskekara & Bagaric, 2004; Anderson, 1993; Andrews, 1996). Many of the theses from Tractatus can be traced back to reflecting on the consequences of Fregean logic. For example, propositions are classified as truth-functions of elementary propositions. Additionally, elementary propositions are seen as functions of names. The meaning of each name then becomes the simple object that it stands for. Wittgenstein suggested that simple objects necessarily exist as a condition of the meaningfulness of language (Hamblin & Somerville, 1991; Hardwig, 1991; Harris, 2003; Harris & Holm, 2002; Harvey & Chadwick, 1992; Hasnas, 1995). Hence, the existence of simple objects was guaranteed by the requirement that sense is determinate in language. This allowed Wittgenstein to reach metaphysical conclusions through rigorously pursuing the implications of his logical views. To that end, the work of Wittgenstein extended from foundational logic to the nature of the world.

Analysis takes us to the ultimate constituents of propositions and the nature of the world according to Wittgenstein (Kaveny, 1991, 2006; Khushf, 1994; Knoppers & LeBris, 1991; Kozłowski, 2021; Lane & Grodin, 1997; Mathieu, 1992). The logical conception was generally accepted despite Wittgenstein not providing examples of simple objects. Moreover, equally definite conclusions were drawn about the thought process. For example, knowing on purely logical grounds that there must be elementary propositions which can be understood by everyone in their un-analyzed forms. The aim of the analysis was to bring out what we only tacitly know even if the claims made may appear to be obviously false.

Interestingly, Wittgenstein later dismantled this logical and metaphysical picture (Waymack, 1991; Weithman, 1999; Whitaker & Edwards, 1990; White, 1990; Wicclair, 1991a, 1991b; Wildes, 1997). For example, he rejected the assumption that Fregean logic provides the logic of language and the world. Instead, Wittgenstein started emphasizing the myriad uses of language. Additionally, Wittgenstein critiqued the notion that names mean that their bearers appeal to tacit processes generating meaning. The same connection with various theses of functionality and compositionality were critiqued.

In his later work, Wittgenstein argued that nothing is hidden (Munzer, 1994; Nelson, 1994; Nobles, 2012; O'Donovan & Gilbar, 2003; Oberman, 1992; Okin, 1990; Oster, 2021; Paliwala, 2016). Indeed, he suggested that philosophy merely involves getting a clearer picture of what is already existent in the public domain. This is what is known as the grammar of our language. The philosophical investigation is therefore a grammatical one shedding light on our problem. This analysis enables us to clear misunderstandings concerning the use of words.

There could be many reasons for our misunderstandings of words according to the later works of Wittgenstein (Lane & Grodin, 1997;

Mathieu, 1992; May, 1999; McConnell, 1991; McCoy, 1992; Meisel, 1992, 1996; Menzel, 1992). For example, these misunderstandings may be caused by certain analogies between forms of expression that occur in different regions of language. Indeed, some of these can be removed by substitution of one form of expression for another. In some ways, this could be called an analysis of our forms of expression. Some see this as taking a thing apart to clarify its meaning and implications.

There is a marked transition away from the earlier conception of analysis as combining the logical with the decompositional in Wittgenstein's work (Anderson, 1993; Andrews, 1996; Arinta et al., 2021; Ayres et al., 1993; Bekrycht & Mańko, 2020; Bianchi, 2017; Blair & Kaserman, 1991). Instead, Wittgenstein now focuses on connective analysis. Because the earlier conceptions in Tractatus had been deeply ingrained, the new approach was seen as a complete rejection of the earlier theses. Hence, some heralded the later work of Wittgenstein as a mark of a new era of post-analytic philosophy. However, others have pointed out that this an extreme interpretation of the nuancing of Wittgenstein's earlier work.

In fact, Wittgenstein does not explicitly repudiate his earlier analysis (Truog et al., 1991; Turrina et al., 2021; van Delden & Laurie, 2004; Van Der Burg, 1997; Van der Burg & Brom, 2000; van Schooten, 2014). This is more a case of interpretations that have taken a different tract from the evolution of Wittgenstein. For example, the new version thinks of analysis primarily in its crude decompositional sense. Hence, logical analysis is important when translating into logical language. This is because it frees us from misleading views of language. Yet, connective analysis is still a form of analysis.

Perhaps, this makes better sense when contextualized in a specific school such as the Cambridge school of analysis which focuses on logical and metaphysical forms (Strauss, 1992; Stroud, 1996; Sullivan & Goldzwig, 1995; Sulmasy, 1989; TÄNnsjÖ, 1992; Thomson, 1999). The Cambridge school of analysis was primarily active in the 1930s based on the educational institution of its name. The school was inspired by the logical atomism of Wittgenstein and Russell. It also took inspiration from the earlier work of Moore. The central figures in the school include Susan Stebbing, Moore, John Wisdom, Austin Duncan-Jones, and Max Black. The journal Analysis was founded in 1933 as part of the school and remains a key collection of philosophy today. At the time when the school was emerging, the primary paradigm of analysis was Russell's theory of descriptions (Hill, 1991b;

Hope & Fulford, 1994; Hylton, 1990; Kadish, 1992; Kahn, 1991; Kalb, 1990; Kamisar, 1993; Kamm, 2001; Kass & Lund, 1996). This created opportunities for rephrasing propositions into a logical order. This would help to avoid the problems that had been created by misleading surface grammatical forms. Hence, this type of analysis allowed for the revelation of deeper structure. The approach was embedded in the metaphysics of logical atomism. Hence, one could engage in analysis for uncovering the ultimate constituents of propositions and any primitive elements of the facts that our propositions present. All these philosophies and standpoints were then translated into the practice and philosophies of law by luminaries such as Hart.

1.4. THE WORK OF HERBERT LIONEL ADOLPHUS HART

One of the leading legal philosophers of the 20th century was Herbert Lionel Adolphus Hart (1907–1992). His professional roles included a professorship of jurisprudence at Oxford University and a college principal at the Brasenose college in Oxford. Hart's seminal work "*The concept of law*" was published in 1961. Many have acknowledged this as one of the most significant legal philosophy books written in that century alongside with works of Hans Kelsen (Munzer, 1994; Nelson, 1994; Nobles, 2012; O'Donovan & Gilbar, 2003; Oberman, 1992; Okin, 1990; Oster, 2021; Paliwala, 2016).

Hart was born to Rose Samson and Simeon Hart on the 18th of July 1907 in Harrogate. The family had moved from the East End to London. Rose was a Jewish tailor with Polish and German ancestry. Hart's mother was a daughter of successful polish traders mainly dealing in clothing and she was responsible for finance and administration in the family firm. Hart was a middle child with an elder brother Albert and a younger sister Sybil. His education encompassed Bradford Grammar School, Cheltenham College, and Oxford University (New College) where he was awarded a first in classical greats in 1929.

Having become a barrister, Hart practiced at the Chancery Bar between 1932 and 1940. Some of his friends included Christopher Cox, Douglas Jay, and Lord Wilberforce. Having received a Harmsworth Scholarship to the Middle Temple, one of Hart's many notable achievements was his authorship of literary journalism for John O'London's Weekly which was a highly regarded periodical. Hart was about the World War II effort when working with MI5, a key section of British military intelligence which helped unearth the spy networks that had penetrated the United Kingdom. During his time in the intelligence services, Hart got the opportunity to renew relationships with the likes of Stuart Hampshire and Gilbert Ryle, major figures in the world of philosophy (Lane & Grodin, 1997; Mathieu, 1992; May, 1999; McConnell, 1991; McCoy, 1992; Meisel, 1992, 1996; Menzel, 1992). Another important connection was Dick White who would go on to lead both the MI5 and MI6. Hart also had experience of working at Bletchley Park and was well acquainted with the now-famous scientist Alan Turing.

During is work with the security agencies, Hart occasionally visited Blenheim palace, the family home of the Dukes of Marlborough. At the time, the palace was the seat of MI5 but was also famous for being the birthplace of Winston Churchill, the venerated wartime leader. During his stay, Hart read the diaries of Sarah Churchill, Duchess of Marlborough by her marriage to John Churchill, 1st Duke of Marlborough. Although these events did not directly relate to Hart's eventually contribution to the philosophy of the law (*see* Figure 1.7 for a graphical example of the links between the law, values, and fact which Hart's work would later interrogate directly and indirectly), they helped to raise his profile and experience of power and influence at the highest echelons.

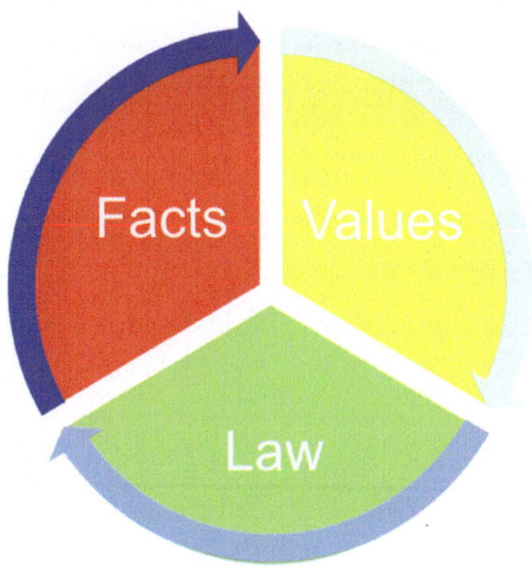

Figure 1.7. Three core components of jurisprudence.

Source: Dr. Jorge's World.

Aside from his impressive philosophical resume, Hart was a personable intellectual whose humanity and wit were considered legendary. In any case, his stay at Blenheim Palace was eventful since he shared offices with Anthony Blunt, one of the notorious Cambridge spies who was later found to be sharing state secrets with the Soviet Union. After the war, Hart opted not to return to his legal profession. Rather, he accepted a teaching post in philosophy at New College. According to Hart, he was heavily influenced by J.L. Austin during this period. For example, both jointly taught a seminar on "*Legal and moral responsibility*" in 1948. Some of the notable publications that Hart released include several essays. Examples include: "*The ascription of responsibility and rights*;" "*Law and fact*;" "*Is there knowledge by acquaintance*?" and "*A logician's fairytale*."

Hart was elected to the professorship of jurisprudence at Oxford in 1952. He was a fellow at University College between that time and 1973. "*The concept of law*" which many consider his most famous work was started in 1952 but was not published until 1961. Together with Tony Honoré, Hart published "*Causation in the law*" in 1959. He also served the Aristotelian Society as President between 1959 and 1960. The Master-Mind Lecture of 1962 was a high point in his career at the time.

Hart's first wife was Jenifer Fischer Williams who worked as a senior civil servant in the Home Office before becoming an Oxford historian at St. Anne's College with a noted specialty in police history. During the 1930s, Jenifer Hart had been a sleeper member of the Communist Party of Great Britain. During the 1960s, Jenifer was interviewed by Peter Wright (principal spy hunter at MI5) about a potential security risk of being a member of the party and being able to pass state secrets to the Soviets. After explaining her position, Wright decided that no further action was necessary. The fact that Jenifer Hart mainly worked in family policy which was of little interest to the Soviets also helped her case.

It was a difficult marriage although it lasted for a lifetime. Nicola Lacey, an LSE law professor, suggested that Hart had confessed to be a suppressed homosexual. Indeed, contemporaries of the couple suggested that Jenifer had a long-standing affair with Isaiah Berlin who was a close friend to her husband. The couple had four children. Interestingly, Mojo Mathers the first deaf member of parliament in Australia (2011) is a granddaughter of Hart. In 1969, Hart retired from the Chair of Jurisprudence. His successor was Ronald Dworkin, another famous philosopher who contributed significantly to the development of law. Eventually, Hart as appointed Principal of the Brasenose College at Oxford. Hart died on the 19th of December 1992 at the age of 85 and was buried at the Wolvercote Cemetery which is incidentally also the resting place of Isaiah Berlin. During his long and illustrious career, Hart had many students who became important figures in intellectual circles (Anderson, 1993; Andrews, 1996; Arinta et al., 2021; Ayres et al., 1993; Bekrycht & Mańko, 2020; Bianchi, 2017; Blair & Kaserman, 1991). These students were significant philosophers in politics, morality, and law. Examples include William Twining, Chin Liew Ten, Joseph Raz, Neil MacCormick, David Hodgson, Peter Hacker, Kent Greenawalt, John Gardner, John Finnis, Ronald Dworkin, and Brian Barry. During the 1950s, Hart was a strong influence on the then young John Rawls who was a visiting scholar at Oxford university having completed his PHD.

One of the key influences and areas of expertise that Hart contributed to academia was his method of philosophy (Truog et al., 1991; Turrina et al., 2021; van Delden & Laurie, 2004; Van Der Burg, 1997; Van der Burg & Brom, 2000; van Schooten, 2014). Hart was a stickler for methods when developing his version of Anglo-American positive law. This has become a major influence in the jurisprudence as well as the philosophy of law in the English-speaking world. His major influences included Hans Kelsen, Ludwig Wittgenstein, and John Austin. To that end, Hart utilized the tools of analytic and linguistic philosophy to address some of the central problems that emerged in legal theory.

An evaluation of Hart's method suggests that it borrows from the 20th century analytic philosophy as well as the jurisprudential traditions of Jeremy Bentham (Strauss, 1992; Stroud, 1996; Sullivan & Goldzwig, 1995; Sulmasy, 1989; TÄNnsjÖ, 1992; Thomson, 1999). Some have compared Hart's conception of law with the pure law theory which had been formulated by Hans Kelsen, a famous Austrian legal philosopher. However, it is notable that Hart rejected several distinguishing features of pure law theory.

Indeed, it is the differentiation of Kelsen and Hart that was at the heart of the British version of positive law theory (Hill, 1991b; Hope & Fulford, 1994; Hylton, 1990; Kadish, 1992; Kahn, 1991; Kalb, 1990; Kamisar, 1993; Kamm, 2001; Kass & Lund, 1996). Hence, Hart defended the British version while critiquing the continental version of positive law theory. The evolution of the distinct arms of the root theory was discussed in an article titled "*Leaving the Hart-Dworkin Debate*" which was published in the University of Toronto Law Journal. That article suggested that "*The concept of law*" by Hart expanded positive law theory so that it could include sociological and philosophical domains. These expanded domains of assessment differed from the more restrictive approach of Kelsen and continental positive law theory which limited the domains of assessment to jurisprudence (Gostin, 1995; Greenberg & Kamin, 1993; Grondelski, 1989; Hamblin & Somerville, 1991; Hardwig, 1991; Harris, 2003). According to received wisdom, Hart was influenced by Glanville Williams who published an article titled "*Language and the law*." Another influential paper by the same author in this circle of influence was "*International law and the controversy concerning the word 'law*.'" In the former paper, the author criticized lawyers and jurists who debate whether international law qualified as real law.

Accordingly, the differences between municipal and international law do not invalidate the latter (Figueira-Mcdonough, 1990; Finer, 1991; Fluss & Zeegers, 1990; Fortin, 1991; Gelman, 1994; Glass & Speyer-Ofenberg, 1996; Glick, 1992; Gormally, 2002). Indeed, it has been suggested that the debate is concerned with verbal usage rather than substantial difference that might disqualify international law from the family of real law. Although individual theorists could opt for conventional verbal usages, they ought to dictate their own preferences to others according to Williams who called these debates a waste of time.

Hart refined those criticisms in the final chapter of his 1961 book "*The concept of law*" (Clark, 2002; Clerkin, 2021; Coady, 2002; Cohen, 1989; Coughlan, 1989; Crigger, 1995; Crossley, 1993; Crouch & Elliott, 1999). This chapter demonstrated how the use of different social phenomena when addressing an abstract word such as "law" reflected the fact that these phenomena were communally shared without necessarily possessing any specific distinctive features. This was an approach that Glanville adopted when editing a student text on jurisprudence. Indeed, this approach can be seen in his work titled "*The definition of crime*."

A lot of academic attention has been focused on the theses in "*The concept of law*" and their implications for jurisprudence (Fentiman, 1989; Field, 1990, 1991; Figueira-Mcdonough, 1990; Finer, 1991; Fluss & Zeegers, 1990; Fortin, 1991; Gelman, 1994). Although the initial edition was published in 1961, a second edition that included a postscript was posthumously published in 1994. The origins of the book emerge from a set of lectures that Hart had started delivering in 1952. The presage is the Holmes lecture titled "*Positivism and the separation of law and morals*" which was delivered at the Harvard Law School. One of the enduring achievements of the work was a sophisticated view of legal positivism (*see* Figure 1.8).

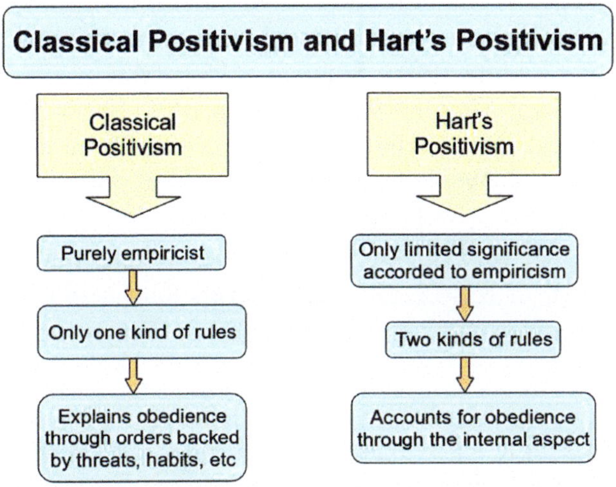

Figure 1.8. Comparing classical positivism to Hart's positivism.

Source: Hindi Sadak.

There are many seminal ideas in the book. For example, there is a critique of John Austin's theory that laws are nothing more than commands from the sovereign with the threat of punishment if there is disobedience (Hope & Fulford, 1994; Hylton, 1990; Kadish, 1992; Kahn, 1991; Kalb, 1990; Kamisar, 1993; Kamm, 2001; Kass & Lund, 1996). Hart sees a distinction between primary and secondary legal rules. Here, the primary rule governs conduct and a case in point is criminal law. The second rule governs the procedural methos through which primary rules are prosecuted and enforced. Hart enumerates three principle secondary rules as follows:

- ***The Rule of Recognition*:** This refers to the rules by which any member of a society ascertains, checks, and discovers the primary rules of that society. Among the simplest societies, this rule might be written in a sacred book or declared by the ruler. According to Hart, this was an evolution from the basic norm that had been suggested by Hans Kelsen.
- ***The Rule of Change*:** This refers to any rules by which existing primary rules are altered, created, or deleted.
- ***The Rule of Adjudication*:** This refers to the rules by which society determines when a rule has been violated. Indeed, this rule will also set out the means through which a remedy can be prescribed for that rule violation.

Another important contribution from the work was the distinction between external and internal points of view with regards to rules and laws (Lane & Grodin, 1997; Mathieu, 1992; May, 1999; McConnell, 1991; McCoy, 1992; Meisel, 1992, 1996; Menzel, 1992). This discussion was influenced and close to the distinction between legal and sociological perspectives that Max Weber had posited in his description of the law. Hart wrote of a concept of open-textured terms in the law. These are conceived along the lines that were set by Waisman and Wittgenstein. In the initial conceptualization, there were defeasible terms that were later disavowed. Indeed, these are ideas which have found a home in artificial intelligence and law.

That is not to say that Hart's version of legal positivism was universally well-received (Blair & Kaserman, 1991; Blustein, 1993; Bonnicksen, 1995; Bradley, 1993; Braithwaite, 1991; Brock, 1991; Brock, 1995). Indeed, his postscript to the second edition of his famous book saw Hart respond to Dworkin. This is notable since Dworkin was a rights-oriented legal philosopher and a successor to Hart at Oxford. Some of the notable critiques can be ford in "*Law's empire*" which was published in 1986; "*A matter of principle*" which was published in 1985; and "*Taking rights seriously*" which was published in 1977.

There is other literature to which Hart contributed in a notable way (Menzel, 1992; Merrick, 1990; Morreim, 1991; Munzer, 1994; Nelson, 1994; Nobles, 2012; O'Donovan & Gilbar, 2003; Oberman, 1992). A case in point is the co-authorship with Tony Honoré in "*Causation in the law*" which was first published in 1959 and a second edition released in 1985. That book is widely considered as a critical academic discussion of causation in legal contexts. Indeed, the early chapters of the work philosophically tackle the conceptualization of cause. A discerning analysis shows that they have a lot of Hart's contribution. The later chapters are more concerned with English Law which was a specialty of Honoré.

Another significant project is "*Law, liberty, and morality*" which was published in 1969 (Kass & Lund, 1996; Kaveny, 1991, 2006; Khushf, 1994; Knoppers & LeBris, 1991; Kozłowski, 2021; Lane & Grodin, 1997). This work was conceived as a result of the famous debate between Hart, Baron Devlin, and Patrick Devlin. The gist of that debate was the role of criminal law in enforcing moral norms. The book itself comprised three lectures that Hart had given at Stanford University. In 1965, Hart wrote "*The morality of the criminal law*" which explored similar themes. According to

Hart, the Devlin reference to Mill's harm principles when discussing the decriminalization of homosexuality was perverse.

Later, Hart stated that he believed that the reforms regarding homosexuality that had been inspired by the Wolfenden report were not sufficient (Harvey & Chadwick, 1992; Hasnas, 1995; Hill, 1990, 1991a, b; Hope & Fulford, 1994; Hylton, 1990). This was not the only foray into political and policy discourse in Hart's career. For example, Hart gave lectures to the Labor Party about closing tax loopholes that were being exploited by the super-rich. When asked about his political leanings, Hart would only admit to being on the non-communist West. Indeed, Hart had expressed hostility to Margaret Thatcher an iconic of the political right in the United Kingdom.

There is a rich body of writings that are credited to Hart. Examples include "*The ascription of responsibility and rights* which was published in the Proceedings of the Aristotelian Society (1949). Another important work is the "*Definition and Theory in Jurisprudence*" (1953). Then there is "The Concept of Law" (1961; 1994; 2012). Another is "*Punishment and Responsibility*" (1968). The later works include "*Essays on Bentham: Studies in Jurisprudence and Political Theory*" (1982) as well as "*Essays in Jurisprudence and Philosophy*" (1983). Overall, Hart is in the same category as other giants of legal philosophy such as Jeremy Bentham.

1.5. CONTRIBUTION OF JEREMY BENTHAM

Jeremy Bentham was born on the 15th of February in 1748 and died on the 6th of June 1832. He was one of the best-known English jurists, philosophers, and social reformers. Many consider him to be the founding father of modern utilitarianism (Sulmasy, 1989; TÄNnsjÖ, 1992; Thomson, 1999; Truog et al., 1991; Turrina et al., 2021; van Delden & Laurie, 2004). One of his contributions was the fundamental axiom which underpinned his philosophy that the greatest happiness is based on a measure of what is right and wrong. As a leading theorist in Anglo-American philosophy of law, Bentham was a political radical whose work greatly inspired welfarism as a social policy concern.

Bentham was a firm advocate for economic and individual freedom (Wilson, 1994; Woliver, 1990; Wyld & Cappel, 1990; Yamada, 2019; Zohar, 1991; Zomerski, 2020). He also called for the separation of the Church from the state. Moreover, Bentham believed in equal rights for women and freedom of expression. Even more interesting at the time was his belief in the right to divorce as well as the decriminalization of homosexual acts. Bentham was one of the voices that were critical of slavery and called for its abolition.

As a social reform, there is a consistent thread of freedom and free will in Bentham's work (Nobles, 2012; O'Donovan & Gilbar, 2003; Oberman, 1992; Okin, 1990; Oster, 2021; Paliwala, 2016; Paris & Poorman, 1995). For example, Bentham called for the abolition of capital and corporal punishment. Moreover, he advocated for the rights of children and for them to be free of oppression that is masked as otherwise acceptable chastisement. As one of the early advocates for animal rights, Bentham was ahead of times by expressing concern about social and political issues that are current today (*see* Figure 1.9 for a summary of his work).

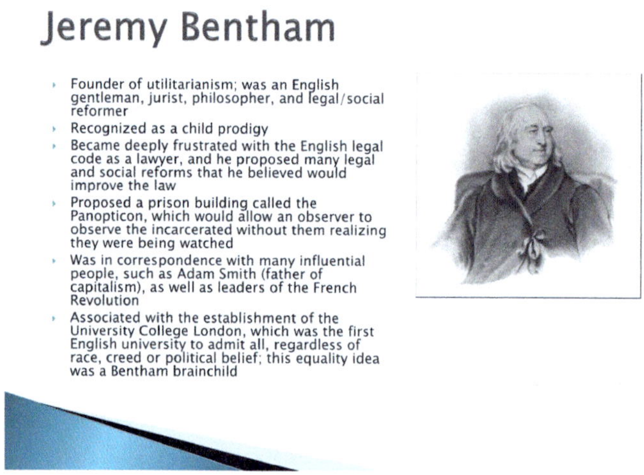

Figure 1.9. Summarizing the work of Jeremy Bentham.

Source: Sorena Nasser (2014) via Slide Serve.

Interestingly, Bentham was opposed to the notion of "God-given" origins for any of the rights that he advocated and therefore set the stage for a human rights culture (Rich, 1997; Rivard, 1992; Robertson, 1996, 1999; Savulescu, 1994; Schneider, 1992; Schuck, 1994; Sevelin, 2019). Similarly, he rejected the notion of natural rights or even natural law. A dismissive term for these rights that he used was "nonsense upon stilts." Additionally, Bentham critiqued legal fictions in their conceptualization and operationalization. Bentham influenced many including his secretary James

Mill and John Stuart Mill. Many count Bentham as a significant influence in their famous work (Shanley, 1990; Sharpe & Pellegrino, 1997; Sheldon & Wilkinson, 1997, 1998; Shepherd, 1995). Examples include John Austin, the famous legal philosopher.

The activist John Neal counted Bentham among his influences. From a policy point of view, Bentham inspired reforms in courts, legislation, and prison. A case in point is the refinement and expansion of the poor laws that had originally been conceived under Elizabeth I. Following his death and wishes, Bentham's body was dissected and preserved as an auto-icon or self-image which is now displayed at the Student Centre of the University College London (UCL). This is in reverence for Bentham's advocacy for greater access to education. Indeed, some consider him its spiritual founder although he only played a limited role in the foundation of the institution.

Bentham's origins did not always portend the kind of reformer he would become. Born to a wealthy family in Houndsditch (London), his family was of Tory persuasion. Early reports indicate a child prodigy who studied Latin at just three years of age. By seven, Bentham could play Handel sonatas at dinner parties. Bentham was close to his surviving sibling Samuel who lived from 1757 to 1831. Having attended Westminster School, Bentham was sent to Queen's College at Oxford when he was only 12. Three years later, he was awarded a bachelor's degree at 15 and a master's when he was 18.

Having trained as a lawyer, he never practiced even though he was called to the bar in 1769. Bentham was frustrated by the complexities of English law. Hence the epithet that it was like the Demon of Chicane. When the American colonies published their Declaration of Independence during July 1776, the British government refused to respond. Instead, it secretly commissioned John Lind, a London-based lawyer and pamphleteer, to publish a rebuttal. That rebuttal was titled a "*Short review of the declaration*" despite its 130 pages. This was credited to Bentham as a "friend of Lind." The document mocked the American philosophy.

For a year starting in 1786, Bentham travelled to Krichev which is based in modern Belarus but was part of White Russia at the time. The purpose of the visit was to visit his brother Samuel who was managing a range of industrial and non-industrial projects for Prince Potemkin. According to Bentham, it was his brother Samuel who conceived the notion of a circular building that could be used as a hub of a larger compound. This would then allow a relatively small number of managers to oversee a much larger unskilled workforce.

Thereafter, Bentham developed the model in as far as it could be applied to prisons. He wrote a series of letters to their father back home to outline his ideas. This later came to be known as the abortive prison project which was closely linked to the Panopticon project. Bentham was supplementing the supervisory principle with contract management. Hence, the protocols would involve the administration of a contract rather than relying on trust. Moreover, the director would have a pecuniary interest in lowering the average rates of mortalities.

The intention between this idea was that the Panopticon would be cheaper than the prisons of the era. This was because of the requirement for fewer staff members. To that end, Betham requested the Committee for the Reform of Criminal Law for permission to construct a model based on the Panopticon. In his request, Bentham said he would be the jailer and would cost nothing to the nation for that service. One of the interesting arguments for the scheme was that since the guards were not seen by prisoners, they could leave their posts at any time without the prisoners knowing. Hence, the watching was being left to those that were being watched.

Prisoners would be used as menial labor under this scheme. They could be walking on wheels to spin looms or running a water wheel. Hence, the idea that this would decrease the costs of running the prison. It could also become a source of income. This was one of the many ideas that Bentham posited for reforming the prison system in England. Having spent 16 years developing his ideas, Bentham hoped the government would appoint him the contract governor of a National Penitentiary designed on these principles.

Ultimately, the prison was not built. However, the concept was influential on other generations of future thinkers (Feinberg, 1991; Fentiman, 1989; Field, 1990, 1991; Figueira-Mcdonough, 1990; Finer, 1991; Fluss & Zeegers, 1990; Fortin, 1991). Michael Foucault, for example, suggested that the panopticon was paradigmatic of 19th century disciplinary institutions. Nevertheless, Bentham was bitter for the rest of his life that the scheme had not been adopted. He blamed the King and aristocracy for secretly undermining his ideas. This sense of frustration led him to conceive the idea of a sinister interest or vested interests that arose because the powerful were conspiring against the wider public interest.

That notion of a sinister interest underpinned Bentham's broader arguments for social, political, and economic reform (Shanley, 1990; Sharpe & Pellegrino, 1997; Sheldon & Wilkinson, 1997, 1998; Shepherd, 1995; Shevory, 1990). When he returned to England following his visit to Russia,

Bentham commissioned Willey Reveley (an architect) to draw his plans. The material was published in 1791 as a book. Nevertheless, the refinement process continued over many years. By this point, Bentham had concluded that he would have the prison built himself rather than relying on the state. When completed, he would be its contractor-governor and would be assisted by his brother Samuel.

Meanwhile, Bentham's idea to raise interest in his ideas from the authorities in France failed despite this being a revolutionary period. At the same, Bentham engaged William Pitt (British Prime Minister) to review the previously abandoned scheme for a National Penitentiary to be constructed as a panopticon. Eventually, Pitt and his advisors were persuaded to the extent that in 1794, £2,000 was advanced for the preliminaries on the project. An act of 1779 had authorized the intended site of the construction.

This site was an earlier ear-marked location at Battersea Rise. The local landowner was Earl Spencer who raised objections about the project and raised technical legal challenges. Consequently, alternative sites were unsuccessfully considered, including Hanging Wood near Woolwich. The final option was Tothill Fields near Westminster which was common land with no known landowner. Nevertheless, there were interested parties such as Earl Grosvenor who owned property on adjacent land and therefore raised objections to the possibility of a prison overlooking his house.

All these problems brought the project to a premature impasse. Hence, Bentham organized to purchase a site at Millbank which adjoined the Thames. Government funds were availed and during November of 1799 the property was bought on behalf of the British crown for £12,000. The intersection between public and private resources was an interesting one given, Bentham's conception of the law (*see* Figure 1.10).

Despite the obstacles that had invariably been placed his way, Bentham still found the new site at Millbank not entirely satisfactory. For example, it was marshy, relatively small, and marshy. He therefore asked the government for more money to acquire additional land. The official response was that this was not supported since he had only been authorized to construct a small-scale experimental prison. Bentham was disappointed by this response which he interpreted as an official approach that lacked commitment to genuine and comprehensive penal reform based on the panopticon.

Despite negotiations continuing, William Pitt resigned from office 1801. The new prime minister Addington abandoned the project. A devastated Bentham was reported to have remarked that they had murdered his best days by this decision. After some years (between 1811 and 1812), the British government once again revived the notion of a National Penitentiary. These ideas specifically included the panopticon as an option. At 63, Bentham was still willing to be governor of such an institution. Nevertheless, it soon became clear that there was no real commitment towards the project.

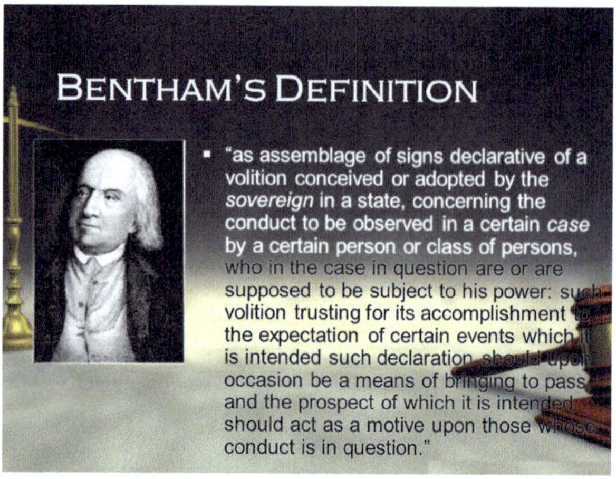

Figure 1.10. Bentham's definition of positive law.

Source: Thomasine Hensley (2015) via Slide Player.

Once Bentham finally recognized this fact, he turned his attention to extracting some form of compensation from the government for his years of effort which had not been rewarded in any meaningful way. To that end, Bentham submitted an initial claim of about £7,00,000. After negotiations, a settlement of £23,000 was agreed. Although only a fraction of the original claim, it was still a substantial amount. By an act of parliament passed in 1812, the land that Bentham had acquired for the project was transferred to the British crown.

A much more successful project was Bentham's cooperation with Patrick Colquhoun with regards to fighting corruption within the Pool of London. Accordingly, the Thames Police Bill of 1798 was eventually given royal assent in 1800. One of the outcomes of the bill was the creation of the Thames River Police. This was the maiden preventative unit in Britain and was an important inspiration for the reforms by Robert Peel that occurred three decades later. Aside from these projects with mixed levels of success, Bentham was an influential writer and philosopher to whom the legal tradition owes a lot. It is notable that Bentham corresponded with many influential figures of the time and some scholars have speculated that these figures contributed towards the development of his philosophy. For example, during the 1780s Bentham corresponded with the now ageing doyen of classic economics Adam Smith. At the time, Bentham was arguing that interest rates should be allowed to freely float even though Smith never accepted this argument. Having corresponded with Mirabeau and other leaders of the French Revolution, Bentham became an honorary citizen of France.

Bentham critiqued the revolutionary discourses concerning natural rights whilst at the same time condemning the violence that broke out in 1792 when the Jacobins took power. He was also in correspondence with Francisco de Miranda, the Latin American revolutionary. Another friendship was struck up with José Cecilio del Valle. These friendships and engagements linked him with some of the most radical and revolutionary thinkers of the time. However, Bentham also had more traditional views which may appear contradictory to the modern gaze.

A case in point were the discourses pertaining to the South Australian colony proposal. On the 3rd of August 1831, a proposal was printed with the approval of the Committee of the National Colonization Society. The gist of the proposal was the establishment of a free colony on the southern coast of Australia. This project would be funded by the sale of appropriated colonial lands. The scheme would be overseen by a joint-stock company. The idea was that this company would eventually be granted self-government. Although many assumed that Bentham was directly involved in this proposal, existing research shows that he was not.

Instead, the proposal had been spearheaded by Anthony Bacon, Charles Grey (2nd Earl), and Robert Gouger. Nevertheless, evidence shows that Bentham was involved in an 1831 draft which had not been published. The paper had been titled "*Colonization Company Proposal*" and was said to have been prepared in August of that year. The gist of that paper was a presentation of Bentham's view on the proposal that had been set out by the National Colonization Society. Many of the ideas that were being discussed would be designated as colonial and exploitative.

Bentham was closely linked to the Westminster Review which he co-founded in 1823. His partner in this project was James Mills. The review was effectively a journal for what were dubbed "philosophical radicals." This comprised a group of younger disciples of the Bentham doctrines. Indeed, the philosophical radicals allowed Bentham to exert considerable influence in British public life. A case in point was John Bowring whom

Bentham described as being like a son. Bentham appointed Bowring the political editor of the journal and eventually he became a literary executor for him. Another important figure among the philosophical radicals was Edwin Chadwick who presented substantial essays on policing, sanitation, and hygiene. One of his major projects was the Poor Law Amendment Act. Eventually Bentham appointed Chadwick his secretary and subsequently bequeathed him a substantial legacy.

CHAPTER 1 SUMMARY

This introductory chapter explores the origins of the analytical school of jurisprudence. That process involved revisiting the development of its philosophy as well as explaining some of its approaches to the law. To provide context for this philosophy, the chapter briefly explored the biography of important contributors in the form of Jeremy Bentham and Herbert Lionel Adolphus Hart. The next chapter attempts to distinguish formal legalism from analytical jurisprudence.

CHAPTER 2

Distinguishing Analytical Jurisprudence From Legal Formalism

Contents

In this second chapter, we will identify the distinguishing features of legal formalism that separate it from analytical jurisprudence. We will start off by conceptualizing legal formalism. This will then be followed by an exploration of the meaning of natural laws. The work of David Hume will be briefly summarized to evaluate the implications of these definitions. The chapter will then analyze the relationships between power and the law as well as between morality and the law. The overall purpose of this chapter is to demonstrate the fact that legal formalism is distinct from analytical jurisprudence even though they may share connections in the larger body of legal philosophy. A good starting point for this discussion is to find out what legal formalism is and is not.

2.1. WHAT IS LEGAL FORMALISM?

In essence, legal formalism comprises a descriptive and normative theory concerning how judges out to decide cases (Truog et al., 1991; Turrina et al., 2021; van Delden & Laurie, 2004; Van Der Burg, 1997; Van der Burg & Brom, 2000; van Schooten, 2014). In essence, legal formalism is a descriptive theory. It is also a normative theory that describes who judges ought to decide cases. The descriptive aspect calls for jurists and judges to reach their decisions by applying uncontroversial principles to the facts presented to them.

That requires an assumption of an underlying logic to decided cases (Downie & Randall, 1997; Draper, 1993; Dresser, 1995, 2003; Dworkin, 1991, 1992; Dyck, 1992; Eisenstat, 1991). Despite the diversity and range of principles that could apply to cases, they are all linked by the fact of logic. Anyone with some legal expertise can understand these principles. Ultimately, the aim of legal formalism is to describe these principles in a determinate and single way. Hence, the principles can be applied in a mechanical way. That is where the term mechanical jurisprudence emerged from.

This is an entirely different take from one that has been adopted by legal realism. Indeed, some scholars argue that formalism is the antithesis of realism (Rich, 1997; Rivard, 1992; Robertson, 1996, 1999; Savulescu, 1994; Schneider, 1992; Schuck, 1994; Sevelin, 2019). Nevertheless, formalism remains one of the most accepted and recognized theories pertaining to the ways in which judges arrive at their decisions in court. To understand formalism, it is necessary to develop an appreciation of some of the different approaches to the law that can be contrasted with it.

There are essentially four approaches to the law that are known in jurisprudence (Munzer, 1994; Nelson, 1994; Nobles, 2012; O'Donovan & Gilbar, 2003; Oberman, 1992; Okin, 1990; Oster, 2021; Paliwala, 2016). These are known as the schools of law. The first is formalism which treats the law as a scientific endeavor. Realism acknowledges the politics of the law, and some have even argued that under this school the law is just another name for politics. Positivism is the third school. This approach posits that law comprises the rules, regulations, and laws that have been enacted and recognized by both the parliament and the government arm of the executive. Naturalism is the fourth and final school. This calls for the law to reflect the eternal principles of morality and social justice. These principles then exist outside any recognition by the state. Figure 2.1 summarizes the basic tenets of these schools.

4 schools of Law:

- **Formalism proposes that law is a science**
- **Realism holds that law is just another name for politics;**
- **Positivism suggests that law must be confined to the written Laws, rules and regulations enacted or recognized by the Parliament & the government.**
- **Naturalism maintains that the law must reflect eternal principles of justice and morality that exist independent of governmental recognition.**

Figure 2.1. Four schools of law.

Source: Yerkin Massanov (2019) via PPT Online.

It is notable that the descriptive conceptualization of legal formalism is extended to normative theory (Sullivan & Goldzwig, 1995; Sulmasy, 1989; TÄNnsjÖ, 1992; Thomson, 1999; Truog et al., 1991; Turrina et al., 2021; van Delden & Laurie, 2004). The tenet of this extension is that judges do no more than apply uncontroversial principles to the facts of the case before them. To that end, sound legal decisions are justified as conclusions of valid deductive syllogism. To the formalists, adjudication does not involve the creative interpretation of the law and its implications.

Formalism has suggested that discerning the relevant principles of the law when deciding a case involves nothing more than surveying existing case law to identify the relevant ones (Resnik, 1997; Rich, 1997; Rivard, 1992; Robertson, 1996, 1999; Savulescu, 1994; Schneider, 1992; Schuck, 1994). Indeed, Christopher Columbus Langdell posited that the science of law could be created with nothing more than access to a well-stocked and relevant library. This is one of the reasons why legal formalism has been referred to as an autonomous discipline. Such a reference emphasizes the notion that judges require nothing more than principles of the law and facts to decide cases.

To that end, the formalists reject the notion that judges can reference politics and morality of the day (Shewmon, 1997; Shultz, 1990; Singleton Jr, 1989; Skene & Parker, 2002; Somerville, 1989; Spurr, 1993; Stacy, 1994). Indeed, it has been argued that anything other than the mechanical application of judicial principles to facts is an overreach and breaches the principle of separation of powers between the judiciary, executive, and legislature. Indeed, the mechanical application of these principles can insulate the judges from criticism. Hence, formalism has been called the official theory of judging.

Yet, legal formalism is not without its critics (Kamisar, 1993; Kamm, 2001; Kass & Lund, 1996; Kaveny, 1991, 2006; Khushf, 1994; Knoppers & LeBris, 1991). For example, some scholars question when the purest forms of legal formalism ever existed. Unlike realists, formalists take the judges and the judgments that they make at face value. They consider that the record of the case reflects the rationale used by the judges and hence pronounces the relevant principles. The means by which the judges arrive at their decisions is not as important as it would be for legal realists.

Formalists have argued that officials including judges must be constrained and restrained in their interpretation of legal texts (Shultz, 1990; Singleton Jr, 1989; Skene & Parker, 2002; Somerville, 1989; Spurr, 1993; Stacy, 1994; Stauch, 2000). Judges merely expose and espouse the law. They have no business opining on what the law should be. A case in point is the Massachusetts Constitution of 1780 which explicitly prevents the judiciary from ever exercising any executive or legislative powers. This is said to mean that the government is one of laws rather than being one of men.

In emphasizing the separation of powers, formalists insist that judges must undertake their roles outside the pressures and demands of social and political institutions (Dresser, 2003; Dworkin, 1991, 1992; Dyck, 1992; Eisenstat, 1991; Eldridge, 2021; Elhauge, 1994; Emanuel, 1999). Such an approach has been compared to legal instrumentalism. Yet, the American legal realism is contrasted with formalism. According to the instrumentalists, there ought to be creativity in the interpretation of legal texts which is aimed to serve social interests and good public policy. In that sense, instrumentalism sees the law as a vehicle for achieving human rights and justice.

The instrumentalists call for and recognize a wide range of judicial discretion (Merrick, 1990; Morreim, 1991; Munzer, 1994; Nelson, 1994; Nobles, 2012; O'Donovan & Gilbar, 2003; (Oberman, 1992). Formalists disagree with this position and argue that judicial discretion undermines the rule of the law. This tension plays out in common law which typically depends on precedents. Nevertheless, those who support common law argue that it is incrementally and gradually improved by judges as they take into consideration the economic, social, and technologies of the communities that come before courts.

Indeed, the realists may suggest that judges may even be better placed than politicians to address some of the gaps in existing laws since they are not beholden to a fickle populace that can vote them out of power (Knoppers & LeBris, 1991; Kozłowski, 2021; Lane & Grodin, 1997; Mathieu, 1992; May, 1999; McConnell, 1991; McCoy, 1992). That is why legal realism or "*relationalism*" has been adopted in certain common law jurisdictions. Here, the codification that is typical of civil law is virtually unknown. Figure 2.2 demonstrates how the tenets of formalism have been in different ways depending on context and the perspectives of the interpreter.

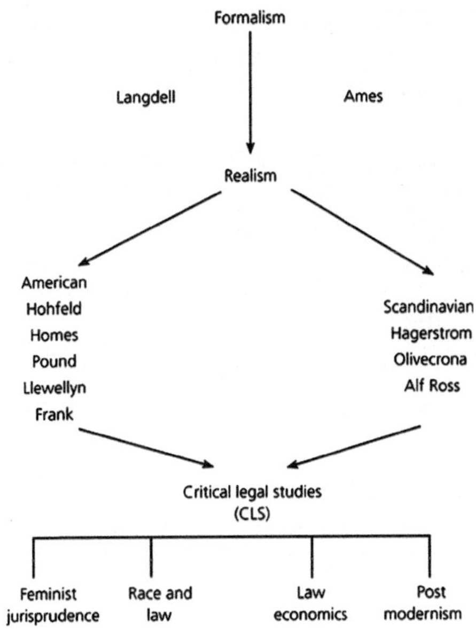

Figure 2.2. Formalism, realism, and pragmatism in law.

Source: Law Explores.

One of the present stars of legal formalism is the late Justice Antonin Scalia of the US Supreme court. The senior jurist was noted for adopting frustratingly formalist views on certain topics that had currency in the social and cultural wars taking place in the USA. For example, Scalia posited that the Constitution should be adopted using an originalist stance despite any conflict with modern liberal sensitivities (Rich, 1997; Rivard, 1992; Robertson, 1996, 1999; Savulescu, 1994; Schneider, 1992; Schuck, 1994; Sevelin, 2019). To that end, Scalia pursued a plain meaning of statutes that were written decades ago or even a century before.

In his rulings, Scalia adopted textualism which was an extension of formalism. This is despite the criticisms that had been levelled at formalism for being too formulaic to address the present-day concerns of American society (Finer, 1991; Fluss & Zeegers, 1990; Fortin, 1991; Gelman, 1994; Glass & Speyer-Ofenberg, 1996; Glick, 1992). Scalia was unabashed in his preference for formalism and even formulaic outcomes. He argued that the rule of law was about form. For him, it is formalism that provided rules of evidence and consistency that raised confidence in the legal system. His essay titled "The rule of law as a law of rules" is a treatise on his philosophy and practice.

Another important figure in this philosophy is Frederick Schauer (Coughlan, 1989; Crigger, 1995; Crossley, 1993; Crouch & Elliott, 1999; Daniels & Sabin, 1997; Den Hartogh, 1997; Downie, 1992). Having served a professorship at the school of law of the University of Virginia, Schauer published a famous article titled "Formalism" in the 1988 edition of the Yale Law Journal. One of his compelling arguments is that there should be a rethinking of the cotemporary aversion to formalism. To that end, Schauer aimed to rescue formalism from what he considered a form of intellectual and philosophical banishment.

According to him, there was a need to conceptually rethink formalism beyond arguments about its goodness or badness (Savulescu, 1994; Schneider, 1992; Schuck, 1994; Sevelin, 2019; Shanley, 1990; Sharpe & Pellegrino, 1997; Sheldon & Wilkinson, 1997). Rather, Schauer suggested that formalism can inform us about how language can and should be used to restrict the power of decision-makers during the process of making decisions. This is very similar to the work that was done by Jan Wolenski.

Wolenski exemplified his philosophy in an essay titled "Formal and informal in legal logic." According to that essay, there are rhetorical functions that are served by metalogical concepts which are used in legal discourses (Kaveny, 1991, 2006; Khushf, 1994; Knoppers & LeBris, 1991; Kozłowski, 2021; Lane & Grodin, 1997; Mathieu, 1992). This allowed for the introduction of the informal into an imperative logic. Additionally, Wolenski reviews Jørgensen's paradox in a way that introduces deontic logic. He also acknowledges the valuable contribution made by the innovations of Georg Henrik von Wright. The formalism of these thinkers is far-removed from the notion of natural laws.

2.2. THE NATURAL LAWS

Natural law comprises a system of rules and regulations that arise from a close observation of human nature (Rae & DeGiorgio, 1991; Ravven, 2016; Raymond, 1999; Resnik, 1997; Rich, 1997; Rivard, 1992; Robertson, 1996, 1999). That observation then leads to a series of assumptions, rules, and regulations that are intrinsic to humanity. Those principles and rules are independent of positive law. In this case, positive law refers to laws that are enacted and recognized by the state through its arms such as parliament, executive, and judiciary. Positive law is expressed and manifested as recognized and recognizable legislation. The tenets of natural law theory are summarized in Figure 2.3.

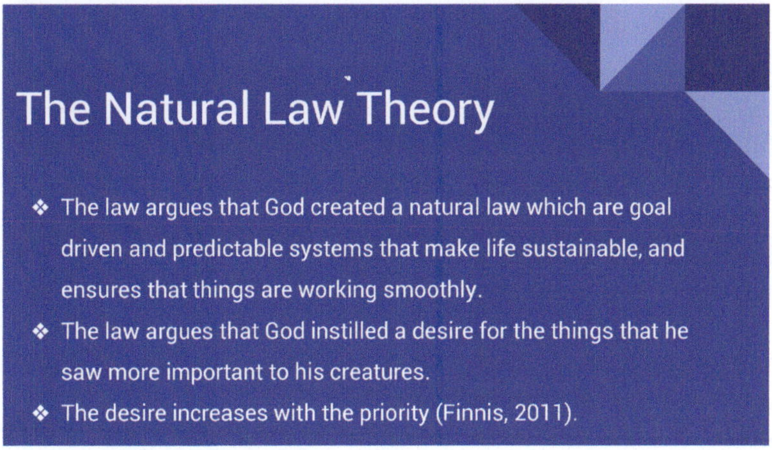

Figure 2.3. Theory of natural law.

Source: Study Pool.

The natural law theory is an important anchor of natural law (Shanley, 1990; Sharpe & Pellegrino, 1997; Sheldon & Wilkinson, 1997, 1998; Shepherd, 1995; Shevory, 1990). This is what is known as jusnaturalism.

One of the assumptions of that theory is that all people have inherent rights. These rights cannot be conferred by legislation alone. Rather, they are conferred by virtue of being part of nature and being created by God or even through reasoning. Hence, natural law theory refers to a range of theories and hypotheses relating to civil life, politics, ethics, norms, values, and religiosity.

The Western tradition still included natural law even before the times of Socrates (White, 1990; Wicclair, 1991a, b; Wildes, 1997; Wilson, 1994; Woliver, 1990; Wyld & Cappel, 1990). For example, there was a search for principles that governed human beings and the cosmos. Ancient Greek philosophy documented the concept of natural law. A case in point was the work of Aristotle. Indeed, natural law was referenced in ancient Roman times. One example of those references is the work of Cicero.

A strong religious element is found in the conceptualization and justification of natural law (Hylton, 1990; Kadish, 1992; Kahn, 1991; Kalb, 1990; Kamisar, 1993; Kamm, 2001; Kass & Lund, 1996; Kaveny, 1991). For instance, there were references to natural law both testaments of the Bible. During the Middle Ages, a series of Christian philosophers expounded of natural law. Examples include Thomas Aquinas and Albert the Great. During the Renaissance, the School of Salamanca emerged as a key example of natural law being centered.

Despite being a key component of the Christian faith and the resultant religiosity from the time of the Roman empire, many scholars believe that Aquinas was the pioneer in setting out a consistent and coherent foundation of natural law (Menzel, 1992; Merrick, 1990; Morreim, 1991; Munzer, 1994; Nelson, 1994; Nobles, 2012; O'Donovan & Gilbar, 2003; Oberman, 1992). Aquinas was credited with curating and synthesizing the ideas from his predecessors before condensing them into "*Lex Naturalis*." According to Aquinas, the reason that humans have reason is a spark of the divine when they perceive an image of Good. The implication therefore is that all human lives are of infinite value and are sacred.

This is particularly poignant when the value of humans is compared to that of objects (Blustein, 1993; Bonnicksen, 1995; Bradley, 1993; Braithwaite, 1991; Brock, 1991, 1995, 1999; Brody, 1998). There is an implicit assumption that all humans are equal because they are created by the same God in the same image. The equality of human beings is expressed by God bestowing certain fundamental rights to humans based on their humanity as opposed to any legislative or executive process. These rights are inalienable, meaning that no human entity or institution can remove those rights.

During the age of enlightenment, modern versions of natural law began to emerge (Brock, 1991, 1995, 1999; Brody, 1998; Cantor, 2005; Capron, 1990, 1999; Chandler, 1990; Chervenak & McCullough, 1991). These laws were a combination of contemporary concepts such as social contract theory. They also borrowed from Christian scholastic philosophy and Roman law. That law was used to challenge the assumed divine right of kings. Over time, it became an alternative justification for the establishment of positive law, social contracts, and the state or government in the form of granting legal rights to people. That is why this natural law led to the early forms of classical republicanism.

During the first part of the 21st Century, we have established a close relationship between natural law and natural rights (Capron, 1990, 1999; Chandler, 1990; Chervenak & McCullough, 1991; Chesterman, 1998; Clark, 2002; Clerkin, 2021). This has given rise to the notion of human rights that are embedded within legislation. Scholars and jurists today use natural law and rights synonymously. Others speak of natural justice to refer to those unbreakable rules of engagement and interpretation that are assumed to exist in law. One of the pertinent examples is that of the right to be heard before being condemned under the law.

Yet, there are those that perceive important differences between natural law and natural rights (Okin, 1990; Oster, 2021; Paliwala, 2016; Paris & Poorman, 1995; Pellegrino & Sharpe, 1989; Ploughman, 1995; Pogge, 1991). The Act of Abjuration (1581) seeks to reconcile and rationalize the intersection between natural law and natural justice. This law was passed in the Netherlands. It mirrors the kind of intersection that was recognized by the Declaration of Independence (1776) of the United States. Similarly, the Declaration of the Rights of Man and of the Citizen (1789) of France enshrined these principles during a time of revolution. More recently, the Universal Declaration of Human Rights (1948) of the United Nations has made these principles relevant to a new generation. At the supranational or regional level, examples include the European Convention on Human Rights (ECHR) (1953).

The distinction between natural and positive law (*see* Figure 2.4) has sometimes created conflicts in contemporary jurisprudence (Daniels & Sabin, 1997; Den Hartogh, 1997; Downie, 1992; Downie & Randall, 1997; Draper, 1993; Dresser, 1995). For example, some argue that natural law has sometimes been captured by religious fanatics to impose certain deprivations on non-believers and those who do not adhere to the strictest versions of the faith. A case in point are the heated debates concerning the feasibility and justification for criminalizing homosexuality. Some of the challenges of linking law to rights have been explored by great thinkers including David Hume.

Reviewing the difference between Natural and Positive Law

Natural Law	Vs.	Positive Law
God	Vs.	The State/Government
Rationalism/justice	Vs.	The law IS just
Morals	Vs.	Control
Universal laws	Vs.	Man made laws
Universal principals	Vs.	Self preservation/law is order
Born rights	Vs.	Majority rules
Common good	Vs.	"General will" the greatest good for the greatest amount of people

Figure 2.4. Differences between natural and positive law.

Source: Eileen Paul (2018) via Slide Player.

2.3. THE WORK OF DAVID HUME

David Hume was a Scottish enlightenment philosopher born on the 7th of May 1711 and lived to the 25th of August 1776. Apart from the contribution to legal theory, Hume was also an economist, historian, essayist, and librarian (Fortin, 1991; Gelman, 1994; Glass & Speyer-Ofenberg, 1996; Glick, 1992; Gormally, 2002; Gostin, 1995). Perhaps his most memorable contribution was to the development of philosophical empiricism as well as naturalism and skepticism. His work started with "*A treatise of human nature*" which was published between 1739 and 1740. Figure 2.5 summarizes his memorable contributions.

Accordingly, Hume sought a naturalistic science of man (Emanuel, 1999; Feinberg, 1991; Fentiman, 1989; Field, 1990, 1991; Figueira-Mcdonough, 1990; Finer, 1991; Fluss & Zeegers, 1990). This allowed him to examine the psychological bases of human nature. Hence, Hume argued against the existence of innate ideas. According to him, all human knowledge is solely and exclusively derived from human experience of it. In that thought, he was joining several empiricists and similarly inclined philosophers such as John Locke, Thomas Hobbes, and Francis Bacon.

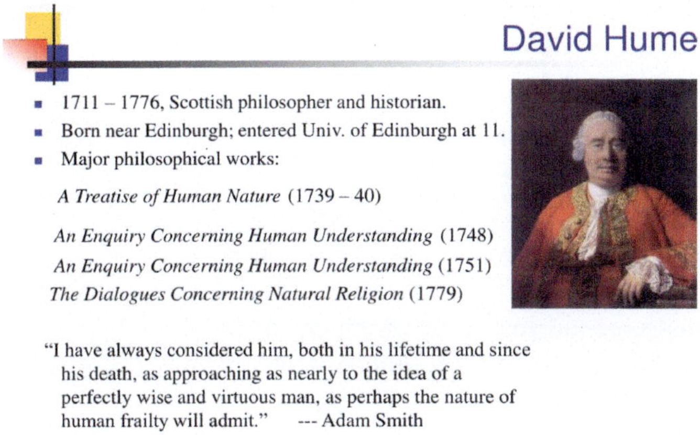

Figure 2.5. Contributions of David Hume.

Source: Rosa Fidel (2019) via Slide Serve.

Hume's view was that belief in causality and inductive reasoning cannot be justified rationally (Chandler, 1990; Chervenak & McCullough, 1991; Chesterman, 1998; Clark, 2002; Clerkin, 2021; Coady, 2002; Cohen, 1989). Rather, beliefs and inductive reasoning are derived from mental habit and custom. Instead of perceiving one event being caused by another, we only experience the constant conjunction of events. It is only if we assume that the future will resemble the first that we can deduce causal inferences based on past experiences. This is a presupposition that cannot be rationally grounded in past experiences.

Hume was an opponent of philosophical rationalists (Blustein, 1993; Bonnicksen, 1995; Bradley, 1993; Braithwaite, 1991; Brock, 1991, 1995, 1999; Brody, 1998; Cantor, 2005). For example, he argued that passions rather than reason govern the ways in which people behave. At the same time, Hume was a sentimentalist who suggested that ethics are based on sentiment and emotion rather than any abstract moral principles. Hence, Hume maintained an early commitment to naturalistic explanations for moral phenomena. According to Hume, a statement of fact alone cannot lead to normative conclusions about what ought to be done.

The philosophical positioning of Hume denied that humans have self-conception (Field, 1990, 1991; Figueira-Mcdonough, 1990; Finer, 1991; Fluss & Zeegers, 1990; Fortin, 1991; Gelman, 1994; Glass & Speyer-Ofenberg, 1996). Instead, he argued that humans experience a bundle of sensations. Moreover, Hume adopted a compatibilist theory of free will. The implication is that causal determinism is compatible with human freedom.

Hume rejected miracles and even the argument from design which supported the existence of God. These were controversial ideas at the time, although they have since found favor among liberals and rationalists.

Through his work, Hume contributed to the development of logical positivism as well as utilitarianism (Okin, 1990; Oster, 2021; Paliwala, 2016; Paris & Poorman, 1995; Pellegrino & Sharpe, 1989; Ploughman, 1995; Pogge, 1991). He was also instrumental in the emergence of the philosophy of science as well as early forms of analytic philosophy. His work was instrumental in the development of theology, cognitive science, and a host of other fields and disciplines. This was why Immanuel Kant said that Hume had inspired him to awaken from his dogmatic life.

The body of literature left behind by Hume has made significant impressions in a multi-disciplinary context (Sullivan & Goldzwig, 1995; Sulmasy, 1989; TÄNnsjÖ, 1992; Thomson, 1999; Truog et al., 1991; Turrina et al., 2021; van Delden & Laurie, 2004). For example, his treatise on human nature argued that all sciences have a relationship with human nature. This included natural philosophy, mathematics, and natural religion. It is the science of man that contributes to and helps in the development of these fields according to Hume. The science of man is therefore the only solid foundation of the other sciences.

Human science requires observation and experience to emerge (Eldridge, 2021; Elhauge, 1994; Emanuel, 1999; Feinberg, 1991; Fentiman, 1989; Field, 1990, 1991; Figueira-Mcdonough, 1990). These were the foundations for logical argument in any meaningful sense. Frederick Copleston (1999), a philosophical historian, has posited that Hume wanted to apply the method of experimental philosophy on the science of man. At the time, experimental philosophy meant natural philosophy. Hence, Copleston argued that Hume wished to extend the methodological limitations of Isaac Newton's physics to philosophy.

Hume has been characterized as being part of the empiricist skepticism group (*see* Figure 2.6). Additionally, he was seen as a forerunner of logical positivism until recently (Savulescu, 1994; Schneider, 1992; Schuck, 1994; Sevelin, 2019; Shanley, 1990; Sharpe & Pellegrino, 1997; Sheldon & Wilkinson, 1997). This was a form of anti-metaphysical empiricism. When summarizing their verification principle, the logical positivists argued that anything that could not be verified by experience as being true or false (tautological or contradictory) was meaningfulness. Hume considered himself a proto positivist.

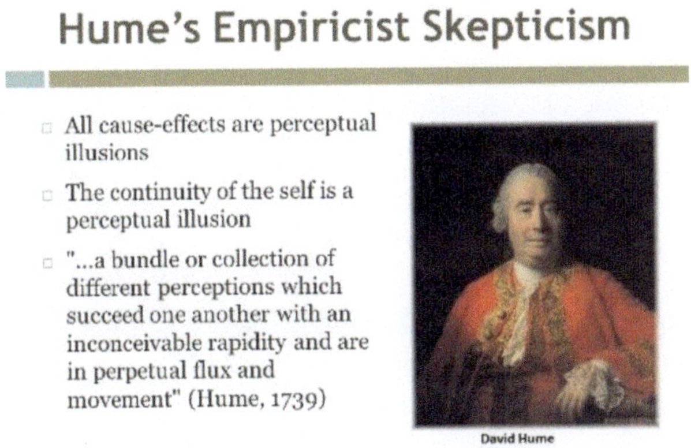

Figure 2.6. David Hume's empiricist skepticism.

Source: Pinterest.

When writing his philosophy, Hume sough to demonstrate the different ways in which ordinary propositions about causal relations, objects, and the self were semantically equivalent to propositions concerning one's experiences (Emanuel, 1999; Feinberg, 1991; Fentiman, 1989; Field, 1990, 1991; Figueira-Mcdonough, 1990; Finer, 1991; Fluss & Zeegers, 1990). Since that time, many scholars have rejected this understanding of Humean empiricism. Instead, they stress an epistemological, as opposed to semantic reading. This alternative view is that Hume was positing that our knowledge is restricted to what can be experienced.

Hence, our ability to conceive goes beyond what can be experienced (Emanuel, 1999; Feinberg, 1991; Fentiman, 1989; Field, 1990, 1991; Figueira-Mcdonough, 1990; Finer, 1991; Fluss & Zeegers, 1990). The underlying idea is that humans can form beliefs that extend beyond the possibilities of experience. This is achieved through the operation of a range of faculties. Examples of these faculties include imagination and custom. Nevertheless, Hume was skeptical about claims to knowledge based on this model. This is one of the many impressions and ideas that were cultivated by Hume.

The very first lines of the "*Treatise of human nature*" broadly sets out the central doctrine of Hume's thinking (Capron, 1990, 1999; Chandler, 1990; Chervenak & McCullough, 1991; Chesterman, 1998; Clark, 2002; Clerkin, 2021). This is the assumption that the mind comprises perceptions and mental objects which are present to that mind. These perceptions are then subdivided into two major categories including ideas and impressions. Hume did not consider it necessary to deploy many words to confirm this distinction. Many commentators have argued that this distinction is equivalent to the one between thinking and feeling.

Hume suggested that the distinction is a matter of degrees, a notion that became controversial (Walters, 1991, 2012; Waymack, 1991; Weithman, 1999; Whitaker & Edwards, 1990; White, 1990; Wicclair, 1991a). Nevertheless, Hume suggested that impressions differ from idea because of their liveliness, force, and vivacity. This is what was referred to as the "*FLV criterion*" by Henry E. Allison (2008). To Hume, ideas are faint impressions. A case in point is how feeling pain is more forceful than thinking about it. The implication is that all human ideas emanate from impressions.

It is this way of thinking that inspired Don Garrett (2002) to posit the term "copy principle." This referred to the notion that all ideas are copied from original impression (Shanley, 1990; Sharpe & Pellegrino, 1997; Sheldon & Wilkinson, 1997, 1998; Shepherd, 1995). This includes sensation and passion which derive from original impressions. The next division of impressions and ideas is based on whether they are simple or complex. In simple perceptions or impressions, there is little distinction between the two. In contrast, complex perceptions and impressions can be distinguished from each other.

An example of this is the ways in which humans experience a variety of color sensations. Hume refers to these as complex impressions. The same can be said of taste, tactile, and smell sensations. Thinking about a concept such as an apple, one will experience a range of complex sensations that may relate to its look, taste, or smell. All these can be broken into smaller parts until a saturation point is where there are no further constituent parts for the concept. At that point, the perceptions become simple.

The principle of association is an important dynamic in the theories espoused by Hume and his followers (Elhauge, 1994; Emanuel, 1999; Feinberg, 1991; Fentiman, 1989; Field, 1990, 1991; Figueira-Mcdonough, 1990; Finer, 1991). One of the underlying dictates of this principle is that regardless of how boundless our imagination seems; it is confined by the ability of the human mind to recombine information and knowledge that has already been acquired through sensory experience. These are ideas that are derived from impression. Hence, our imagination takes the most basic ideas in our leads and then combines them to form new ideas. There are three major principles of association including contiguity, resemblance, and cause-effect. Resemblance refers to ideas becoming associated with objects they represent (Pogge, 1991; Purdy, 1990; Quante, 1999; Rae & DeGiorgio, 1991; Ravven, 2016; Raymond, 1999; Resnik, 1997). For example, an illustration of a flower triggers a notion of a physical flower because the illustrated object has been associated with its physical version. Contiguity describes the tendency of ideas to become more associated with certain objects they represent when they are near to each other in space and time. An example is of associating biscuits when looking at a tin that typically holds biscuits.

The cause-and-effect principle arises out of the tendency for ideas to become associated if the objects they represent are causally related (Field, 1991; Figueira-Mcdonough, 1990; Finer, 1991; Fluss & Zeegers, 1990; Fortin, 1991; Gelman, 1994; Glass & Speyer-Ofenberg, 1996; Glick, 1992). For example, a bullet wound will make one think of the bullet and gun that caused it. Despite the vividness of the examples provided for these principles, they can become rather abstract for those that are interested in analytical jurisprudence. However, the underlying expectation is that these principles will then be understood and appropriately applied to real life law and cases. That is essentially, the same expectation when considering the relationship between the law and power.

2.4. THE RELATIONSHIP BETWEEN LAW AND POWER

The rule of law is a longstanding maxim in liberal democracies which are often the hegemonies of contemporary life, with the notable exceptions of the likes of China (McConnell, 1991; McCoy, 1992; Meisel, 1992, 1996; Menzel, 1992; Merrick, 1990; Morreim, 1991; Munzer, 1994). Nevertheless, even the most dictatorial countries aspire to or pretend to believe in the rule of law. The rule of law implies that the people are sovereign and hold all power. Their will is supreme, and it is expressed in laws that are not arbitrary.

The rule of law has become an abstraction since in practice there are institutions and people that capture and exercise this power (Glick, 1992; Gormally, 2002; Gostin, 1995; Greenberg & Kamin, 1993; Grondelski, 1989; Hamblin & Somerville, 1991). Some pretend to represent the will of the people when they clearly do not. A case in point are those quasi democracies in which elections are so rigged that it is impossible for the opposition to ever win them. Nevertheless, an attempt at the imperfect practice of the rule of law is often taken to be sufficient to be classified a liberal democracy.

That does not mean that there are glaring gaps (Hamblin & Somerville, 1991; Hardwig, 1991; Harris, 2003; Harris & Holm, 2002; Harvey & Chadwick, 1992; Hasnas, 1995). A case in point is the notion that the rules apply to everyone equally. This is contrary to the reality that often the wealthy and politically connected have a much wider leeway for breaking rules when compared to those that are poor and marginalized. We cannot speak of the rule of law when issues such as sexism, racism, homophobia, and classism ensure that those on the margins are unlikely to ever achieve true justice. These problems often occur in liberal democracies that profess the rule of law. For example, Figure 2.7 shows that the Australian Constitution calls for the rule of law despite the differential experiences of indigenous communities such as the aboriginals when they meet the justice system.

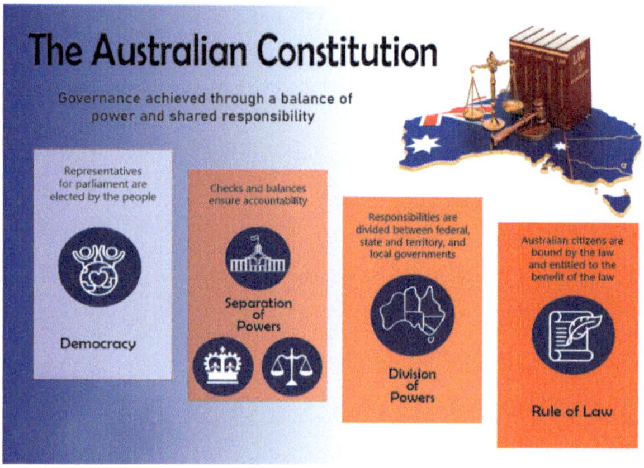

Figure 2.7. The Australian constitutional settlement.

Source: Rule of Law Education – Australia.

Two aspects of the rule of law have been characterized as being revolutionary by scholars (Bradley, 1993; Braithwaite, 1991; Brock, 1991, 1995, 1999; Brody, 1998; Cantor, 2005; Capron, 1990). First, is the notion that the people rather than the king are sovereign. This is an overturning of the divine right of monarchs or the hegemonic power of a combination of commons, lords, and kings to rule the people. Written constitutions allow the populace to determine how it is to be governed. Those that are given power exercise it subject to the will of the people and within the confines or limits that have been set by the people.

In these cases, the law is not arbitrary but is set up by the people for their own benefit (Stacy, 1994; Stauch, 2000; Stein, 1998; Steinbock & McClamrock, 1994; Strauss, 1992; Stroud, 1996; Sullivan & Goldzwig,

1995). This then leads to the second revolutionary element in which the power of a legitimate government is limited by the will of the people. The rule of law is applied in a consistent manner across the populace and includes even the politicians, representatives, or judicial officers that comprise the government. The state machinery is designed to enact and enforce the law that is willed by the people.

Many consider these two innovations to be decisive in changing the nature of political science (Kaveny, 2006; Khushf, 1994; Knoppers & LeBris, 1991; Kozłowski, 2021; Lane & Grodin, 1997; Mathieu, 1992; May, 1999). They are also a blueprint for various forms of self-government. Because the people oversee the government, they determine how the rules are made. This can be achieved through elections and regular changing of political leaders. The universality of the law means that politicians, bureaucrats, and judicial officers are limited to creating important exemptions for themselves. All the rules are meant to apply equally to everyone.

The people as a community are the fountain of authority even though all individuals in that community are subject to that authority as expressed by the rules, regulations, and laws pertaining (Truog et al., 1991; Turrina et al., 2021; van Delden & Laurie, 2004; Van Der Burg, 1997; Van der Burg & Brom, 2000; van Schooten, 2014). The United States of America prides itself on being an exemplar of democracy and the rule of law. The blueprint for the rule of law pertaining the USA was not directly imported from its former colonial master of Great Britain. Nevertheless, British constitutionalism was referenced when Americans were fashioning their own brand of democracy. Interestingly, even the United Kingdom which is a monarchy prides itself on the rule of law.

This pride and reconfiguration are based on the notion that the British monarch is a constitutional one rather than an absolute one. In that sense, the people still hold power although the head of state and head of the nation is placed in that position by accident of birth rather than elections (Hylton, 1990; Kadish, 1992; Kahn, 1991; Kalb, 1990; Kamisar, 1993; Kamm, 2001; Kass & Lund, 1996; Kaveny, 1991). King George III who was notorious for losing America had inherited a monarchy that was significantly limited by a constitutional revolution. The Glorius Revolution of 1688–1689 had forever changed the locus of sovereignty in the UK. For example, the king ruled by the will of the people and not through divine right.

The implication was that monarchical government was no longer arbitrary or absolute. The representatives of the people in parliament made laws and were custodians of justice as administered by the judiciary rather than the king and his ministers (Sheldon & Wilkinson, 1997, 1998; Shepherd, 1995; Shevory, 1990; Shewmon, 1997). The ultimate authority in the United Kingdom and its empire was parliament. This parliament comprised the king as the sovereign, the house of commons as primary legislators, and the house of lords as the reviewing entity in parliament. Initially, the revolution as welcomed in the USA as a colony whose members felt proud to be part of a reformed monarchy.

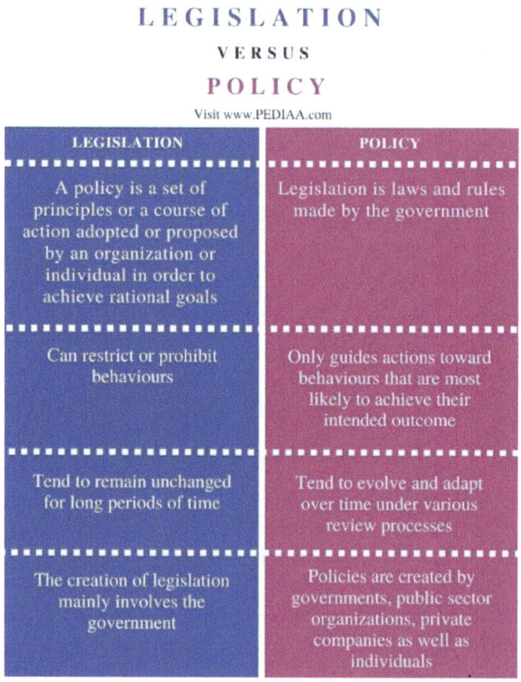

Figure 2.8. Differences between policy and legislation.

Source: Pediaa.

That support soon dissipated as power was centralized in the Westminster parliament to the detriment of the colonial authorities and decentralized powers. Other areas of contention were taxes, declarations of parliamentary will which were not harmonized with the colonies, the rebellion of the tea parties, and the quartering of troops in private homes. These are often the disputes concerning the intersection of the law and power (Field, 1990, 1991; Figueira-Mcdonough, 1990; Finer, 1991; Fluss & Zeegers, 1990; Fortin, 1991; Gelman, 1994). Nevertheless, the US constitution benefitted from some of the lessons learned from the mother of parliaments in Westminster.

For example, the fine distinctions between legislation and policy (*see* Figure 2.8) were a necessary clarification once countries like America had to break away and develop their own constitutional arrangements.

One of the relatively novel ideas that the Americans adopted from the British monarchy after the revolution was the location of sovereignty within a body that would represent all the people of the realm or nation (Viljoen, 2012; Walters, 1991, 2012; Waymack, 1991; Weithman, 1999; Whitaker & Edwards, 1990; White, 1990). That power was then linked to the legislative role of parliament which had been traditionally recognized even during the Tudor times when the monarch was unquestionably absolute in their powers.

Nevertheless, there are challenges of trying to locate and deploy this people's sovereignty (Shewmon, 1997; Shultz, 1990; Singleton Jr, 1989; Skene & Parker, 2002; Somerville, 1989; Spurr, 1993; Stacy, 1994). The USA, for example, went through a challenging period of experimentation between 1770 and 1790 before settling on any form of constitutional settlement that could last decades and even centuries. Indeed, many countries are continuing the struggle as they seek a more perfect form of government. One of the prevailing contentions is the role of morality in the law.

2.5. THE RELATIONSHIP BETWEEN LAW AND MORALITY

The relationships between morality and law are controversial because of the diversities of moralities (Abrams, 1996; Agich & Spielman, 1997; Allen, 1990, 1992; Alward, 2002; Amaraskekara & Bagaric, 2004; Anderson, 1993). Something that is religiously correct for one community may be perceived to be a form of barbarism by another. Hence, issues such as sexuality and gender have become focus points for this debate. For example, one may ask whether it is moral to call for the death penalty whilst simultaneously advocating for the right to life for unborn fetuses. Indeed, some laws are obeyed only grudgingly because they contravene personal and community morals.

The theory of morality and law has dominated discourses and attracted significant research interest (Kamisar, 1993; Kamm, 2001; Kass & Lund, 1996; Kaveny, 1991, 2006; Khushf, 1994; Knoppers & LeBris, 1991). These debates have existed since the revival of a scientific study of jurisprudence and its connections with morality as well as the law. The discussion is ongoing, and some experts argue that it may never be settled at all due to the sensitivities of the people and issues involved. There is a wide variety of opinion that has been tolerated and even accepted in ongoing discourses.

The perspectives on the links between morality and law run on a spectrum (Sulmasy, 1989; TÄNnsjÖ, 1992; Thomson, 1999; Truog et al., 1991; Turrina et al., 2021; van Delden & Laurie, 2004). The extreme ends of the doctrine are perhaps troubling for many who are in the middle. For example, Austin lies on the extreme end which sees no morality in the law. Indeed, this perspective suggests that the law is so independent of morality that the two concepts may become diametrically opposed. A good jurist, according to this perspective, therefore, ignores any considerations of morality in deciding what the law is and how it should be applied to the cases they are dealing with.

Another extreme are the perspectives in theocracies such as Iran where the law is a moral process (Eldridge, 2021; Elhauge, 1994; Emanuel, 1999; Feinberg, 1991; Fentiman, 1989; Field, 1990, 1991; Figueira-Mcdonough, 1990). On this end of the spectrum, the law is sometimes derived from Holy texts such as the Koran, Torah, or Bible. Increasingly, the liberal democracies of North America and Western Europe are rejecting the role of religion in the law. They argue that examples such as the Spanish Inquisition demonstrate the fact that religious authorities are never good custodians of law and justice.

In any case, there may exist certain connections and distinctions between the law and morality as demonstrated in Figure 2.9. For instance, the law emanates from the sovereignty of the people and therefore applies to them regardless of their moral situation (Kass & Lund, 1996; Kaveny, 1991, 2006; Khushf, 1994; Knoppers & LeBris, 1991; Kozłowski, 2021; Lane & Grodin, 1997). Hence, a priest may be tried in ecclesiastical courts for breaking a moral and vocational code but that does not negate the reality of legal proceedings in the secular court where the punishments might be even more consequential than would be the case if they were tried by fellow priests.

Countries like France have developed a civil code which studiously avoids discussion of moralities, especially those moralities that pertain to religious affiliation (TÄNnsjÖ, 1992; Thomson, 1999; Truog et al., 1991; Turrina et al., 2021; van Delden & Laurie, 2004; Van Der Burg, 1997). The debates about morality in the law have been practical, pertinent, and contextualized. One of the more popular views is that the law exists to promote morality as well as preserving specific conditions that make it possible to lead a moral life. In other words, the law is designed to help people lead industrious and sober lives. However, those views may not be readily acceptable in modern liberal democracies where personal choice and freedom are highly valued.

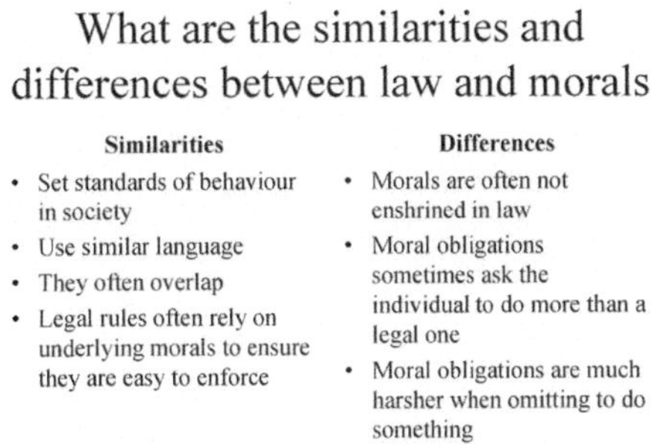

Figure 2.9. Linkages and divergencies between law and morality.

Source: Stella Dawson via Slide Player.

Nevertheless, the perceptions and experiences of the law may rise questions about its role in a supposedly moral life (Fluss & Zeegers, 1990; Fortin, 1991; Gelman, 1994; Glass & Speyer-Ofenberg, 1996; Glick, 1992; Gormally, 2002). For example, during apartheid and Jim Crow obedience to the law meant accepting unequal treatment and violation of the rights of others based on their race or ethnicity. For some, these were unjust laws because they violated their own personal ethics of justice and acceptance. Others argued that the laws during apartheid and Jim Crow were invalidated by their arbitrary nature. This latter group sidestepped the discussions about personal morality.

Unsurprisingly, contextual matters are important when determining what is lawful or moral (Rich, 1997; Rivard, 1992; Robertson, 1996, 1999; Savulescu, 1994; Schneider, 1992; Schuck, 1994; Sevelin, 2019). For instance, it would be a brave person to argue for atheism during the days of religious intolerance. Currently, most people regard the law as being systematized. However, justice is less systematic and may comprise a chaotic mass of moral principles that are self-contradictory and often irrational. Moralists always run into trouble when critics ask for consistency in the application of the principles that they claim to hold so dear. Others speak of hypocrisies that allow the well-connected elite to excuse themselves from the laws that they impose on others. Meanwhile positive law is perceived as a code of rules (Walters, 2012; Waymack, 1991; Weithman, 1999;

Whitaker & Edwards, 1990; White, 1990; Wicclair, 1991a, b). These rules may correspond to a code of moral laws. Such laws derive their authority from the obligatory nature of moral laws. Some of these laws may be just or unjust but they are considered necessary for the moral wellbeing of the populace. The decision on whether a law is unjust and just is therefore a function of subjective perceptions of whether the law agrees with the moral values of the perceiver. For example, the pedophile may perceive the law as being oppressive since they consider certain minors capable of consent.

Meanwhile, the law will continue to operate regardless of these views which may be considered socially deviant (Merrick, 1990; Morreim, 1991; Munzer, 1994; Nelson, 1994; Nobles, 2012; O'Donovan & Gilbar, 2003; Oberman, 1992; Okin, 1990). Those who break the law are liable to punishment regardless of whether they consider the laws just or unjust. It is why, for example, political dissidents are often convicted of treason when they critique entrenched governments. It is not considered yet a legitimate defense to express moral disagreements with the charge sheet for such cases and indeed convictions take place with the resultant punishment being meted out.

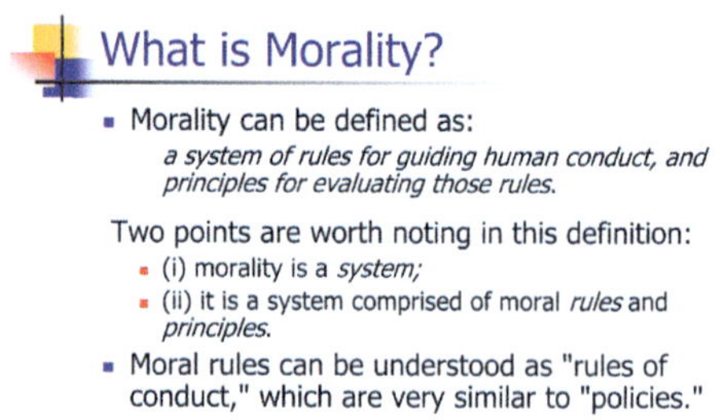

Figure 2.10. Conceptualizing morality.

Source: "Dan" via Slide Serve.

In any case the question of what morality is (*see* Figure 2.10) can be complicated through subjectivity and misconceptions. Indeed, the notion that just laws are the ones that one morally agrees with has been found to be scientifically inadequate (Glass & Speyer-Ofenberg, 1996; Glick, 1992; Gormally, 2002; Gostin, 1995; Greenberg & Kamin, 1993; Grondelski, 1989). This is the same criticism that has been levelled at other popular misconceptions in public discourses as well as in existing literature. As jurists and scientists, many practitioners have necessarily abandoned this view of morality and justice. The idea that the only just laws are the ones which are in agreement with one's personal morals is faulty because it goes against the tenets of positive law (Ravven, 2016; Raymond, 1999; Resnik, 1997; Rich, 1997; Rivard, 1992; Robertson, 1996, 1999; Savulescu, 1994). Indeed, one of the strengths of positive law is that it does not rest on the capricious morals of individual members of a community. Nevertheless, there is some validity to the notion that laws typically reflect the morality of the society that constructs them. For example, common notions of justice may influence the legislative process. However, once the laws are enacted it becomes more difficult to subject them to arbitrary moralities.

Additionally, there will be no further appeal on positive laws beyond the highest courts in a jurisdiction (Somerville, 1989; Spurr, 1993; Stacy, 1994; Stauch, 2000; Stein, 1998; Steinbock & McClamrock, 1994; Strauss, 1992). For instance, it would not make sense to suggest that the law will be adjudicated by God. For the lay person, there is a process that confounds any links between morality and law because it is abstracted into a set of rules that must be obeyed lest the members of the community face sanction. These objections do not even touch on questions about the probity of those who claim to determine what is moral and immoral in the law.

The examples of theocracies like Iran have demonstrated the dangers of linking morality to the law. This is because of the subjectivity of the notion of morality (Schuck, 1994; Sevelin, 2019; Shanley, 1990; Sharpe & Pellegrino, 1997; Sheldon & Wilkinson, 1997, 1998; Shepherd, 1995). Some of the traditions and norms that are referenced when determining morality are obsolete or speak to values that are no longer relevant. This is particularly important for those communities that may not adhere to the mainstream understanding of morality. For instance, there may be certain minorities that are ostracized by the mainstream of society. Where the morality of the mainstream is imposed, it can lead to further deprivations against vulnerable minorities.

CHAPTER 2 SUMMARY

This chapter has sought to distinguish analytical jurisprudence from legal formalism. The chapter has developed a working definition of legal formalism. It has introduced the contrasts between formalism and natural law. We have seen the work of David Hume and its influence on the development of jurisprudence. The chapter also explored the controversial relationships that may exist or not exist between law, power, and morality. The next chapter considers the role of language in the development of the law.

CHAPTER 3

Language and the Law in Development

Contents

This chapter considers how language can impact on the development of analytical jurisprudence. The discussion begins with the linguistic turn. This then leads us to an exploration of British idealism as a philosophical stance. The chapter will highlight the effects of logical holism on the law. We then consider the possibilities and limitations of an ideal language philosophy in the law. The chapter will conclude with the implications of ordinary language philosophy. Overall, this chapter aims to demonstrate the possibilities of a sophisticated use of language to advance analytical jurisprudence. The linguistic turn is a good starting point to this discussion.

3.1. THE LINGUISTIC TURN

During the first part of the 20th century, the linguistic turn emerged as one of the most important developments in Western philosophy (Singleton Jr, 1989; Skene & Parker, 2002; Somerville, 1989; Spurr, 1993; Stacy, 1994; Stauch, 2000; Stein, 1998). Its most crucial characteristic was the focusing of philosophy and clarifying its relationships with the other arms of humanities. For instance, the linguistic turn explored the relationships that exist between the users of language, the language itself, and the world in which they exist. In the present day, the linguistic turn has been associated with thesis-antithesis model (*see* Figure 3.1).

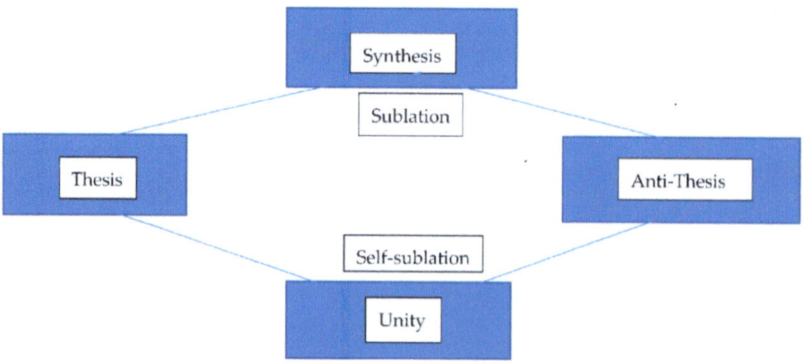

Figure 3.1. Development of knowledge from thesis and antithesis through synthesis and unity.

Source: Claviez (2019).

There have been different intellectual movements that have been associated with the linguistic turn (Morreim, 1991; Munzer, 1994; Nelson, 1994; Nobles, 2012; O'Donovan & Gilbar, 2003; Oberman, 1992; Okin, 1990; Oster, 2021). For example, the term linguistic turn was popularized by Richard Rorty in his anthology titled "*The linguistic turn*" which was published in 1967. The central thesis of the work was the turn towards linguistic philosophy. Later, Rorty would associate himself with analytic philosophy generally and linguistic philosophy specifically. However, the true origins of the phrase are from Gustav Bergmann who was a notable philosopher.

The associations with analytic philosophy have attracted research and practice interest (Andrews, 1996; Arinta et al., 2021; Ayres et al., 1993; Bekrycht & Mańko, 2020; Bianchi, 2017; Blair & Kaserman, 1991). From the traditional perspective, the linguistic turn has been associated with the birth of analytic philosophy. For example, it was the linguistic tur that increased interest and research focus on the philosophy of language as well as its logic. Additionally, it has been associated with the acknowledgment of the cleavage that exists between ordinary language philosophy and ideal language philosophy.

Frege was one of the philosophers who was associated with these developments (Kamisar, 1993; Kamm, 2001; Kass & Lund, 1996; Kaveny, 1991, 2006; Khushf, 1994; Knoppers & LeBris, 1991). Michael Dummett has suggested that the first recorded reference to the linguistic turn was in "*The foundations of arithmetic,*" a book by Gottlob Frege and published in 1884. The specific reference is where Frege is exploring the identity of a numerical proposition. This was designed to answer a Kantian question about numbers.

The question was: "*How are numbers given to us, granted that we have no idea or intuition of them?*" To respond, Frege relies on the context principle. This had been stated at the start of the book. The overall principle is that propositions only have meaning in a specific context (Kaveny, 2006; Khushf, 1994; Knoppers & LeBris, 1991; Kozłowski, 2021; Lane & Grodin, 1997; Mathieu, 1992; May, 1999). Bearing in mind such a supposition, we can find a solution to queries about a sense of a proposition which includes a number word.

Researchers have characterized this as an epistemological and ontological problem (Gormally, 2002; Gostin, 1995; Greenberg & Kamin, 1993; Grondelski, 1989; Hamblin & Somerville, 1991; Hardwig, 1991). The solution to it has traditionally been found among the idealists. However, the emergence of the linguistic turn meant that this problem could now be reasonably resolved by linguistics and its philosophy. One of the key figures in these developments are Russell and Wittgenstein. They expressed a concern for the logic of propositions as well as their relationship to facts.

A case in point was the work titled "*On denoting*" which was published by Bertrand Russell. This work played an important role in the beginning of logical atomism (Crouch & Elliott, 1999; Daniels & Sabin, 1997; Den Hartogh, 1997; Downie, 1992; Downie & Randall, 1997; Draper, 1993). Ludwig Wittgenstein was an associate of Russell and contributed to the emergence of the linguistic turn. The treatise was explored in "*Tractatus Logico-Philosophicus*." This work explored some of the philosophical issues that could arise when there is a misunderstanding of the logic underpinning language. Later, these points were emphasized in Wittgenstein's remarks on language games.

There is something of a departure from the common tenets of analytic philosophy that can be detected in the later works of Wittgenstein (Blustein, 1993; Bonnicksen, 1995; Bradley, 1993; Braithwaite, 1991; Brock, 1991, 1995, 1999; Brody, 1998; Cantor, 2005). Others have argued that his later work has significant affinity with post-structuralism. Nevertheless, other contributors expanded our understanding of the linguistic turn. Examples include Quine and Kripke. For example, W.V.O. Quine has described the historical continuity of the linguistic turn when considering an earlier philosophy. This was in his work titled "*Two Dogmas of Empiricism*." According to this work, mean is an outcome of essence when divorced from the object of reference whilst being wedded to a word.

Saul Kripke was a later philosopher in the 20th century who wrote "*Naming and necessity*." That work drew metaphysical conclusions from the close analysis of language. Similar developments were taking place in what came to be known as continental philosophy (Finer, 1991; Fluss & Zeegers, 1990; Fortin, 1991; Gelman, 1994; Glass & Speyer-Ofenberg, 1996; Glick, 1992). This was a form of structuralism which had decisive effects on the development of the linguistic turn within the wider family of humanities. One of the leading exponents of this type of philosophy was Ferdinand de Saussure. The core text for his treatise was "*Cours de linguistique Générale*" which was posthumously published in 1916.

According to Saussure, language comprises a system of symbolic rites which can be systematically studied (Finer, 1991; Fluss & Zeegers, 1990; Fortin, 1991; Gelman, 1994; Glass & Speyer-Ofenberg, 1996; Glick, 1992). These systems are comparable to writing systems which are used by specific communities such as those with hearing difficulties. Language comprises representational symbols that are organized according to specific and discernible patterns. Moreover, Saussure posited a new science known as semiology. This effectively meant the study of signs. Later the science was acknowledged as semiotics (Lane & Grodin, 1997; Mathieu, 1992; May, 1999; McConnell, 1991; McCoy, 1992; Meisel, 1992, 1996; Menzel, 1992). This was a new development to existing notions of language and science. For example, at the dawn of the 20th century, etymology was the prevailing concern of linguistics. This comprises an historical analysis which was also referenced as diachronic analysis. The process involved tracing the history of the meanings that are associated with individual words.

It could be argued that Saussure was an innovator that went against the grain (Schneider, 1992; Schuck, 1994; Sevelin, 2019; Shanley, 1990; Sharpe & Pellegrino, 1997; Sheldon & Wilkinson, 1997, 1998). For example, he was a notable critic of the comparative philologists that had held sway in the 19th century. One of those criticisms was the exclusive focus on Indo-European languages and yet coming up with conclusions that were not rooted. During that period, there was a belief that language would become the fourth natural kingdom.

The approach to language that was adopted by Saussure involved examining the present functioning of language (Brock, 1999; Brody, 1998; Cantor, 2005; Capron, 1990, 1999; Chandler, 1990; Chervenak & McCullough, 1991; Chesterman, 1998). This would be a synchronic analysis which involved a relational approach. That involved considering the system of relations that exist between words as sources of meaning. According to Saussure, the synchronic is the static side of the science of linguistics. This is different from the diachronic which focused on evolution. Some have borrowed these notions when considering the third linguistic turn (*see* Figure 3.2).

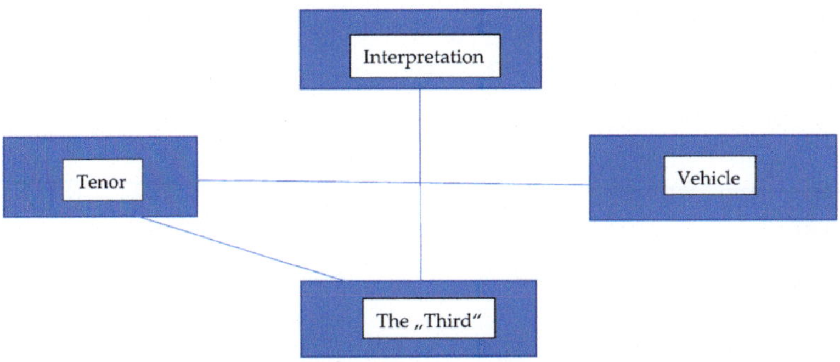

Figure 3.2. Tenor, interpretation, vehicle, and the "third" in the linguistic turn.

Source: Claviez (2019).

In comparing a range of languages, Saussure found that there is no fixed bond between that which is signified and that which signifies (Bonnicksen, 1995; Bradley, 1993; Braithwaite, 1991; Brock, 1991, 1995, 1999; Brody, 1998; Cantor, 2005). For instance, there is no fixed bond between "dress" and "attire." There are no natural forces that dictate any spontaneous expressions of reality. Additionally, Saussure showed the grammatical consequences of a phonetic evolution. This was achieved by illustrating the ways in which diachronic facts appear in different forms. For instance, attire might appear as a scarf-attire, glove-attire, blouse-attire, etc.

Moreover, Saussure posited that conceptual definitions cannot exist independently of a linguistic system (Hill, 1991b; Hope & Fulford, 1994; Hylton, 1990; Kadish, 1992; Kahn, 1991; Kalb, 1990; Kamisar, 1993; Kamm, 2001; Kass & Lund, 1996). This system is defined through focusing on differences. Hence, it is argued that a concept of something may not exist without being named. There can be no differences between our perceptions and meanings structure. To that end, it is argued that real attire does not exist when manipulating symbolic systems.

Any concept cannot be truly recognized until it is differentiated from everything else (Hill, 1990, 1991a, b; Hope & Fulford, 1994; Hylton, 1990; Kadish, 1992; Kahn, 1991; Kalb, 1990; Kamisar, 1993). Using the example of attire, we cannot fully understand what it is until we can say that it is not a vehicle or furniture. Objects and concepts are a collection of characteristics which have been defined in specific ways. All these layers of definition and meaning are located within the overall structure of a symbolic system of language. It is argued that the differences between meanings are instrumental in structuring our perceptions. Hence, for instance, there is no real attire unless we are manipulating symbolic systems. Humans are not able to recognize objects and concepts without also recognizing the differences they have with everyone else.

One of the first outcomes of the linguistic turn suggested by Saussure was the birth of structuralism (Arinta et al., 2021; Ayres et al., 1993; Bekrycht & Mańko, 2020; Bianchi, 2017; Blair & Kaserman, 1991; Blustein, 1993). Later, this turned into poststructuralism based on the ideas of Friedrich Nietzsche. Some of the most influential poststructuralists include Luce Irigaray, Judith Butler, Michel Foucault, Gilles Deleuze, Jacques Derrida, and Julia Kristeva. These poststructuralists were interested in the power of language. Key examples include Hayden White's exploration of certain metahistorical tropes that occurred in historical discourse.

The various philosophical movements that have existed in time have created an impression that language constitutes a form of reality (Abrams, 1996; Agich & Spielman, 1997; Allen, 1990, 1992; Alward, 2002; Amaraskekara & Bagaric, 2004; Anderson, 1993). This is a position that has been critiqued for being counterintuitive and not consistent with much of Western traditional philosophy. Derrida referred to the metaphysical core of Western thought when writing about the traditional views of language. In that perspective, words functioned as labels that could be attached to concepts. Hence, for instance, there is real attire which exists in an external reality which roughly corresponds with a concept that is born and processed within human thought. The linguistic word "attire" refers to this reality. The issue of reality is one which is explored in British idealism.

3.2. LEARNING FROM BRITISH IDEALISM

British idealism emerged as a subject of absolute idealism (McCoy, 1992; Meisel, 1992, 1996; Menzel, 1992; Merrick, 1990; Morreim, 1991; Munzer, 1994; Nelson, 1994). This philosophical movement was influential in the middle of the 19th century within Great Britain. Indeed, British idealism persisted right up to the middle of the 20th century. Some of the leading figures in this movement include Bradley (1846–1924), Green (1836–1882), and Bosanquet (1848–1923). A second generation of philosophers in this movement includes Collingwood (1889–1943), Taylor (1869–1945), Joachim (1868–1938), Roman Ingarden (1893–1970), and McTaggart (1866–1925).

The last significant event in British idealism was the work of Mure (Stein, 1998; Steinbock & McClamrock, 1994; Strauss, 1992; Stroud, 1996; Sullivan & Goldzwig, 1995; Sulmasy, 1989; TÄNnsjÖ, 1992). Having explored the basic tenets of the Mure doctrines, two Cambridge philosophers decided to start a new philosophical movement. This was known as analytic philosophy. The two pioneers were Bertrand Russell and G. E. Moore. Their collective work and that of their disciples has remained important in the development of analytical jurisprudence.

It could be argued that the 20th century was an important decade for much of the philosophy that is applied regularly (Steinbock & McClamrock, 1994; Strauss, 1992; Stroud, 1996; Sullivan & Goldzwig, 1995; Sulmasy, 1989; TÄNnsjÖ, 1992). Such an assertion holds true regardless of the specific discipline that is being examined. Figure 3.3 highlights some of the key philosophical movements of the 20th century.

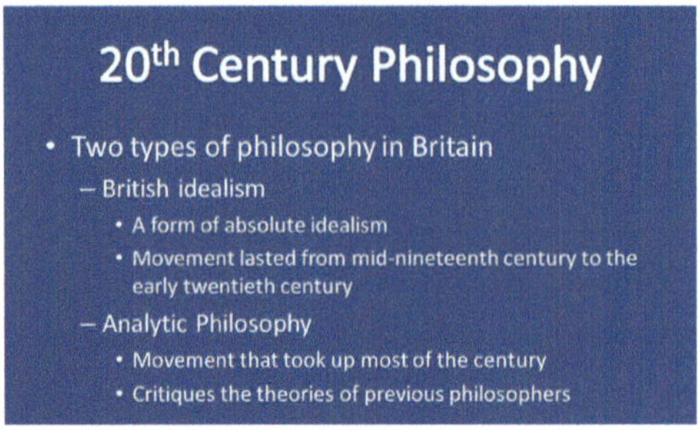

Figure 3.3. Two philosophies in 20th century Britain.

Source: April Stanley (2016) via Slide Player.

One of the marked characteristics of British idealism was the presence of broad tendencies (Hardwig, 1991; Harris, 2003; Harris & Holm, 2002; Harvey & Chadwick, 1992; Hasnas, 1995; Hill, 1990, 1991a, b). For example, there was a belief in an absolute truth which possessed a single and all-encompassing reality. This formed some sense of an inclusive and coherent system of ideas. British idealism as also marked by the assignment of a high place to reason. This was because reason was perceived to be a faculty by which the absolute structure can be grasped. Additionally, reason was assumed to be the structure of truth itself. British idealism refused to accept any dichotomy between an object and thought.

Another important characteristic of British idealism is the conceptualization of a reality that comprises a thought and object combination in a strongly coherent unit (Blustein, 1993; Bonnicksen, 1995; Bradley, 1993; Braithwaite, 1991; Brock, 1991, 1995, 1999; Brody, 1998). Moreover, it is acknowledged that British idealism emanates from the German counterpart which included philosophers such as Hegel and Kant. Writers like Green have characterized the relationships between German and British idealism as a salvation for the latter following the perceived demise of empiricism.

One of the key voices in bringing German idealism to English philosophers was Thomas Carlyle (Sullivan & Goldzwig, 1995; Sulmasy, 1989; TÄNnsjÖ, 1992; Thomson, 1999; Truog et al., 1991; Turrina et al., 2021; van Delden & Laurie, 2004). Addressing an English-speaking world, Carlyle has been credited with fostering British idealism. Others suggest that this was a reaction to the works presented by the likes of Henry Sidgwick, John Stuart Mill, David Hume, and John Locke. Apparently, all these voices were either utilitarian or empiricist in their philosophies. These form part of the philosophies of science and language (*see* Figure 3.4).

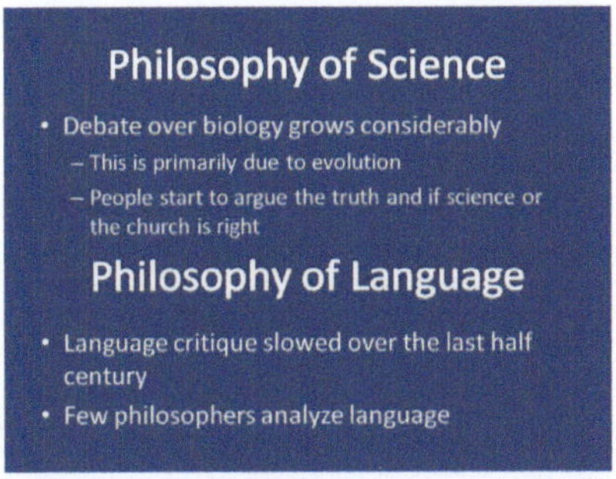

Figure 3.4. Philosophies of science and language.

Source: April Stanley (2016) via Slide Player.

Notably, Hegel influenced the emergence of British idealism (Ayres et al., 1993; Bekrycht & Mańko, 2020; Bianchi, 2017; Blair & Kaserman, 1991; Blustein, 1993; Bonnicksen, 1995). Certainly, this happened in terms of a broad outline of philosophies. Indeed, there is evidence to suggest that British idealism had adopted some of the doctrines and terminology that had been used by Hegel. Some of the examples include the notion of the absolute as well as the doctrine of internal relations.

Hegel also contributed the notion of a coherent theory of truth as well as that of conceptualizing a concrete universal reality (Ayres et al., 1993; Bekrycht & Mańko, 2020; Bianchi, 2017; Blair & Kaserman, 1991; Blustein, 1993; Bonnicksen, 1995). Certain researchers have identified a form of dialectical structure that has been inherited by British idealists from Hegel. A classic case in point are the writings of Bradley. Nevertheless, it is notable that only a few British idealists adopted Hegel's philosophy in all its fullness. Certainly, some only adopted the parts that were logically consistent with their own philosophical leanings.

Whereas Hegel wrote extensively on logic, it seems that British idealists simply ignored his ideas on this point (van Delden & Laurie, 2004; Van Der Burg, 1997; Van der Burg & Brom, 2000; van Schooten, 2014; Viljoen, 2012; Walters, 1991). Nevertheless, there were writer such as Mure who were considered deep students of Hegel especially with regards to the central ontological thesis that had been posited by Hegel. Yet, British idealists extended beyond philosophical boundaries and were involved in policy debates that could potentially have a significant impact on society.

From a political standpoint, the British idealists refuted what they considered the atomistic and brittle forms of individualism that were prevalent at the time (Steinbock & McClamrock, 1994; Strauss, 1992; Stroud, 1996;

Sullivan & Goldzwig, 1995; Sulmasy, 1989; TÄNnsjÖ, 1992). One of the philosophers or writers that was strongly critiqued by the British idealists was Herbert Spencer. To the British idealists, humans are fundamentally social in their manner and being. However, Spencer and his followers had failed to adequately recognize the sociability of human existence which could be construed as a direct attack on the notions of strict individuality.

Hegel had notably reified the state in his writings (Shewmon, 1997; Shultz, 1990; Singleton Jr, 1989; Skene & Parker, 2002; Somerville, 1989; Spurr, 1993; Stacy, 1994). British idealists did not accept this position. For instance, Green spoke of the individual as the locus of value. He further posited that the state and its existence could only justified to the extent that it contributed to the realization of value the lives of individuals. These were ides that could potentially transform the ways in which policy was conceived and executed.

The change of heart on the part of Bertrand Russell and GE Moore was fatal to the prospects of British idealism (Stroud, 1996; Sullivan & Goldzwig, 1995; Sulmasy, 1989; TÄNnsjÖ, 1992; Thomson, 1999; Truog et al., 1991; Turrina et al., 2021). Certainly, this was the case in the United Kingdom which had provided the base for British idealism. Moore eventually delivered conclusive and decisive arguments against British idealism. In 1958, Mure published "*Retreat from truth*" which included criticisms of Wittgenstein and Russell. The criticism extended to analytic philosophy from an idealist lens. The influence of British idealism in the USA was limited in many ways (Hardwig, 1991; Harris, 2003; Harris & Holm, 2002; Harvey & Chadwick, 1992; Hasnas, 1995; Hill, 1990, 1991a, b). For example, some have argued that the early thought of Josiah Royce had some resemblance to what neo-Hegelian thought might have looked like. The same can be said of Royce's less illustrious contemporaries. Brand Blanshard was a rationalist from the American branch who was influenced by Green, Bosanquet, and Bradley.

This limited influence of British idealism in the USA eventually disappeared in the latter part of the 20th century (Downie & Randall, 1997; Draper, 1993; Dresser, 1995, 2003; Dworkin, 1991, 1992; Dyck, 1992; Eisenstat, 1991). Nevertheless, it is notable that during the 1990s there was something of a revival of interest in British idealism. A case in point is the foundation of the Michael Oakeshott Association. Similarly, many scholars revisited the writings of Bosanquet, Green, and Collingwood which had been hitherto neglected. This type of evolution and transition is experienced elsewhere. A case in point are the effects of logical holism.

3.3. EFFECTS OF LOGICAL HOLISM

Logical holism is a philosophical positioning based on the belief that the world operations in ways that require that the entire whole is known before knowing the individual constituent parts (Glick, 1992; Gormally, 2002; Gostin, 1995; Greenberg & Kamin, 1993; Grondelski, 1989; Hamblin & Somerville, 1991). Theoretical holism is part of a philosophy of science which posits that knowledge can only be understood in its entirety. The pioneer for theoretical holism is Pierre Duhem. It is notable that there is a range of scientific theories that are accessed through making them commensurable.

This is achieved by allowing statements in one theory to be converted into sentences in another (Chesterman, 1998; Clark, 2002; Clerkin, 2021; Coady, 2002; Cohen, 1989; Coughlan, 1989; Crigger, 1995; Crossley, 1993). This is understood to be a process of making theories commensurable. According to Richard Rorty, the incompatibility between theories necessitates a process of hermeneutics. Martin Heidegger includes practical holism in his work which posits that it is impossible to produce a complete understanding of one's experiences of reality. This is because our existence must necessarily embed within our cultural practice. This constrains the tasks of understanding our experiences fully.

Other writers have explored the conceptualization of "*meaning holism*" (Okin, 1990; Oster, 2021; Paliwala, 2016; Paris & Poorman, 1995; Pellegrino & Sharpe, 1989; Ploughman, 1995). This is a term that is applied to the different views that applied to meaning. For instance, there is an assumption that the words of a language are interdependent. The interconnections between and among the different ways in which words are used is one of the appeals of meaning holism. However, this notion of holism can be contradictory and controversial when closely examined. For example, some argue that the meanings of individual words are stable and shared for the most part. These discussions of language philosophy are not merely limited to abstract. As Figure 3.5 shows, philosophy can impact on societal dynamics such as production (Shultz, 1990; Singleton Jr, 1989; Skene & Parker, 2002; Somerville, 1989; Spurr, 1993; Stacy, 1994; Stauch, 2000). Similarly, the use of language in areas such as meaning holism can impact on the ways in which the law is conceived and interpreted. Certainly, an understanding of language is of the essence for all those who operate in any legal system. A critical examination of meaning holism is therefore part of the debates which can lead to important policy adjustments.

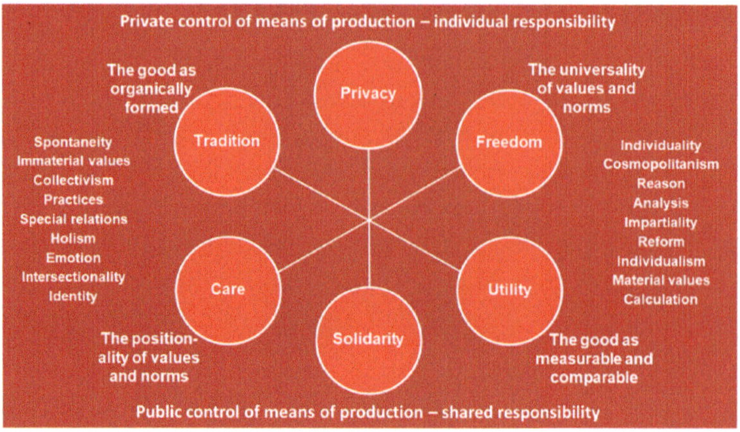

Figure 3.5. How philosophical positioning impacts on control of production?

Source: Matti (2022).

Several arguments have emerged to support or critique meaning holism (Amaraskekara & Bagaric, 2004; Anderson, 1993; Andrews, 1996; Arinta et al., 2021; Ayres et al., 1993; Bekrycht & Mańko, 2020). When we use the words meaning holism, for example, the implication is that meanings of words are neither stable nor independent. Rather, they share a network of similarities and associations. Some writers have suggested that the opposite of meaning holism is atomism which suggests that the meaning of each word is separate from the meanings of other words.

Another contrasting perspective is that of molecularism in which the meanings of certain words are tied to a specific subset of the language (Clark, 2002; Clerkin, 2021; Coady, 2002; Cohen, 1989; Coughlan, 1989; Crigger, 1995; Crossley, 1993; Crouch & Elliott, 1999). It is argued that the cognitive meaning of statements in an empirical language is reflected in the total logical relationships that exist with all the other statements that exist in that language. Such understandings can be constructed through culture. Figure 3.6 shows a case in point how learning engineering is constructed in Indian culture.

The interdependence that has been associated with meaning holism is considered an indicator that the usage of a word is tied to its meaning (Whitaker & Edwards, 1990; White, 1990; Wicclair, 1991a, b; Wildes, 1997; Wilson, 1994; Woliver, 1990). The use in this case can be tied to several factors. For example, it might comprise the beliefs that could be expressed using those words. It could also relate to all the inferences that are involved when utilizing the word. This has created a dichotomy of belief-focused and inference-focused characterizations. Indeed, holism suggests that these ways can be interchangeable. It is often easier to treat them as interchangeable unless their distinction is contextually important. The challenges in meaning holism have raised the possibilities of resolving them through an ideal language philosophy.

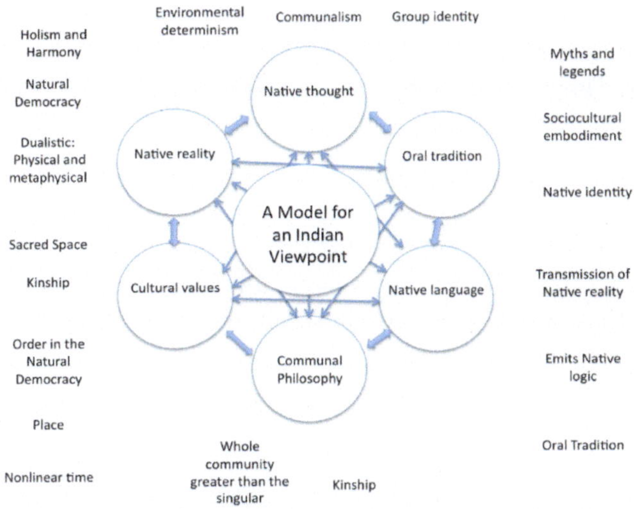

Figure 3.6. Example of an Indian perspective on learning engineering.

Source: Foster et al. (2014) via Semantic Scholar.

3.4. IDEAL LANGUAGE PHILOSOPHY

Ideal language philosophy is contrasted with ordinary language philosophy in existing literature (Fluss & Zeegers, 1990; Fortin, 1991; Gelman, 1994; Glass & Speyer-Ofenberg, 1996; Glick, 1992; Gormally, 2002). Between 1910 and 1930, analytic philosophers (e.g., Bertrand Russell and Ludwig Wittgenstein) emphasized creating an ideal language. This would be useful for philosophical analysis. Indeed, this was the type of language philosophy that would be free from the ambiguities of natural language.

The critics of natural language often argued that it was susceptible to philosophical error (Van Der Burg, 1997; Van der Burg & Brom, 2000; van Schooten, 2014; Viljoen, 2012; Walters, 1991, 2012). Hence, Russell and Wittgenstein sought to understand language and its philosophical problems. This goal could be achieved by using formal logic to formalize the way in which philosophical statements are made. To that end, Wittgenstein developed a comprehensive system of logical atomism in 1921 using his publication titled "*Tractatus Logico-Philosophicus*."

According to Wittgenstein, the universe is the totality of facts rather than being a totality of things (Thomson, 1999; Truog et al., 1991; Turrina et al., 2021; van Delden & Laurie, 2004; Van Der Burg, 1997; Van der Burg & Brom, 2000). These are actual states of affairs. Moreover, these states of affairs can be expressed by the language of first-order predicate logic. To that end, a picture of the universe can be construed by means of expressing atomic facts. This is done in the form of atomic propositions. A further step is linking them using logical operators.

According to many researchers, Wittgenstein's Tractatus was composed as an elaborate work of philosophical irony or "nonsense" (Fortin, 1991; Gelman, 1994; Glass & Speyer-Ofenberg, 1996; Glick, 1992; Gormally, 2002; Gostin, 1995). Those who support this view argue that Wittgenstein was demonstrating how such a way of thinking is absurd. Nevertheless, his work remains important in the emergence of philosophy. It also in certain disciplines such as the law because it encourages practitioners to think about the logic of their expression.

Ordinary Language philosophy is sometimes referred to as 'Oxford' philosophy (Grondelski, 1989; Hamblin & Somerville, 1991; Hardwig, 1991; Harris, 2003; Harris & Holm, 2002; Harvey & Chadwick, 1992). This is a kind of 'linguistic' philosophy. Alternatively, linguistic philosophy may be characterized as the view that a focus on language. Such a focus is crucial to the content and method of the discipline of philosophy in its entirety. Philosophy is also distinguished from the philosophy of language in this way. Linguistic philosophy includes both Ordinary Language philosophy and Logical Positivism. This area of study was developed by the Vienna Circle of philosophers.

There are many outputs from ordinary language philosophy including the development of translation theory (*see* Figure 3.7). These two schools are inextricably linked historically and theoretically in existing literature (Wicclair, 1991a, b; Wildes, 1997; Wilson, 1994; Woliver, 1990; Wyld & Cappel, 1990; Yamada, 2019). Indeed, this conclusion is one of the keys to understanding Ordinary Language philosophy. It also helps in understanding the relationship it bears to Logical Positivism. The idea of philosophies that are interlinked is inescapable in these circumstances.

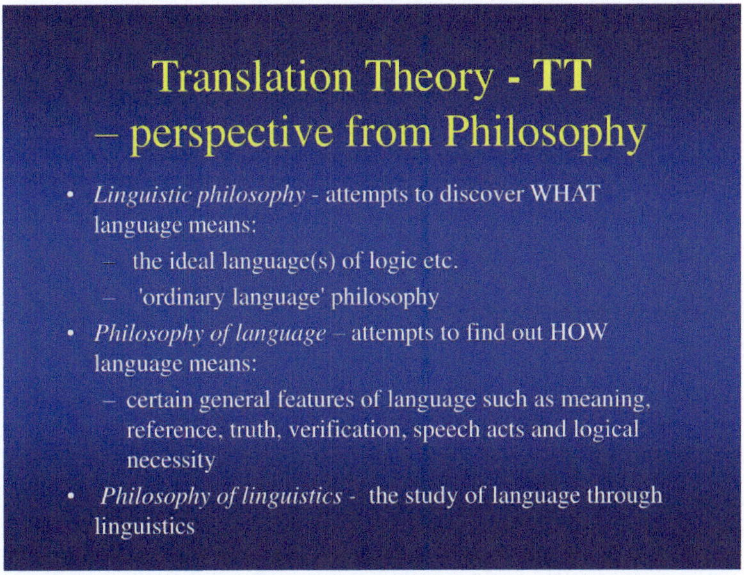

Figure 3.7. Translation theory from a philosophical perspective.

Source: "Leo" via Slide Serve.

It is notable that Ordinary Language philosophy and Logical Positivism share the conviction that philosophical problems are 'linguistic' problems (Van der Burg & Brom, 2000; van Schooten, 2014; Viljoen, 2012; Walters, 1991, 2012; Waymack, 1991; Weithman, 1999). Additionally, both logical positivism and ordinary language philosophies posit that the method proper to philosophy is 'linguistic analysis.' Nevertheless, they posit significantly different ideas as to what such analysis amounts to as well as answering questions as what the aims of carrying it out are. An ideal language is also known as philosophical or a priori language. It comprises any constructed language that is built up out of first principles.

A case in point of ideal language or language philosophy is logical language (Lane & Grodin, 1997; Mathieu, 1992; May, 1999; McConnell, 1991; McCoy, 1992; Meisel, 1992, 1996; Menzel, 1992). Such languages are contrasted with ordinary or spoken languages which are known as natural languages. Natural languages (e.g., French, English, Japanese, Cantonese, Urdu, Patois, Shona, Luganda, etc.) have within them a great deal of fuzziness. These languages may also experience overlap as well as vagueness. The idea is that ideal language will address some of these gaps and challenges of natural language. There will several challenges that make ordinary language less suitable for the philosophical purposes that are envisaged by ideal language (Greenberg & Kamin, 1993; Grondelski, 1989; Hamblin & Somerville, 1991; Hardwig, 1991; Harris, 2003; Harris & Holm, 2002). One of those problems is ambiguity which can lead to the emergence of multiple meanings. Natural language also suffers from indeterminacy of meaning for words and phrases. That means that it has been associated with unclarity as well as inherent contradictions.

Natural language faces challenges in clarifying the difference between intension and extension of terms (May, 1999; McConnell, 1991; McCoy, 1992; Meisel, 1992, 1996; Menzel, 1992; Merrick, 1990; Morreim, 1991). Some experts have suggested that this is not necessarily a defect of natural languages. Rather, they posit that it may constitute a strength of natural language. Nevertheless, the implication is that those who want clarity and precision of language will not be satisfied with natural or ordinary languages.

Similarly, natural language may not be useful for those who construct an ideal language to eliminate all the limitations described above (Rivard, 1992; Robertson, 1996, 1999; Savulescu, 1994; Schneider, 1992; Schuck, 1994; Sevelin, 2019; Shanley, 1990). An ideal language entails a stronger claim of absolute perfection. It may also claim a level and purity of truth that is transcendent or mystical truth. This is different from that truth that is based on pragmatic principles.

Natural languages have dominated discourses on language in recent times (Chandler, 1990; Chervenak & McCullough, 1991; Chesterman, 1998; Clark, 2002; Clerkin, 2021; Coady, 2002; Cohen, 1989). However, philosophical languages were popular in Early Modern times. This trend was partly motivated by the goal of recovering what was thought to be the lost Divine or Adamic language. Yet, there is still interest in philosophical languages particularly when determining processes of analysis in contemporary disciplines.

In a philosophical language, words are constructed from a limited set of morphemes (Coady, 2002; Cohen, 1989; Coughlan, 1989; Crigger, 1995; Crossley, 1993; Crouch & Elliott, 1999; Daniels & Sabin, 1997). These are then treated as "elemental" or fundamental. It is suggested that philosophical language resembles taxonomic language. The vocabularies of oligosynthetic languages are made of compound words. These words are coined from a small set of morphemes which is theoretically minimal. These discussions of these various languages can be incorporated into philosophical inquiry which serves different purposes (*see* Figure 3.8).

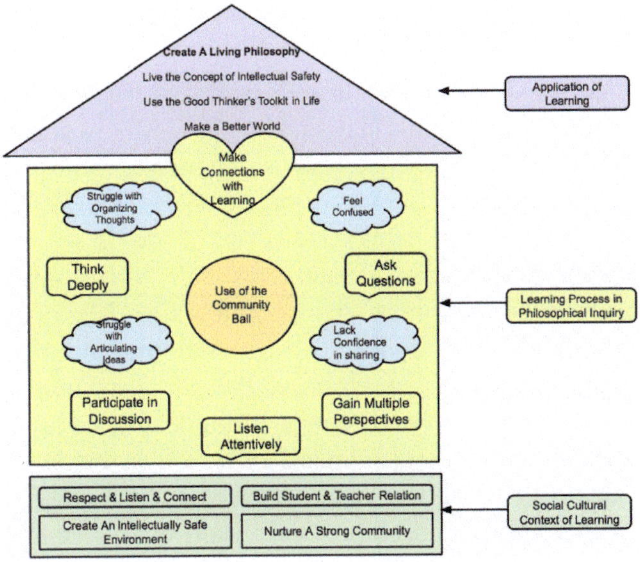

Figure 3.8. The role and function of philosophical inquiry.

Source: Lu Leng (2020) Front. Psychol. doi.org/10.3389/fpsyg.2020.00449.

Different languages may serve different purposes (Kozłowski, 2021; Lane & Grodin, 1997; Mathieu, 1992; May, 1999; McConnell, 1991; McCoy, 1992; Meisel, 1992). One of the examples is "Láadan" by Suzette Haden Elgin is designed to grammaticalize and lexicalize the concepts. In this case, the distinctions are important to women. Such an assumption is based on muted group theory. Another example is Toki Pona by Sonja Elen Kisa. This is based on minimalistic simplicity. It is also notable for incorporating elements of Taoism. Another important category of languages is the a priori languages. These are constructed languages where the vocabulary is invented directly as opposed to being derived from other existing languages. Yet, there is also an ordinary language philosophy which provides contrasts to the languages listed above.

3.5. ORDINARY LANGUAGE PHILOSOPHY

Ordinary Language philosophy is acknowledged to be associated with the later works of Ludwig Wittgenstein (Daniels & Sabin, 1997; Den Hartogh, 1997; Downie, 1992; Downie & Randall, 1997; Draper, 1993; Dresser, 1995). It is a category that is also associated with the work done by the philosophers of Oxford University between 1945 and 1970 (approximately). The origins of Ordinary Language philosophy go back to 1945. This was a time when work was done at Cambridge University. Nevertheless, a lot of literature suggests that ordinary language philosophy started as late 1929.

This is a period that coincided with the return of Wittgenstein, who had spent some time away from the Cambridge faculty. G. E. Moore was a great influence on the early development of ordinary language philosophy (Stauch, 2000; Stein, 1998; Steinbock & McClamrock, 1994; Strauss, 1992; Stroud, 1996; Sullivan & Goldzwig, 1995). However, Moore is not considered an ordinary Language philosopher himself. However, Moore initiated a focus on and interest in 'commonsense' views about reality. Major figures of Ordinary Language philosophy include Norman Malcolm, John Wisdom, J. L. Austin, Morris Lazerowitz, Alice Ambrose, P. F. Strawson, and Gilbert Ryle. Ordinary Language philosophical view was not developed as a unified theory based on existing literature (Sulmasy, 1989; TÄNnsjÖ, 1992; Thomson, 1999; Truog et al., 1991; Turrina et al., 2021; van Delden & Laurie, 2004). Neither was it an organized program when closely examined by the contemporary glaze of science. Moreover, 'Ordinary Language' philosophers did not refer to themselves as such. Indeed, this was originally a term of derision which was dismissively used by its detractors. Yet interest in this philosophy has survived many decades and is discussed in a range of disciplines including analytical jurisprudence.

Ordinary Language philosophy can be conceived as a historical movement (Eisenstat, 1991; Eldridge, 2021; Elhauge, 1994; Emanuel, 1999; Feinberg, 1991; Fentiman, 1989; Field, 1990, 1991). However, most experts agree that it is foremost a methodology. This specific methodology is committed to the close and careful study of the uses of the expressions of language. It is especially interested in the philosophy of the more problematic ones. Those that aspire to Ordinary Language philosophy must be committed to its approaches and principles.

The discipline of philosophy pays credence to Ordinary Language philosophy as a core component of its existence (Den Hartogh, 1997; Downie, 1992; Downie & Randall, 1997; Draper, 1993; Dresser, 1995, 2003; Dworkin, 1991). One of the advantages of Ordinary Language philosophy is its ability to unify different views despite their diversity. In Figure 3.9, it is contrasted with comparative language.

Ordinary Language philosophy explores the use of the expressions of language (Hope & Fulford, 1994; Hylton, 1990; Kadish, 1992; Kahn, 1991; Kalb, 1990; Kamisar, 1993; Kamm, 2001; Kass & Lund, 1996). However, this analysis is not limited to their use of expressions in and of themselves.

Hence, the focus is not on distinguishing ordinary from technical words. Moreover, this is not about a distinction based on the language used in various areas of discourse. The implication is that ordinary uses of language occur in all discourses. Here the expression may have both a lay and a scientific use. However, both uses may count as ordinary.

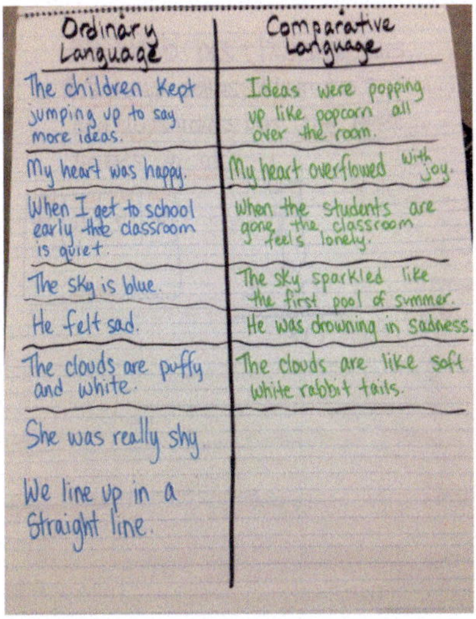

Figure 3.9. Ordinary and comparative language.

Source: Hillary Webb via Pinterest.

The caveat is that it must be quite clear which discourse is in play (Agich & Spielman, 1997; Allen, 1990, 1992; Alward, 2002; Amaraskekara & Bagaric, 2004; Anderson, 1993; Andrews, 1996). This implies clarity about which of the distinct uses of the expression is in play. Even though the various uses of expressions are connected, the difference in use of the expression in different discourses signals a difference in the sense with which it is used. This assertion is based on the Ordinary Language view as opposed to the everyday understanding of language.

Hence, one form of use of a word in a specific discipline may be distinct from its use in the lay sense (Hasnas, 1995; Hill, 1990, 1991a, b; Hope & Fulford, 1994; Hylton, 1990; Kadish, 1992; Kahn, 1991). A case in point is the use of the word "blank space" in terms of physics as well as in the lay sense. In the sense that is used in physics, the phrase "blank space" is synonymous with a vacuum. However, the lay sense is much more flexible in terms of referencing a room without visible objects or even a plot of land that does not have trees or constructed buildings.

The lay and technical uses of phrases in Ordinary Language serves differentiated, but nonetheless valid purposes (Knoppers & LeBris, 1991; Kozłowski, 2021; Lane & Grodin, 1997; Mathieu, 1992; May, 1999; McConnell, 1991; McCoy, 1992). The example of the phrase "empty space" is illustrative. Although the physics use of the phrase is more precise, it is not a replacement of the lay sense. For instance, when describing land without buildings it would be inappropriate to talk of a vacuum. Despite its apparent imprecision, the lay sense is quite adequate to the purposes it is used for. It would be inappropriate to exchange these uses.

It could therefore be argued that the bay way of understanding the *ordinary use of language* is to contrast it with non-ordinary or non-standard usage (Okin, 1990; Oster, 2021; Paliwala, 2016; Paris & Poorman, 1995; Pellegrino & Sharpe, 1989; Ploughman, 1995). Contrasting the ordinary use of language with its technical counterpart is not useful in these instances. Indeed, the ordinary usage of phases encompasses both lay and technical usage. The non-ordinary uses underpin many aspects of philosophical theorizing based on Ordinary Language dictates. This is particularly true if the theorizing creates meanings and perceptions that conflict with what might be ordinarily said of a situation in which the specific phrase is used.

Hence, an argument can be made that philosophical uses of language create philosophical problems that are then resolved through theorizing (Van Der Burg, 1997; Van der Burg & Brom, 2000; van Schooten, 2014; Viljoen, 2012; Walters, 1991, 2012). The emergence of this theorizing is mainly because the ordinary uses of language may miss these non-ordinary nuances by dismissing them as imprecision, inaccuracy, or approximations of the ordinary usage. Additionally, theorizing may arise when the ordinary use of language is considered a less precise use than the non-ordinary usage.

Theorizing helps to clarify this point by highlighting the fact that the non-ordinary use is distinct and worthy of differentiated analysis and theorizing (Van Der Burg, 1997; Van der Burg & Brom, 2000; van Schooten, 2014; Viljoen, 2012; Walters, 1991, 2012). In other words, the theorizing rejects the notion that the ordinary use of language is deficient in any way. Nevertheless, the Ordinary Language position is that non-ordinary uses of expressions simply introduce new uses of expressions. In some instances, the criterion for their use is provided. That means that there is no reason to rule them out. This is a very different debate from one about plain and complex language (*see* Figure 3.10).

Figure 3.10. Tips for plain writing.

Source: Write Girl.

In terms of methodology, using ordinary language is diametrically opposed to any philosophical project (Braithwaite, 1991; Brock, 1991, 1995, 1999; Brody, 1998; Cantor, 2005; Capron, 1990, 1999). One such project is the one started by logical atomists. This movement was later adopted by the logical positivists. The outcome of these explorations was an ideal language philosophy. The underpinning expectation was that the ideal language would be more precise than ordinary language when representing realities.

The emergence of ordinary language was in reaction to a series of views about ideal languages (Oberman, 1992; Okin, 1990; Oster, 2021; Paliwala, 2016; Paris & Poorman, 1995; Pellegrino & Sharpe, 1989; Ploughman, 1995). Specifically, there was interest in the so-called ideal language doctrine which had achieved its maturity during the era of logical positivism. Indeed, the ideal language doctrine perceives ordinary language as a barrier to seeing reality. This is because ordinary language was considered vague, opaque, and misleading hence necessitating its reform through an ideal language. All this reform was necessary to deliver philosophical truths.

CHAPTER 3 SUMMARY

This chapter has explored the role of language in philosophy which indirectly or even directly relates to the development of the law as a thinking profession. Some of the areas that have been covered in the chapter include the linguistic turn, British idealism, logical holism, ideal language, and ordinary language. The next chapter provides an overview of general jurisprudence which involves the application of some of the debates in this chapter.

CHAPTER 4

Overview of General Jurisprudence

Contents

This chapter considers the emergence and relevance of general jurisprudence. The chapter explores general, normative, empirical, and conceptual generations of the law. The chapter also considers the implications of legal generalizations. In many ways, this chapter established the means through which truth id defined, determined, and operationalized within the context of legal philosophy. The notion of conceptual generalization is an excellent starting point for this exploration.

4.1. CONCEPTUAL GENERALIZATIONS IN THE LAW

Generalization in argumentation is an important consideration when practicing law (Spurr, 1993; Stacy, 1994; Stauch, 2000; Stein, 1998; Steinbock & McClamrock, 1994; Strauss, 1992; Stroud, 1996). In these cases, the categories will emerge as linguistic generalizations of the form. For example, one might argue that "all men lie to their girlfriends." When listeners are evaluating this form, they will refer to the features of the category typologies. Hence, any prototype features will block the interpretation of features that are distinct within the category.

The effect of conceptual generalizations is to replace specific information with less specific information (Paliwala, 2016; Paris & Poorman, 1995; Pellegrino & Sharpe, 1989; Ploughman, 1995; Pogge, 1991; Purdy, 1990; Quante, 1999). When activates the category-protype, they ignore the category-instance. This could explain the differential persuasiveness of any generalization arguments. A radial prototype effect may emerge. This refers to a shift between instance and the prototype.

Another potential outcome is the halo evaluation effect (Spurr, 1993; Stacy, 1994; Stauch, 2000; Stein, 1998; Steinbock & McClamrock, 1994; Strauss, 1992; Stroud, 1996). This is also known as a bias towards the prototype. There is an implicit criticism of the problematic inference that members of a category share the same characteristics. In a court room, this can take the form of the assumption that certain types of witnesses (e.g., children, people who take alcohol, teenagers, old people, etc.), are unreliable or reliable witnesses without giving regard to the variability in the ways in which they belong to that category. For instance, someone who has taken one beer may have better recall than someone who has taken 15 beers.

Nevertheless, there are specific characteristics that will qualify or disqualify one in a focal category (Paliwala, 2016; Paris & Poorman, 1995; Pellegrino & Sharpe, 1989; Ploughman, 1995; Pogge, 1991; Purdy, 1990; Quante, 1999). It could therefore be argued that these characteristics will already have predetermined a threshold at which the differential aspects of membership no longer have as much importance as before. For instance, witnesses who are considered alcohol-intoxicated will have consumed a certain threshold of alcohol at which their testimony becomes unreliable even if someone that is more intoxicated is even more unreliable as a witness.

These contextually defined boundaries are important for setting the category and hence it may be a waste of time trying to focus on the minute differentials between those that are already in the category (May, 1999; McConnell, 1991; McCoy, 1992; Meisel, 1992, 1996; Menzel, 1992; Merrick, 1990; Morreim, 1991). As we have seen in the example above, even significant differences may no longer matter once the threshold has been achieved. If one was to ignore the minimum threshold for the category, then it is considered a category transgression. This type of rigor may have other applications including the legal research process (*see* Figure 4.1).

Figure 4.1. The key steps in legal research.

Source: I Edu Note.

The prototype in this case only exists above the boundary characteristics (Harvey & Chadwick, 1992; Hasnas, 1995; Hill, 1990, 1991a, b; Hope & Fulford, 1994; Hylton, 1990). A descriptive baseline may exist to allow a meaningful comparison. This is particularly true of cases where the audiences find that the argument's generalized version is as persuasive as the specific version. In normative terms, where the category-instance is below the boundary quantity then the corresponding argument is less persuasive than would be the case if the instances were above the category boundary.

The dependence on audiences to decide the veracity of categories and qualifications means that there is cultural, individual, and contextual diversity (Bradley, 1993; Braithwaite, 1991; Brock, 1991, 1995, 1999; Brody, 1998; Cantor, 2005; Capron, 1990). The same set of circumstances can be categorized differently depending on the context. A case in point is how the age of consent can vary significant and lead to catastrophic results for those that do not understand the restrictions in specific contexts. The USA is illustrative where the age of consent can be as high as 21 or as low as 16 depending on the state and the relative ages of the participants in a sexual encounter.

Since both effects depend on how audiences understand the category prototype, the effect size may differ across individuals, cultures, or contexts (Fehr, 1988; Horowitz & Turan, 2008; Hovland & Sherif, 1980; Martz, Strohmer, Fitzgerald, Daniel, & Arm, 2009). Even within a single judicial system within a seemingly homogenous society, there can be differences. Sweden is one such society and its judicial system highlights the relevance of diversities and a range of interpretations within the law.

The context within which jurisprudence is applied will significantly impact on how conceptual generalizations are operationalization (Gormally, 2002; Gostin, 1995; Greenberg & Kamin, 1993; Grondelski, 1989; Hamblin & Somerville, 1991; Hardwig, 1991). A case in point is Sweden which has faced the conundrum of harmonizing the work of professional and lay judges. This is because the Swedish courts have allowed this type of duality. Yet, regardless of whether they are professional or otherwise, these judges each have a single vote.

It is important to bear in mind the ways in which courts are comprised and structured when considering the relevance of conceptual generalizations (Wicclair, 1991a, b; Wildes, 1997; Wilson, 1994; Woliver, 1990; Wyld & Cappel, 1990; Yamada, 2019). Here, the Swedish case is instructive. The number of judges sitting in a court will be dependent on the purpose of the court, the level of the court within the judicial hierarchy, and the nature of the case at hand within the Swedish jurisdictions. On page 70 of the 1974 Swedish Code of Judicial Procedure, there are specific guidelines. A professional judge in Sweden is expected to have received a minimum standard of education, training, and experience in the field. These are requirements that are virtually universal regardless of the specific jurisdiction (Capron, 1999; Chandler, 1990; Chervenak & McCullough, 1991; Chesterman, 1998; Clark, 2002; Clerkin, 2021; Coady, 2002). Professional judges will have received instruction and experimented with different legal arguments before they are called to serve as jurists. The employment for life ensures security of tenure and theoretically guarantees impartiality. The lay judges in Sweden are much more unique because they come from diverse professional backgrounds. Each is appointed to serve a fixed term of four years.

In selecting these lay judges, there is an expectation of broad-based inclusion in areas such as political affiliations. This is a democratization and inclusion process that has sadly eluded many other jurisdictions (White, 1990; Wicclair, 1991a, b; Wildes, 1997; Wilson, 1994; Woliver, 1990; Wyld & Cappel, 1990). For example, in the USA the judges tend to reflect the political proclivities of those that have appointed them. Hence, seemingly sacrosanct issues such as the right to abortion are only protected by virtue of the political leanings of judges.

Despite the apparent de-professionalization of the judicial system, Sweden has maintained a central role for qualified and experienced judicial officers. The rationale for this pattern is based on an assumption that professional judges are better than lay people when it comes to overriding intuitive impulses or reactions to complex cases that would otherwise require deliberative thought (May, 1999; McConnell, 1991; McCoy, 1992; Meisel, 1992, 1996; Menzel, 1992; Merrick, 1990; Morreim, 1991). To that end, professional judges are better equipped to handle nuanced arguments that may escape a lay person. Indeed, some scholars have raised concerns that lay people in the judicial system may be easily dissuaded by emotion and intuition.

Interestingly, research has demonstrated a differential perception of the generalization argument when professional jurists are compared to lay people (Gelman, 1994; Glass & Speyer-Ofenberg, 1996; Glick, 1992; Gormally, 2002; Gostin, 1995; Greenberg & Kamin, 1993). Whenever one group is in the majority, then these differentials are crucial to the conduct and eventual outcome of the case. Because generalization is a key aspect of legal reasoning, this is an area that has attracted research and policy interest. One of the key texts for understanding generalization was "*Profiles, probabilities, and stereotypes*" by Frederick Schauer (2003). Even then there are mixed reviews concerning the extent to which such texts can finetune the arguments that are involved in conceptual generalization.

Traditionally, it has been assumed that generalization is an inescapable but undesirable aspect of legal thinking (Glass & Speyer-Ofenberg, 1996; Glick, 1992; Gormally, 2002; Gostin, 1995; Greenberg & Kamin, 1993; Grondelski, 1989). Therefore, jurists were presumed to always find ways of minimizing the effects of generalization. For example, there is an expectation that someone that has been convicted of a crime before is more likely to commit another crime or the same crime than someone who has never been convicted of that crime. However, the courts may not allow criminal history to form part of the prosecution because it could taint juries so that people are judged for sins of the past rather than the present accusation.

This then raises arguments about the extent to which generalization should inform policy, legislation, and even practice in the legal system (Paris & Poorman, 1995; Pellegrino & Sharpe, 1989; Ploughman, 1995; Pogge, 1991; Purdy, 1990; Quante, 1999; Rae & DeGiorgio, 1991). Many scholars argue that generalizations are based on an accumulation of facts and should therefore have some role to play in policy, practice, and legislation. However, there is disagreement about the exact nature and extent of the role that they ought to play. This is particularly concerning given the risk of discrimination and oppression if inaccurate generalizations are relied on to make judicial decisions. Such debates also have relevance for concept-based learning (*see* Figure 4.2) which may be utilized in legal education.

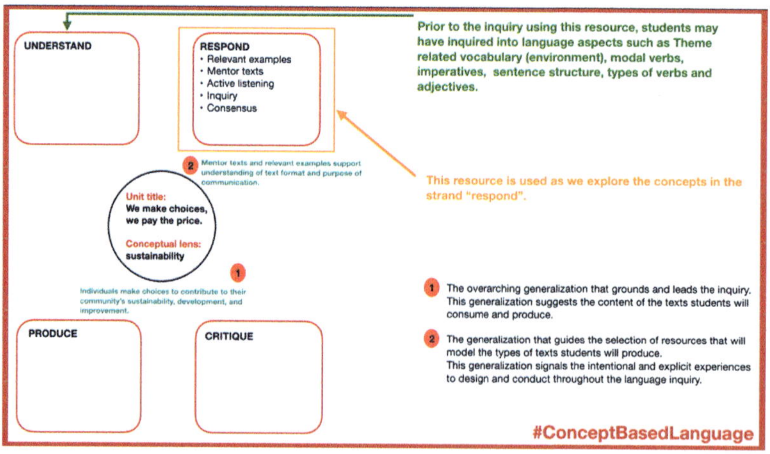

Figure 4.2. Example of concept-based learning.

Source: Rafangel via WordPress.

The potential for catastrophic mistakes based on conceptual generalizations has inspired many legal minds to rethink their reliance on these generalizations (Pellegrino & Sharpe, 1989; Ploughman, 1995; Pogge, 1991; Purdy, 1990; Quante, 1999; Rae & DeGiorgio, 1991; Ravven, 2016). As has been the case when there is prejudice in the judicial system, private biases (which may be conscious or unconscious) can be translated into practice and oppress those that are wrongly stereotyped. The racist tropes of the big black male thug and the frail innocent white woman had a lot to do with lynching during the Jim Crow era of American history.

According to Schauer, the way that lawyers use generalization is different from everyday usages and therefore has certain controls against prejudice. Yet, the justice system has often been used to oppress those that are already marginalized and stereotyped through unfair generalizations (Fluss & Zeegers, 1990; Fortin, 1991; Gelman, 1994; Glass & Speyer-Ofenberg, 1996; Glick, 1992; Gormally, 2002). Putting too much faith in lawyers to exercise discretion and moderation may be based on expectations and evidence that does not always apply in every case. Moreover, the jurists who have interacted with each other over a long period may be subject to bounded rationality that does not allow them to make radical decisions that go against the grain. We must also consider the possibility that generalizations are contextually tainted as is the case with normative generalizations in the law.

4.2. NORMATIVE GENERALIZATIONS IN THE LAW

There is a normative complex that the law seeks to control and subjugate under its own rules, principles, and values (Feinberg, 1991; Fentiman, 1989; Field, 1990, 1991; Figueira-Mcdonough, 1990; Finer, 1991; Fluss & Zeegers, 1990; Fortin, 1991). In theory, the generalization of the normative complex can be placed outside the political structures of a community and even the law. The rule of "*vectura*" is considered special enough to allow for the transportation of rules and norms to an existing legal system that sits within a wider political structure. This same approach has been used in economics (*see* Figure 4.3).

Underpinning the normative generalization is the notion of the law and its role in the factual regulation of a legal system (Spurr, 1993; Stacy, 1994; Stauch, 2000; Stein, 1998; Steinbock & McClamrock, 1994; Strauss, 1992; Stroud, 1996). Jurists and other officers of the court are mean to have a law concept that allows them to conceptualize and operationalize the norms and rules of the law as derived from the legal system. That means being able to differential a system of legal norms from the concept of the law as provided by justices and judges.

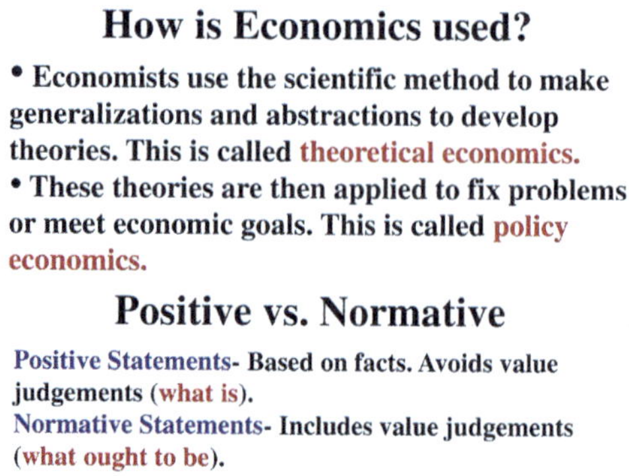

Figure 4.3. Contrasting positive and normative economics.

Source: Ada Shaw (2018) via Slide Player.

It is nearly impossible to reduce the complexity of the law into a group of rules of any specific system (Shewmon, 1997; Shultz, 1990; Singleton Jr, 1989; Skene & Parker, 2002; Somerville, 1989; Spurr, 1993; Stacy, 1994). The penalty for trying to do is vacuous voluntarism that is attributed to a political structure. Nevertheless, rules and norms in the legal system can only have veracity and value if they arise from a thesis about the law. The genesis of a system ought therefore not to be confused with the origins of law. For instance, the origins of law do not equate to the development of constitutional law which is a constituent power in the legal system.

It is also misleading to proclaim that there is only one correct and unique theoretical construction of law (Sheldon & Wilkinson, 1997, 1998; Shepherd, 1995; Shevory, 1990; Shewmon, 1997). Similarly, it is inappropriate to assume that only specific functionaries have the exclusive right and ability to give practical answers to a theory about the law. Typically, such roles are assigned to legal philosophers and theorists. Hence, the state may or may not be able to impose a determined idea. The implication is that correctness involves reducing rules to a single group that may be deemed a form of comprehension or theory.

Presenting a theory about law or dealing with the inherent contradictions of that theory is an onerous task (Okin, 1990; Oster, 2021; Paliwala, 2016; Paris & Poorman, 1995; Pellegrino & Sharpe, 1989; Ploughman, 1995; Pogge, 1991). Rather, some writers have opted to present a series of elements that can be estimated by jurists to interpret or understand the law. Such presentations include guidelines about what might comprise a conceptualization of the law. This involves special regard to the duties, roles, and responsibilities of judges.

Judges are expected to develop a comprehension of law to resolve cases that involve a conceptualization of the law (Downie, 1992; Downie & Randall, 1997; Draper, 1993; Dresser, 1995, 2003; Dworkin, 1991, 1992). Jurists require a notional minimum for ensuring that their judicial actions are undertaken with efficacy which is a combination of effectiveness and efficiency. One of the minimum standards is not confusing an understanding of rules and norms from the legal system with the law. Although a seemingly obvious consideration, it can be hard to operationalize.

First, it is important to recognize that norms and rules emanate from the law (Sulmasy, 1989; TÄNnsjÖ, 1992; Thomson, 1999; Truog et al., 1991; Turrina et al., 2021; van Delden & Laurie, 2004; Van Der Burg, 1997). However, the law does not emanate from rules and norms. A serious and effective jurist should have a concept of law outside the rules and norms of the judicial system under which they operate. The concept of law has many characteristics which have been variably covered by different authors in existing literature. One of the principal considerations in that discussion is that law comprises a special form of reasoning. It is also a technique or reasoning method.

The philosophy of science has already recognized its normativity (*see* Figure 4.4). Hence, knowledge of law does not imply complete ignorance of the norms, values, and rules that underpin the legal system (Stroud, 1996; Sullivan & Goldzwig, 1995; Sulmasy, 1989; TÄNnsjÖ, 1992; Thomson, 1999; Truog et al., 1991; Turrina et al., 2021). Rather have a concept of law is a form of esoteric knowledge that may distinguish the jurist from a lay person. Having a blueprint of what law is allows jurists to engage in legal reasoning. Moreover, it could be argued that law comprises a generalization of a series of normative complexes.

Using law as a technique yields certain results (e.g., judicial decisions) whilst paying heed to norms that have been developed in a political structure (Singleton Jr, 1989; Skene & Parker, 2002; Somerville, 1989; Spurr, 1993; Stacy, 1994; Stauch, 2000; Stein, 1998). Indeed, some writers suggest that these norms and rules require the political structure to become legal. The normative law results are fully integrated into a political structure to allow the judicial system to function as intended. The genesis of the judicial system corresponds to the rule of vectura which is a legal rule.

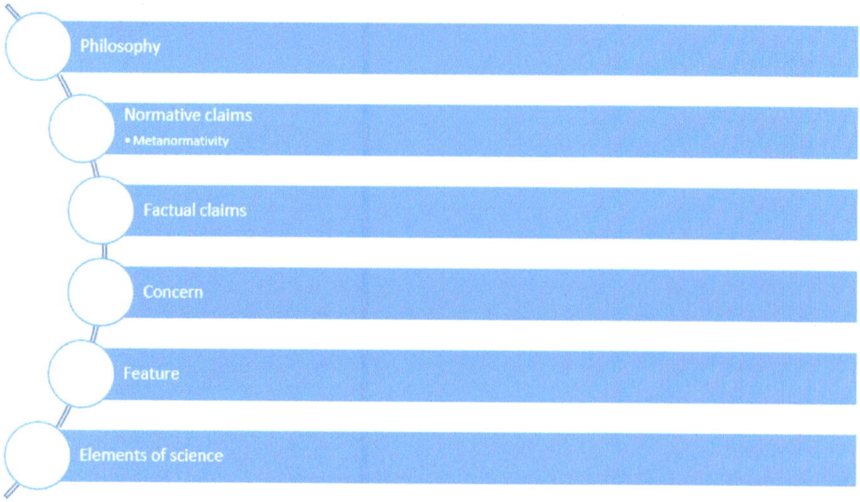

Figure 4.4. Normativity in the philosophy of science.

Source: Adopted from: Kaiser (2019) via Wiley Online.

That is a foundational rule that determines the other rules that are necessary when delimitating the legal system (Hamblin & Somerville, 1991; Hardwig, 1991; Harris, 2003; Harris & Holm, 2002; Harvey & Chadwick, 1992; Hasnas, 1995). The rules that are explored are necessary for the identification of the vectura norms. Additionally, there are unique presentations of legal validity that may not mirror a lay understanding of the law and these rules. Here, validity is based on techniques which imply law. These techniques involve the generalization of normative complexes.

4.3. EMPIRICAL GENERALIZATIONS IN THE LAW

Empirical generalizations are mainly used in marketing. However, some of the principles that underpin them may have relevance to analytical jurisprudence (Rivard, 1992; Robertson, 1996, 1999; Savulescu, 1994; Schneider, 1992; Schuck, 1994; Sevelin, 2019; Shanley, 1990). The start of modern marketing science during the 1960s including the strategic use of empirical generalizations. Figure 4.5 uses similar generalizations for price elasticity.

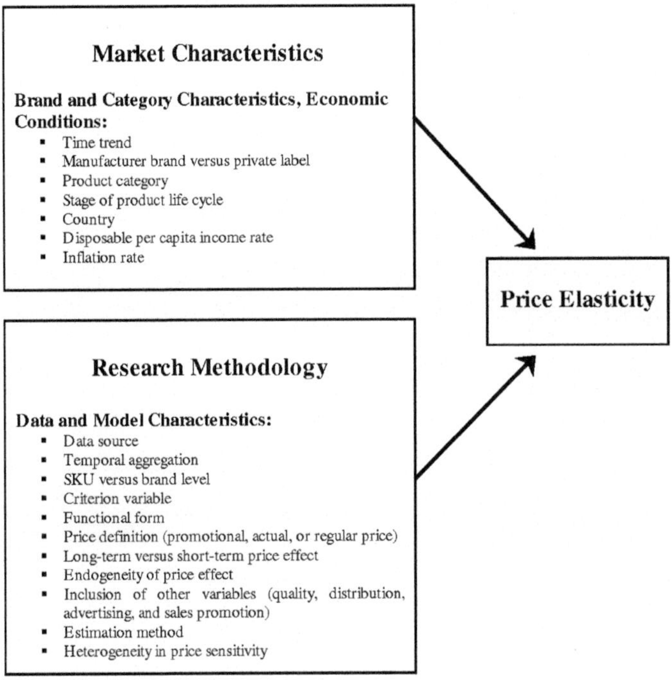

Figure 4.5. New empirical generalizations on the determinants of price elasticity.

Source: Bijmolt et al. (2005) via Semantic Scholar.

One of the key texts in this development was a book by Kristian Palda (1964) which focused on the econometric measurement of the effects of advertising on sales. Like law, marketing borrows from a range of disciplines including statistics, mathematics, economics, and psychology (Capron, 1990, 1999; Chandler, 1990; Chervenak & McCullough, 1991; Chesterman, 1998; Clark, 2002; Clerkin, 2021). A case in point is consumer choice modelling, structural modelling, and decision-making theories. This is a knowledge base that can assist decision-makers.

Jurists make decisions with significant implications for those that are affected by them (Raymond, 1999; Resnik, 1997; Rich, 1997; Rivard, 1992; Robertson, 1996, 1999; Savulescu, 1994; Schneider, 1992). Empirical generalizations rely on existing evidence which is then applied to current circumstances which may not have an exact replica of the circumstances under which the generalization was made. The vulnerabilities of decision-making reflect faulty evidence or faulty interpretations of that evidence. No matter how significant or substantial evidence is it may not be relevant to the current circumstances. Often, the disputes in a court session focus on the extent to which current circumstances can be distinguished from a precedent or empirical generalization that is established in practice (Kaveny, 2006; Khushf, 1994; Knoppers & LeBris, 1991; Kozłowski, 2021; Lane & Grodin, 1997; Mathieu, 1992; May, 1999). Judges may develop knowledge through experience which allows them to finetune their empirical generalizations in line with the facts of the case that they are currently resolving. These generalizations must have a scientific basis. Hence, the decision-maker can project certain likely outcomes based on actions or strategies that have been used before.

One of the areas where empirical generalizations may be appropriate is in deciding the level of sanction that can create a deterrent or punishment (Ayres et al., 1993; Bekrycht & Mańko, 2020; Bianchi, 2017; Blair & Kaserman, 1991; Blustein, 1993; Bonnicksen, 1995). Sentencing guidelines may have an aspect of empirical generalizations since they aggregate knowledge about the dictates of the law and the practical responses to those dictates. For instance, a certain crime may become prevalent and hence necessitate new forms of punishment to ensure that others are deterred from that type of crime.

Although the law has often been considered a qualitative experience, it does have significant quantitative aspects as well (Coady, 2002; Cohen, 1989; Coughlan, 1989; Crigger, 1995; Crossley, 1993; Crouch & Elliott, 1999; Daniels & Sabin, 1997). For example, there are formulas for calculating the seriousness of offending and the commensurate punishment. At the same time, there are qualitative issues such as the perceptions of the parties that are before the court and inferences that are made about their past, present, and future behavior.

Judicial officers who are better qualified and more experienced will already have a baseline of information that gives them a competitive advantage over lay people and less experienced or less qualified jurists (Wicclair, 1991b; Wildes, 1997; Wilson, 1994; Woliver, 1990; Wyld & Cappel, 1990; Yamada, 2019; Zohar, 1991; Zomerski, 2020). A lot of this information will have been gleaned from empirical generalizations. The knowledge is used to ensure efficacy in judicial decisions. Indeed, the review and appeals process are meant to guarantee that any mishaps are corrected before they can cause serious damage to public confidence in the judicial system. Research processes such as the one illustrated in Figure 4.6 will also rely on certain empirical generalizations to develop a theory surrounding the topic at hand. In some ways, lawyers and judges are researchers of the law who then apply it to specific cases (Bekrycht & Mańko, 2020; Bianchi, 2017; Blair & Kaserman, 1991; Blustein, 1993; Bonnicksen, 1995; Bradley, 1993). Some critics argue that knowledge alone is not sufficient to ensure the right judicial decisions. In fact, some of the pre-existing knowledge may be inadequate when addressing the complexities of the law. Hence, those who practice the law may rely on experience and a sense of judgement that allows them to arrive at the right decisions and then support them through logical reasoning.

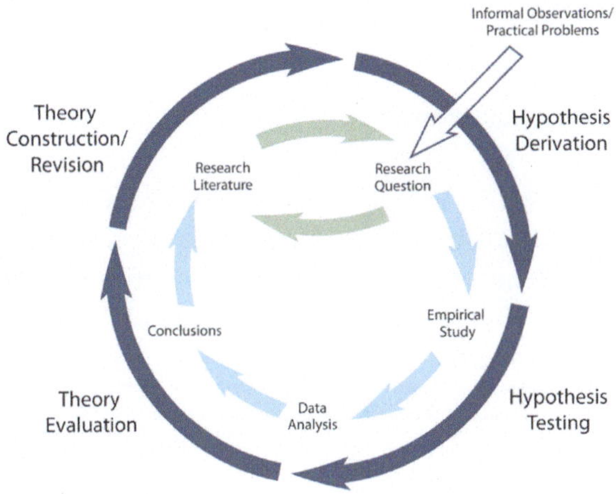

Figure 4.6. Using theories in psychological research.

Source: Lumen Learning.

The idea of experimentation might be suitable for research, but it is not entirely appropriate for judicial decisions that have long term and sometimes irreversible impacts on communities (Gormally, 2002; Gostin, 1995; Greenberg & Kamin, 1993; Grondelski, 1989; Hamblin & Somerville, 1991; Hardwig, 1991).

There may be competing interest groups such as community leaders, politicians, the media, and academics who may act as checks and balances on some of the worst excesses of judicial power. However, the legal system itself must develop means of exercising its own self-control and critiquing some of the empirical generalization that inevitably creeps into judicial decisions and practice. To that end, the application of conceptual generalizations in the law has emerged as a key point of interest.

4.4. APPLYING CONCEPTUAL GENERALIZATIONS IN THE LAW

The legal system may use conceptual generalizations as a form of abstraction (Blustein, 1993; Bonnicksen, 1995; Bradley, 1993; Braithwaite, 1991; Brock, 1991, 1995, 1999; Brody, 1998). In this case, there is an assumption that common properties of specific instances can be formulated in such a way as to develop general claims or concepts. Hence, those that rely on conceptual generalization posit that there is a set of elements that comprise a domain in which one or more characteristics are shared. The conceptual model is therefore created from the elements that share these characteristics.

Generalization forms a valid deductive inference which is relevant to science, mathematics, and logic (Singleton Jr, 1989; Skene & Parker, 2002; Somerville, 1989; Spurr, 1993; Stacy, 1994; Stauch, 2000; Stein, 1998). A process of verification is of the essence to determine the extent to which the generalization holds true in a range of circumstances. Another conceptualization of generalization involves identifying the various parts that make the whole. This allows the analyst to identify the parts that belong to the whole. Those parts that are unrelated to the whole are ignored in that specific instance.

Nevertheless, the parts that do not immediately belong to the whole may become part of the whole when they establish a common relationship with each other (Hamblin & Somerville, 1991; Hardwig, 1991; Harris, 2003; Harris & Holm, 2002; Harvey & Chadwick, 1992; Hasnas, 1995). A common relationship between all parts be first established before they can be considered part of a whole. However, that requirement should not imply that the parts are necessarily unrelated. Hence, parts may be related but without being part of a whole until a common relationship among them is established.

Generalization as a concept can have multidisciplinary and transdisciplinary application (Rivard, 1992; Robertson, 1996, 1999; Savulescu, 1994; Schneider, 1992; Schuck, 1994; Sevelin, 2019; Shanley, 1990). Typically, the disciplines that use the term are interconnected in some way. However, the term may have a more specialized and esoteric meaning within a specific context. For instance, the psychologists see generalization as a technical term. Similarly, education as a profession and discipline has utilized the term.

To demonstrate the meaning and understanding of generalization, the example of two or more concepts has been used in existing literature

(Capron, 1990, 1999; Chandler, 1990; Chervenak & McCullough, 1991; Chesterman, 1998; Clark, 2002; Clerkin, 2021). The starting point are two related concepts that for illustrative purposes are named as "A" and "B." Here, A is a generalization of B meaning that B is a special case of A. However, that relationship has some prerequisites without which it does not hold. First, every instance of B is also an instance of A. Secondly, there are instances of A which are not instances of B. Hence, the concept "*Friesian*" is a generalization of the concept "*Bovine*" because every Friesian is a bovine but not all bovines are Friesians.

Such a model can be transported to other fields based on its principles (Raymond, 1999; Resnik, 1997; Rich, 1997; Rivard, 1992; Robertson, 1996, 1999; Savulescu, 1994; Schneider, 1992). Figure 4.7 demonstrates automated generalization as a case in point. There is a link between specialization and generalization. In this case, specialization is also known as particularization. Such a relationship is reflected in the contrasting words "*hyponym*" and "*hypernym*." Here, the hypernym comprises generic strands of a group or class of items that are equally ranked. A case in point is how the term Bovine stands for equally ranked items such as Friesian, New Jersey, and Zebu.

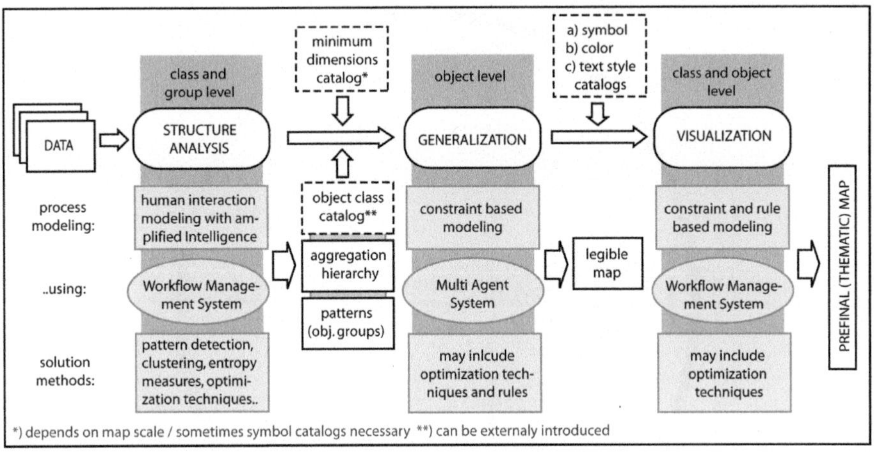

Figure 4.7. Example of a concept map for automated generalization.

Source: Steiniger & Weibel (2005) via Semantic Scholar.

In contrast, a hyponym has items that are included in the generic (Kaveny, 2006; Khushf, 1994; Knoppers & LeBris, 1991; Kozłowski, 2021; Lane & Grodin, 1997; Mathieu, 1992; May, 1999). For example, station wagon and sedan are included in vehicles. Ultimately, the hypernym is superordinate to the to the hyponym. At the same time, the hyponym is subordinate to the hypernym. When a human mind generalizes, it will extract the essence of a concept. This extraction is based on an analysis of the similarities that exist among different discrete objects. This results in a simplification that allows for higher level thinking.

Indeed, such higher-level thinking is essential to concept-based learning (*see* Figure 4.8). This is not a new concept or approach, regardless of how novel its definitions might seem (Ayres et al., 1993; Bekrycht & Mańko, 2020; Bianchi, 2017; Blair & Kaserman, 1991; Blustein, 1993; Bonnicksen, 1995). For example, cartography has historically utilized generalization for creating maps which are on a different scale from the actual figure that is being represented. Hence, one way to define cartography is a process of selecting and representing information. This is done on a map which involves some limitations in terms of scale. Therefore, the display must be adjusted to the scale of the map. It could be argued that maps are generalized to match the display criterion of where they are displayed. That approach is also used for small cartographic scale maps. Based on these relatively straightforward principles, generalization can be applied in specific disciplines such as the law.

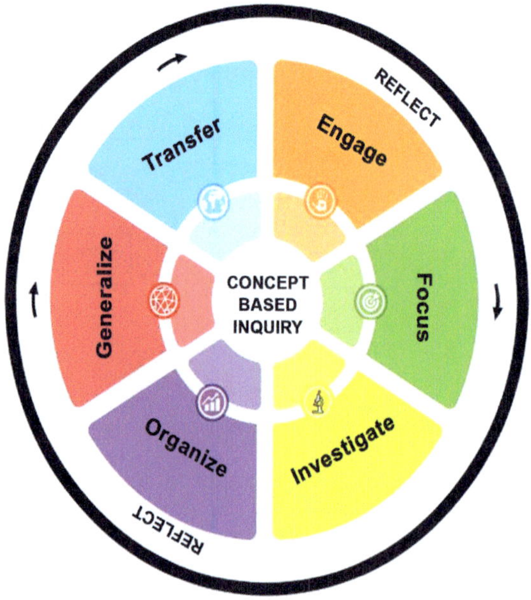

Figure 4.8. Overview of concept-based inquiry.

Source: Professional Learning International.

4.5. LEGAL GENERALIZATIONS AND THEIR EFFECTS

There is a universal law of generalization which has relevance to analytical jurisprudence (Coady, 2002; Cohen, 1989; Coughlan, 1989; Crigger, 1995; Crossley, 1993; Crouch & Elliott, 1999; Daniels & Sabin, 1997). When people have experienced similar circumstances with an objective, they can decipher similar objects or ones that share the characteristics to inform behavior. One of the famous examples of this phenomenon is how a bird uses a previous experience with a worm-like creature to determine whether a worm is edible.

Depending on the circumstances, generalized may be utilized in operational activities and considerations (Wicclair, 1991b; Wildes, 1997; Wilson, 1994; Woliver, 1990; Wyld & Cappel, 1990; Yamada, 2019; Zohar, 1991; Zomerski, 2020). For example, the evolution of litigation (*see* Figure 4.9 for a graphical illustration of this evolution) may reference and rely on generalization to make its assertions and practices. For this to happen, there must be some understanding of the universal law of generalization. This is based on a theory of cognition under which there is an assumption that the probability of a response to one stimulus being generalized to another is a function of the "distance" between the two stimuli. All this happens in a psychological space (Shepard 1987).

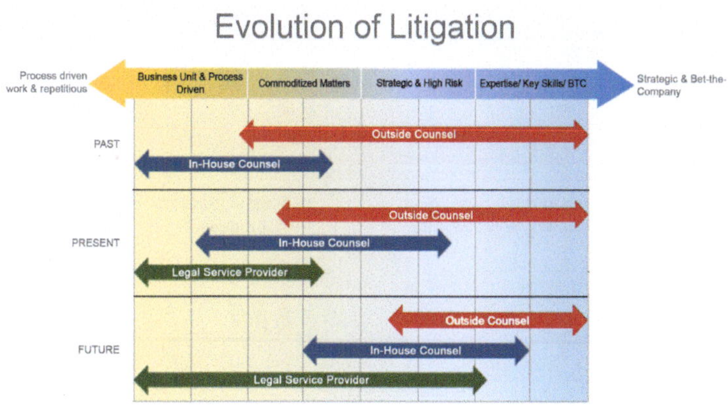

Figure 4.9. Evolution of litigation.

Source: Bill Hendeson via Legal Revolution.

The proponents of this universal law of generalization argue that the problem of generalization is fundamental to the development of learning theories (Bekrycht & Mańko, 2020; Bianchi, 2017; Blair & Kaserman, 1991; Blustein, 1993; Bonnicksen, 1995; Bradley, 1993). This is even more important bearing in mind the possibility that we rarely encounter identical situations. A theory of learning is therefore incomplete without developing a law that governs how what is learned in one situation can be generalized to another.

These generalizations do not necessarily lead to positive or helpful outcomes (Sulmasy, 1989; TÄNnsjÖ, 1992; Thomson, 1999; Truog et al., 1991; Turrina et al., 2021; van Delden & Laurie, 2004). In Figure 4.10, we see how generalization can transition into stereotypes. For some critics, stereotypes are a form of cognitive and intellectual laziness in which people and institutions will not bother to find out more about the nature of the object, subject, or environment they are facing. Instead, it seems easier to go back to a stereotype to undercut any serious considerations of what the new set may bring differently to the table than other similar situations in the past.

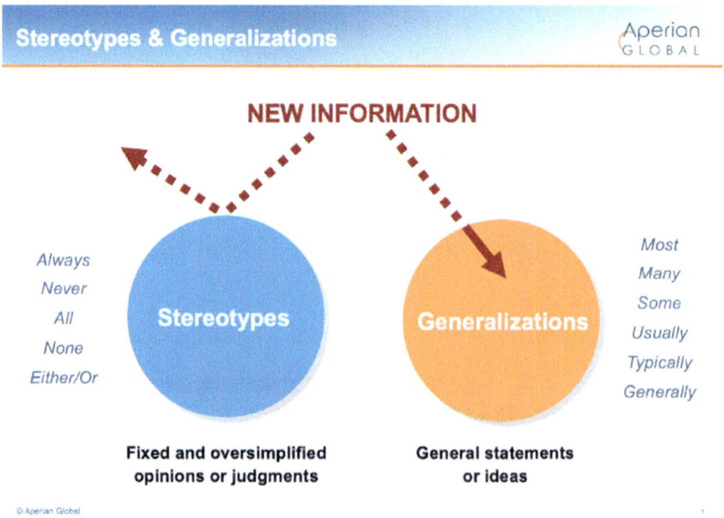

Figure 4.10. Linking generalizations to stereotypes.

Source: Aperian Global Smart.

There are conceptual and practical complexities that must be clarified before fully understanding the effect of legal generalizations (Gormally, 2002; Gostin, 1995; Greenberg & Kamin, 1993; Grondelski, 1989; Hamblin & Somerville, 1991; Hardwig, 1991). Those that engage with the justice system will appreciate the fact that generalizations can become a double-edged sword. On the one hand, they can facilitate the judicial process by ignoring some of the tedious processes involved in establishing facts and comparing them to precedents. On the other hand, generalization might mean that people are pre-judged regardless of their present circumstances.

As we have seen in previous chapter, this can have practical implications on pertinent issues such as the selection of a jury and even the veracity of jury trials (Blustein, 1993; Bonnicksen, 1995; Bradley, 1993; Braithwaite, 1991; Brock, 1991, 1995, 1999; Brody, 1998). Nevertheless, critics argue that those who treat generalization as if it were a bad thing fail to understand the humanity of all people that are involved in the judicial system. By not recognizing the frailties of humanity, one might fail to implement some of the controls that are in-built to ensure better outcomes.

We must also understand the processes and elements that are involved in legal generalizations (Dworkin, 1991, 1992; Dyck, 1992; Eisenstat, 1991; Eldridge, 2021; Elhauge, 1994; Emanuel, 1999; Feinberg, 1991). For example, the psychological space is an interesting concept that merits further exploration. This is defined as an established dimension comprising a set of stimuli that determine metric distances between the stimuli and the probability that a learned response to any stimulus will lead to the generalization of any other invariant. Such a process is also known as a monotonic function of the distance between stimuli and generalized response.

Significant experimentation has taken place among humans and non-humans to ascertain the nature and impact of generalizations (Sheldon & Wilkinson, 1997, 1998; Shepherd, 1995; Shevory, 1990; Shewmon, 1997). Writers like Shepard (1987) have hypothesized that the probability of generalization reduces exponentially with the distance measured by one of two specific metrics. This rule is then taken as being universal due to evolutionary internalization. Here the aim is to identify the generalization as well as its effects.

That does not mean that the universal law of generalization is taken at face value or universally accepted (Mathieu, 1992; May, 1999; McConnell, 1991; McCoy, 1992; Meisel, 1992, 1996; Menzel, 1992; Merrick, 1990). For example, Danie Ennis of the Phillip Morris Research center responded to Shepard in 1988 by questioning the relevance of the theory. To advance this counter-thesis, Ennis highlighted the work of Nosofsky which has created significant exemptions to the rule that had been promoted by Shepard. Nevertheless, Shepard responded to defend his work by distinguishing it from the work of Nosofsky. There are some distinctions in form and focus between Shephard and Nosofsky which could explain the divergence in terms of interpreting the rules of generalization (Lane & Grodin, 1997; Mathieu, 1992; May, 1999; McConnell, 1991; McCoy, 1992; Meisel, 1992, 1996; Menzel, 1992). For example, Shephard points out the fact that Nosofsky focused on specific and precise locations of the psychological space of an individual stimulus. Yet, Shephard experimented with the size, location, and shape of the region of the psychological space that corresponded with a set of stimuli. Shephard had posited that this space would have the same important consequences as a training stimulus. Despite these broad and narrow disagreements, other researchers have continued to explore the implications of generalization in their own field.

One of those researchers is Ken Cheng of the Macquarie University who experimented on the appearance of generalization among honeybees. His findings were then compared with similar research with birds and humans. Cheng gives the example of a bird that has found food in a container that is in one place. The problem arises when the animal is faced with a new container in a different location and must make a bet on whether they are likely to find food in that container so that it flies down to pick it up. The law would not work if the bird were not able to distinguish between the stimuli which are the differentially located food containers. Generalizations have continued to be applied to a range of spheres that reflect their complexities and limitations in each case.

CHAPTER 4 SUMMARY

This chapter has provided an overview of generalizations in jurisprudence. The typologies that are touched on include conceptual, normative, empirical, and legal generalizations. The overriding message from the chapter is that generalization is a trait that is common to animals including humans depending on the context. The fact that it is then transported to a specific discipline and profession such as the law is a testament to the diverse abilities of humans. At the micro level, generalization may contribute to the development of analytical jurisprudence. The next chapter considers the geopolitical dynamics of analytical jurisprudence as a specific context of application.

CHAPTER 5

Geopolitical Dynamics in the Law

Contents

This chapter explores the geopolitical dynamics of the law. It starts with an overview of human rights and religious law. Then it considers the impact of culture on legal interpretations. Two case studies of insolvency and copyright law provide insights into the application of these dynamics. The chapter closes by illustrating the limits and possibilities of commercial law which is geopolitically influenced in many ways. Overall, this chapter demonstrates the importance of location when interpreting the law. A good starting point for the discussion is the intersection of differences between human rights and religious law.

5.1. HUMAN RIGHTS AND RELIGIOUS LAW

Human rights have recently come into conflict with religious law because the latter is considered regressive (Morreim, 1991; Munzer, 1994; Nelson, 1994; Nobles, 2012; O'Donovan & Gilbar, 2003; Oberman, 1992; Okin, 1990; Oster, 2021). However, those who are interested in protecting religious freedom have turned religiosity into a human rights issue. Freedom of religion or belief is guaranteed by Article 18 of the Universal Declaration of Human Rights. It is also mentioned in Article 18 of the International Covenant on Civil and Political Rights. Religiosity and its impact have been considered in the Declaration on the Elimination of All Forms of Intolerance and of Discrimination Based on Religion or Belief.

The work of the mandate of the Special Rapporteur on the freedom of religion or belief has emerged as an important aspect of human rights legislation and practice (Hasnas, 1995; Hill, 1990, 1991a, b; Hope & Fulford, 1994; Hylton, 1990; Kadish, 1992; Kahn, 1991). This mandate is also guided by the relevant articles of the International Covenant on Economic, Social, and Cultural Rights. The emergence of the International Convention on the Elimination of All Forms of Racial Discrimination highlighted some of the ambiguities and challenges of mixing religiosity with pure human rights cultures across the globe.

Similarly, the Convention on the Rights of the Child has tried to protect children from being harmed based on the misguided notion of religious adherence (Eldridge, 2021; Elhauge, 1994; Emanuel, 1999; Feinberg, 1991; Fentiman, 1989; Field, 1990, 1991; Figueira-Mcdonough, 1990). The Convention on the Elimination of All Forms of Discrimination against Women highlighted the gendered nature of cultural interpretations that are so powerful in community life. Perhaps reflecting on the history of religious intolerance and persecution, the Convention against Torture and Other

Cruel, Inhuman or Degrading Treatment or Punishment makes it clear that human rights are universal and inalienable regardless of religious affiliation or otherwise.

New areas of human rights legislation are emerging, even without a specific stance towards protecting religious freedom (Khushf, 1994; Knoppers & LeBris, 1991; Kozłowski, 2021; Lane & Grodin, 1997; Mathieu, 1992; May, 1999; McConnell, 1991). Yet, duty-bearers and implementers often pay heed to the impact of these human rights issues on religious freedom. Examples of the emergent international law regime include the International Convention on the Protection of the Rights of All Migrant Workers and Members of Their Families. This legislation is specifically relevant to many industrialized nations that are increasingly hostile to migrants from the development. Additionally, the Convention on the Prevention and Punishment of the Crime of Genocide and the Convention relating to the Status of Refugees addresses some of the instances where religious intolerance can lead to the wholescale and forcible eviction of communities or sections of the community.

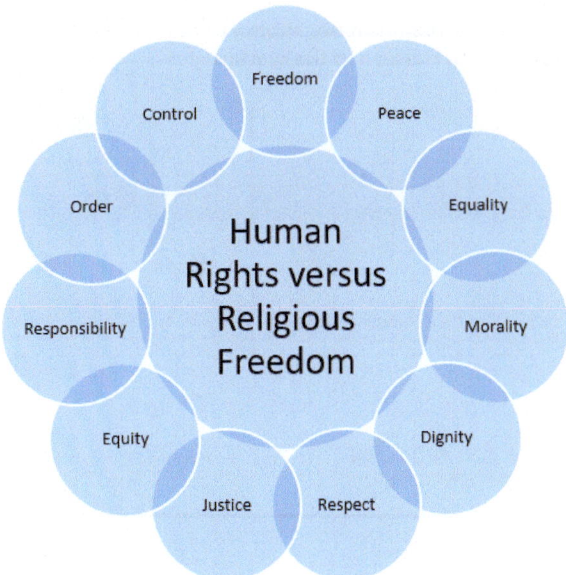

Figure 5.1. Key areas of debate around religious freedom and human rights.

Source: Adapted from: Islam City.

Ultimately, several areas of debate around human rights and religious freedom as demonstrated in Figure 5.1. These include equity, responsibility, freedom, and respect (Abrams, 1996; Agich & Spielman, 1997; Allen, 1990, 1992; Alward, 2002; Amaraskekara & Bagaric, 2004; Anderson, 1993). There are generalized mandates to respect religious and human rights by a range of bodies that are known as duty-bearers. For instance, many institutions are guided by relevant resolutions of the Human Rights Council as well as the General Assembly together with other organs of the United Nations.

On a practice level, there will be reference to relevant jurisprudence of the treaty bodies (Wicclair, 1991a, b; Wildes, 1997; Wilson, 1994; Woliver, 1990; Wyld & Cappel, 1990; Yamada, 2019). Certainly, those specializing in international law must be conversant with the provisions of international humanitarian law. The Special Rapporteur also takes into account relevant human rights instruments and jurisprudence at the regional level. This is done in reference to the extent to which human and religious freedom rights are respected within that context. The generation of appropriate reports acts as a form of control and supervision since the entities within the jurisdiction will not want a bad reputation for being a persistent human rights violator.

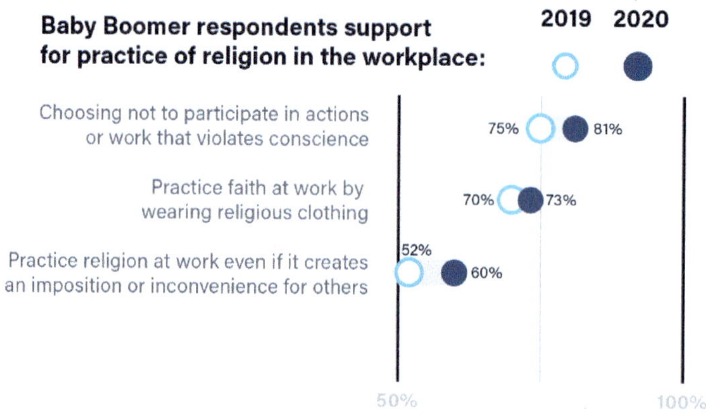

Figure 5.2. Support for religiosity in the workplace among Baby Boomers 2019–2020.

Source: Becket Law.

Freedom of religion or belief has many dimensions which can be complex and far-reaching (Kozłowski, 2021; Lane & Grodin, 1997; Mathieu, 1992; May, 1999; McConnell, 1991; McCoy, 1992; Meisel, 1992). Some of these dimensions intersect with other human rights. There is literature and documentation that points towards these relationships. A case in point is the "*Digest on freedom of religion or belief.*" The principles within this framework include the freedom to change, adopt, or renounce a belief or religion. That can be relevant to those people that are at risk of being put to death for "betraying" their religion by denouncing it or rejecting it (Figure 5.2).

The freedom of religion also entails being protected from being curtailed into joining any or all religions (Shultz, 1990; Singleton Jr, 1989; Skene & Parker, 2002; Somerville, 1989; Spurr, 1993; Stacy, 1994; Stauch, 2000). This rule is relevant to those people that are required to join cults or mainstream religious under the pain of violence or being shunned. In some areas, it is controversial to display any signs of religious affiliation and those who infringe on these conventions may even face violence. Others require the outward demonstration of religious adherence such as dressing in a certain way or speaking in a certain way.

This then raises questions about seemingly liberal democracies such as France which have banned wearing the Burqa as a sign of oppression (Turrina et al., 2021; van Delden & Laurie, 2004; Van Der Burg, 1997; Van der Burg & Brom, 2000; van Schooten, 2014; Viljoen, 2012). Critics may argue that this represents a form of hypocrisy and a sign of Western imperialism in which only their own forms of religion are given credence while other religions are oppressed. It also raises questions about where the boundaries lie between the role of the state and personal freedom when engaging with religious issues. Such debates are specifically relevant to appreciating the role of culture in interpreting law.

5.2. IMPACT OF CULTURE AND CONDITIONS ON INTERPRETATIONS OF THE LAW

Law and culture are often interchanged in discourses despite them being acknowledged as distinct entities (Dyck, 1992; Eisenstat, 1991; Eldridge, 2021; Elhauge, 1994; Emanuel, 1999; Feinberg, 1991; Fentiman, 1989). The law of the land may be a cultural reference for example. Some theorists have argued that this close relationships are based on the similarity of imposing certain rules and dictates on human behavior. The law can coerce human behavior in much the same way as a culture can. For example, incest is illegal and culturally unacceptable.

Nevertheless, it is important to acknowledge that the law and culture have distinctions and demarcations that should not be confused with each other (Merrick, 1990; Morreim, 1991; Munzer, 1994; Nelson, 1994;

Nobles, 2012; O'Donovan & Gilbar, 2003; (Oberman, 1992). If one takes, the example of inheritance law it is possible to understand how the law can conflict with culture. It could be the cultural norm that cross-gender inheritance is frowned upon. Yet, the law could make provisions that ensure the veracity and protection of cross-gender inheritance. Hence, the girl child can be an heir to their father's property.

The overall structures of culture and law as well as their intentions may be similar, but their inherent differences impact on the way that they are differentially enforced (Van Der Burg, 1997; Van der Burg & Brom, 2000; van Schooten, 2014; Viljoen, 2012; Walters, 1991, 2012). That does not mean that cultural enforcements cannot be as powerful as legal enforcement. For instance, cultural rejection may be so significant that it exceeds even the punishment in form of imprisonment which can be meted out by the state.

The fact that law and culture have enforcement mechanisms has implications for human behavior in specific contexts (Bianchi, 2017; Blair & Kaserman, 1991; Blustein, 1993; Bonnicksen, 1995; Bradley, 1993; Braithwaite, 1991; Brock, 1991). Law and culture control the environment and those actors within the environment. These two elements impact on our knowledge, thoughts, lives, and livelihood. We are socialized to anticipate rules and regulations because they are part of our lives and for fear of the consequences of non-compliance.

In these instances, rules can be defined as directives pertaining to acceptable and unacceptable human behavior (Andrews, 1996; Arinta et al., 2021; Ayres et al., 1993; Bekrycht & Mańko, 2020; Bianchi, 2017; Blair & Kaserman, 1991). These laws and cultural rules are enforced by other humans. The differences between law and culture include the identity of those that initiate the rules. The second difference relates to the underlying purpose and values of laws and culture. The third difference relates to the ways in which culture and laws are initiated, developed, expressed, and enforced. The fourth difference relates to the level of acceptance for culture and laws by the people and communities to whom they apply.

A cultural lens (such as the one demonstrated in Figure 5.3) is often used when analyzing the structures, institutions, and practices within the legal sector (Capron, 1990, 1999; Chandler, 1990; Chervenak & McCullough, 1991; Chesterman, 1998; Clark, 2002; Clerkin, 2021). For example, culture may impact on reactions to rules and regulations. This bears in mind that the subjects of law and culture differ in their personalities and experiences. Hence, it is possible for some to fully comply while others are happy to engage in deviance. There is an underlying assumption that people tend to follow rules that are consistent with their own values and are demonstrably for their own wellbeing.

Figure 5.3. A cultural perspective on law firms.

Source: Edge International (2016).

At the same time, people may follow rules because they create a better society for everyone else (Hill, 1991a, b; Hope & Fulford, 1994; Hylton, 1990; Kadish, 1992; Kahn, 1991; Kalb, 1990; Kamisar, 1993; Kamm, 2001). That is why, for example, many abled persons frown upon anyone abled using parking space that is designated for people with disabilities. The interplay between personal and community interests can be problematic, hence leading to ethical dilemmas when exploring the intersection between law and culture. Many people struggle with the notion of adhering to laws that they consider immoral or unjust.

In many instances, culture has been studied as part of the profiling of institutions and organizations (Schuck, 1994; Sevelin, 2019; Shanley, 1990; Sharpe & Pellegrino, 1997; Sheldon & Wilkinson, 1997, 1998; Shepherd, 1995). Figure 5.4 represents one such example. Nevertheless, the intersection and conflicts between law and culture have relevance that goes beyond the fate of institutions and organizations. For example, it can go to the nature of society and how it is organized. The interplay between law and culture does not just impact on its subjects but those who create the law. That is why a culturally insensitive legal regime can lead to civil disobedience. Yet a culturally relevant law may be followed even without having to resort to some of the more extreme forms of coercion. This interplay between law and culture can be experienced in areas of jurisprudence such insolvency law.

Figure 5.4. Elements of an organizational cultural profile.

Source: Barry Law Library.

5.3. A CASE OF GEOGRAPHICAL DIVERSITY IN INSOLVENCY LAW

There is significant diversity in terms of the ways that insolvency law is understood and operationalized (Oster, 2021; Paliwala, 2016; Paris & Poorman, 1995; Pellegrino & Sharpe, 1989; Ploughman, 1995; Pogge, 1991; Purdy, 1990). For example, some culture considers indebtedness to be immoral and exploitative. Hence, those that are unable to clear their debts are imprisoned as civil offenders. Others see insolvency as a necessary social intervention to prevent the financial system from exploiting the citizenry. These are the jurisdictions in which bankruptcy is not treated as a social failure.

At the heart of all bankruptcy is the inability to pay off one's debts (*see* Figure 5.5). There will be specific criterion for deeming an individual or enterprise bankrupt (Hylton, 1990; Kadish, 1992; Kahn, 1991; Kalb, 1990; Kamisar, 1993; Kamm, 2001; Kass & Lund, 1996; Kaveny, 1991). These criteria are meant to protect creditors from the machinations of unscrupulous borrowers with no intention of every repaying what they owe. The different priorities that are given to creditors can lead to significant wrangling as well as public distaste for the ways in which insolvency is handled (Blair & Kaserman, 1991; Blustein, 1993; Bonnicksen, 1995; Bradley, 1993; Braithwaite, 1991; Brock, 1991; Brock, 1995). The law seeks to minimize the scope and depth of the damage that is caused by this event. The applicant under bankruptcy law must undergo certain tests as well as commit to certain actions to ensure that the process is fair and legitimate. For instance, they may be banned from running a company for a specific period or even from holding public office in some instances. At other times, there is a requirement for the disclosure of assets under the pain of substantial imprisonment.

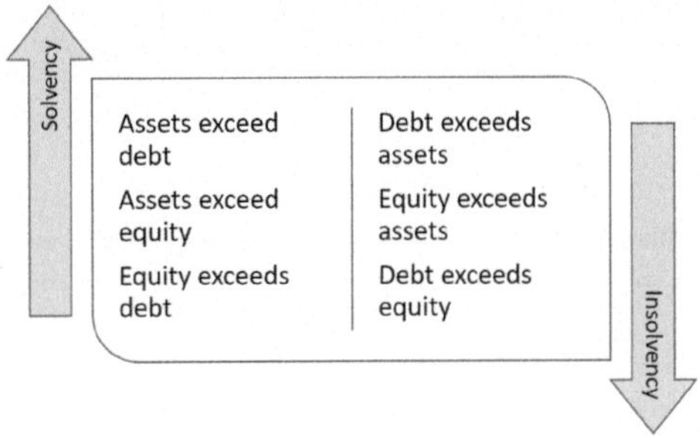

Figure 5.5. Key features of insolvency.

Source: Adapted from: Tax Guru.

Two core problems have emerged in the administration of insolvency cases (Meisel, 1996; Menzel, 1992; Merrick, 1990; Morreim, 1991; Munzer, 1994; Nelson, 1994; Nobles, 2012; O'Donovan & Gilbar, 2003). The first problem is determining the criterion under which an enterprise or person is deemed bankrupt. This is a precondition for the triggering and execution of insolvency law otherwise the entire system could be open to abuse. For instance, there are entrepreneurs that routinely exploit insolvency law to avoid paying their bills. Indeed, for some insolvency has become something of a business strategy.

The second problem is the priority that is granted to the various creditors who may all have an interest in getting paid first before everyone else (Hasnas, 1995; Hill, 1990, 1991a, b; Hope & Fulford, 1994; Hylton, 1990; Kadish, 1992; Kahn, 1991). The law will complement rules and regulations that determine the priority creditors when attempting to dispose of the bankruptcy. Moreover, there is an expectation that creditors have certain rights and responsibilities that will be protected throughout the process. The law is continuously revised to reflect new challenges and aspirations by the community. Moreover, the reform agenda seeks to address loopholes that may not become apparent until the law is being operationalized.

Countries like China have their own regimes which may not comply with international law. However, there is a consensus that a standard is necessary to ensure smooth management of bilateral business (Savulescu, 1994; Schneider, 1992; Schuck, 1994; Sevelin, 2019; Shanley, 1990; Sharpe & Pellegrino, 1997; Sheldon & Wilkinson, 1997). This is particularly relevant in an era where internet communications have rendered some of the old geographical barriers practically irrelevant. Some countries have approached these issues by trying to harmonize international and local law. Others have emphasized international law and made amendments to ensure that they are compliant. Then there are those countries that perceive any international standards as infringing on their own rights to self-determination.

The countries that are not engaging with international standards may suffer the consequences which are manifested through a lack of interest in doing business within jurisdictions that are seemingly lawless on issues of bankruptcy (Hill, 1991b; Hope & Fulford, 1994; Hylton, 1990; Kadish, 1992; Kahn, 1991; Kalb, 1990; Kamisar, 1993; Kamm, 2001; Kass & Lund, 1996). The big multinational corporations may influence legislation and government responses through their threats to abandon those territories without a robust insolvency law. Besides, local consumers may also be concerned that they are vulnerable to unscrupulous institutions if there is no clear insolvency law that can contribute to appropriate regulation.

The criterion for insolvency may trigger a voluntary or involuntary bankruptcy (Meisel, 1996; Menzel, 1992; Merrick, 1990; Morreim, 1991; Munzer, 1994; Nelson, 1994; Nobles, 2012; O'Donovan & Gilbar, 2003). Creditors can also apply for the insolvency where payment is not being made for goods and services or even loans, yet the borrower is not taking any reasonable steps to deal with the problem. Depending on the state, the specific circumstances that predetermine whether insolvency criterion are met will reflect local norms and values.

A reform agenda, such as the one exemplified in Figure 5.6 will consider existing gaps and try to fill them based on the needs of the community as well as the advisory support provided internationally (Rich, 1997; Rivard,

1992; Robertson, 1996, 1999; Savulescu, 1994; Schneider, 1992; Schuck, 1994; Sevelin, 2019). There may be specific conditions on the ground which call for a modification of international standards. For instance, during the COVID-19 pandemic many businesses became insolvent. It would have been imprudent to insist on full bankruptcy measures for all these businesses since the entire economy was in effective lockdown.

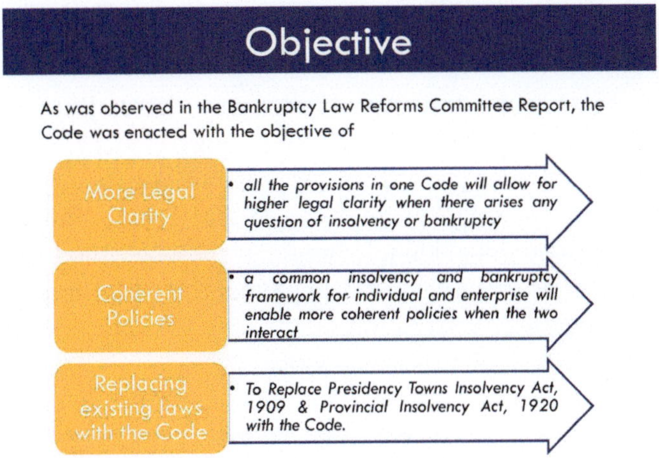

Figure 5.6. Example of a reform agenda for insolvency laws.

Source: Obtained via Slide Player.

There can be surprising profound differences when interpreting criterion for bankruptcy across the globe (Brock, 1995, 1999; Brody, 1998; Cantor, 2005; Capron, 1990, 1999; Chandler, 1990; Chervenak & McCullough, 1991). For example, the inability to pay is not entirely universal as a condition meaning that people who can pay over a long period may still be subject to insolvency in some countries. Other countries forbid companies to offset their debts with assets. This means that it is likely that many who may pay later will end in insolvency today. The decisions about whether this is fair or not depends on context and circumstances.

5.4. CASE STUDY OF GLOBAL DISPUTES ON COPYRIGHT LAW

Similar issues of cultural diversities have arisen when seeking consensus on copyright law (Hill, 1990, 1991a, b; Hope & Fulford, 1994; Hylton, 1990; Kadish, 1992; Kahn, 1991; Kalb, 1990; Kamisar, 1993). Recently, there has been concern that China is not taking issues of copyright seriously. Some suspect that the Chinese ignores Western concerns about this issue because the status quo allows Chinese businesses to steal intellectual property without any significant consequences to them. Implementing a strict copyright law as suggested by the USA might be detrimental to the Chinese economy in the short run. Nevertheless, disputes about copyright highlight the international nature of legal issues that were previously exclusively domestic.

Yet, as Figure 5.7 demonstrates shows, countries like the USA still have many cópyright claims denied on procedural and substantive grounds (Field, 1990, 1991; Figueira-Mcdonough, 1990; Finer, 1991; Fluss & Zeegers, 1990; Fortin, 1991; Gelman, 1994; Glass & Speyer-Ofenberg, 1996). One of the key emergent debates relates to the role of private international law when attempting to harmonize this type of legislation. National law and sovereignty may conflict with international aims and modalities leading to disagreements and even delays in implementing an appropriate regime. There are international conventions that have accepted the notion that copyright law is territorial rather than global.

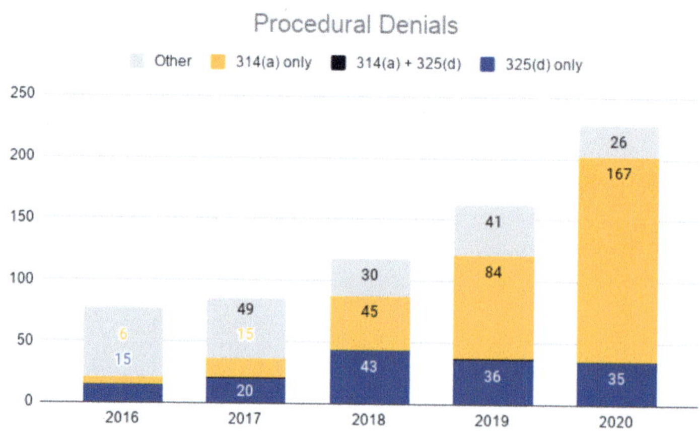

Figure 5.7. Procedural denial of patents in USA 2016–2020.

Source: Unified Patents.

Each country may recognize copyright law, but the exact nature of interpretation and consequences may differ significantly (Okin, 1990; Oster, 2021; Paliwala, 2016; Paris & Poorman, 1995; Pellegrino & Sharpe, 1989; Ploughman, 1995; Pogge, 1991). For example, local artists may have a genuine grievance against their home state for not doing enough to stop pirated work being distributed without any benefit being given to the creator. Yet, these artists may be competing on a global stage where some countries have specific protections within their constitution for artists so that they are not exploited.

Additionally, there is a layer of jurisprudence that covers multinational copyright disputes (Sulmasy, 1989; TÄNnsjÖ, 1992; Thomson, 1999; Truog et al., 1991; Turrina et al., 2021; van Delden & Laurie, 2004; Van Der Burg, 1997). This calls for a careful balancing of local laws and the international regime. Litigants and judicial officers must be cognizant of the power differentials which might mean that either local or international laws are impractical for specific cases. The localization of international law may also lead to further disputes about the sanctity of sovereignty and the independence of the judiciary under the traditional structure of the state. The advent of the internet has made all analysis and comparison that much harder than before.

There is a wealth of literature concerning copyright, even though it is not harmonized so that there is a single international standard (Kamisar, 1993; Kamm, 2001; Kass & Lund, 1996; Kaveny, 1991, 2006; Khushf, 1994; Knoppers & LeBris, 1991). As we have seen with the copyright disputes between the USA and Chia, the failure to resolve these matters can escalate into more serious conflicts such as trade wars. Some of this literature addresses the different ways in which the courts might interpret and operationalize the law. Hence, it is possible that there is diversity of interpretation even within the same jurisdiction.

Other researchers question whether there is any legitimate or enforceable role of international norms when operationalizing copyright law (Bekrycht & Mańko, 2020; Bianchi, 2017; Blair & Kaserman, 1991; Blustein, 1993; Bonnicksen, 1995; Bradley, 1993). Indeed, some have even wondered whether there is a truly international community since most decisions are dominated by a few hegemonic powers which already have a history of colonization. Moreover, there are questions as to the right approach for judges who are faced with a diverse range of complex options when dealing with copyright cases.

The substantive law method as posited by Fritz Juenger can provide useful insights to judges who are dealing with copyright cases in this climate (Anderson, 1993; Andrews, 1996; Arinta et al., 2021; Ayres et al., 1993; Bekrycht & Mańko, 2020; Bianchi, 2017; Blair & Kaserman, 1991). The principle of territoriality may also be considered when judges are being asked to localize international norms that may not be fully embraced by the local populace. Underpinning all these debates is the sense that creators should not be deprived the fruits of their work through negligent or disorganized copyright rules, regulations, and laws. At the same time, judges cannot be expected to make up laws as they go because that would not be sustainable in the long run.

These misgivings notwithstanding, there is a vibrant and growing market for copyright litigation and a lot of the applications have been granted (*see* Figure 5.8). One of the emergent debates is the extent to which private international law has a horizontal effect in areas such as patents, trademarking, and industrial property (Strauss, 1992; Stroud, 1996; Sullivan & Goldzwig, 1995; Sulmasy, 1989; TÄNnsjÖ, 1992; Thomson, 1999). Moreover, the existence of different rules and focus points can become controversial if it is perceived to lead to injustices or otherwise emphasize inequalities. Others question whether the trans-substantive approach is ideal for managing conflicts within copyright law.

Figure 5.8. Patent filings and grants 1991–2012.

Source: The IPKat.

Overall, there is a perception that is sometimes empirically supported that a convergence in copyright law is emerging (Gormally, 2002; Gostin, 1995; Greenberg & Kamin, 1993; Grondelski, 1989; Hamblin & Somerville, 1991; Hardwig, 1991). This is despite the resistance of powerful countries like China which fail or refuse to protect intellectual property owners from rival nations like the USA and members of the European Union. Additionally, there are potential benefits of harmonization in as far as there will be less confusion about what copyright law is and is not. Those that operate in a trans-national sphere would appreciate certainty and predictability when dealing with copyright issues.

Nevertheless, consistency at any cost is also perceived to be a mistake because of the implications for localization (Coady, 2002; Cohen, 1989; Coughlan, 1989; Crigger, 1995; Crossley, 1993; Crouch & Elliott, 1999; Daniels & Sabin, 1997). For instance, an international standard may not fully appreciate the localized dynamics and powerplay among those that are involved in copyright litigation. Some industries are so symbiotic that a rigid application of copy right law would not only be unfair but could lead to significant negative effects on the industry itself. Copyright law is there to make life easier for content and product creators as opposed to putting them out of business. These challenges reflect the limits as well as possibilities of commercial law in society.

5.5. THE LIMITS AND POSSIBILITIES OF COMMERCIAL LAW

One of the most lucrative forms of judicial work is that which relates to commercial law (Lane & Grodin, 1997; Mathieu, 1992; May, 1999; McConnell, 1991; McCoy, 1992; Meisel, 1992, 1996; Menzel, 1992). This is also known as trade law or mercantile law. The law in this area comprises rules, regulations, and conventions that mediate the relationships between people and institutions that are engaged in business or any other commercial enterprise. That list may include sales, trading, merchandizing, and recently it also includes eCommerce.

This branch of the law falls within the civil sphere, although no less important than criminal law for the good order of society (Clark, 2002; Clerkin, 2021; Coady, 2002; Cohen, 1989; Coughlan, 1989; Crigger, 1995; Crossley, 1993; Crouch & Elliott, 1999). The civil law segment also deals with public and private law. One of the key areas that are considered under commercial law is that of titles with reference to agents and principles. The law also deals with carriage by sea or land. Hence, it is responsible for litigation concerning merchant shipping as well as guarantees.

Commercial law has proved critical for the management of the insurance sector on a range of risks such as accidents, death, fires, and marine incidents (Field, 1991; Figueira-Mcdonough, 1990; Finer, 1991; Fluss & Zeegers, 1990; Fortin, 1991; Gelman, 1994; Glass & Speyer-Ofenberg, 1996; Glick,

1992). It has also helped in resolving dispute between and among business partners by way of contracts, letters of association, negotiable instruments, and bills of exchange for example. In fact, many of these aspects can also be classified under financial law. This is a branch of commercial law that focuses on financial markets and financing.

Those that practice commercial law must be conversant with legislation as it pertains to hiring practices, corporate contracting, marketing, and consumer protection (Stein, 1998; Steinbock & McClamrock, 1994; Strauss, 1992; Stroud, 1996; Sullivan & Goldzwig, 1995; Sulmasy, 1989; TÄNnsjÖ, 1992). Many jurisdictions have adopted and adapted civil codes. These codes create specific and comprehensive statements concerning how commercial law is to be governed and operationalized. Although not always as high profile as criminal law, commercial law can be equally compelling in terms of the impact that it has on the relationships that exist between and among community members.

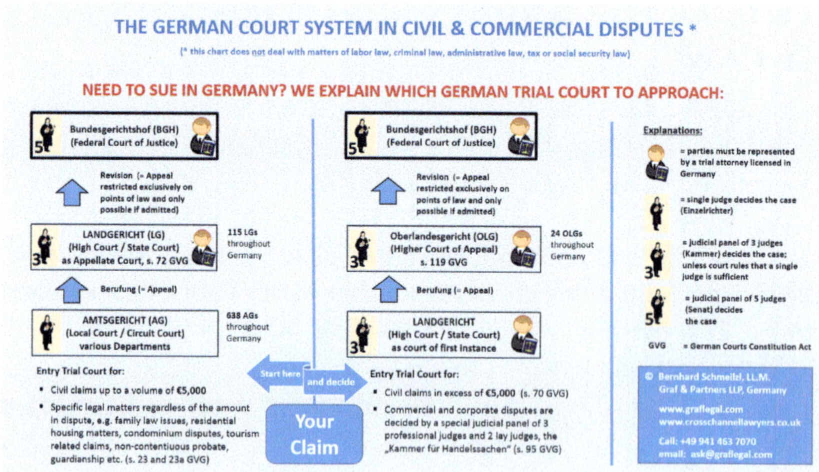

Figure 5.9. Structure of the German civil court system.

Source: German Civil Procedure.

One of the areas of interest has been how the locality impacts on the differences that exist between commercial regimes across the globe (Quante, 1999; Rae & DeGiorgio, 1991; Ravven, 2016; Raymond, 1999; Resnik, 1997; Rich, 1997; Rivard, 1992; Robertson, 1996). This is an implicit acknowledgement of the diversity of commercial law so that no single rule is allowed to dominate communities. Of course, various countries may adopt best practice when they see fit following recommendations or empirical evidence. Figure 5.9 shows the structure of the civil and commercial dispute resolution process in Germany which has been a source of good practice in this way.

The USA is another country which has contributed to the development of commercial law (Abrams, 1996; Agich & Spielman, 1997; Allen, 1990, 1992; Alward, 2002; Amaraskekara & Bagaric, 2004; Anderson, 1993). Under the American regime, Congress is given the mandate to regulate interstate commerce. However, the states are given broad discretion to regulate commercial law within their own boundaries. That means that there can several tiers of law with disputes about which takes precedence. The states have used their police power to regulate trade and industry within their boundaries.

Given the unity of the nation and the need for harmonization, there have been several attempts to create a uniform form of commercial law in the USA (Hamblin & Somerville, 1991; Hardwig, 1991; Harris, 2003; Harris & Holm, 2002; Harvey & Chadwick, 1992; Hasnas, 1995). However, those efforts have been challenged on the basis that the independence of the states is sacrosanct to many who are fearful of the overreaching power of the federal government. Many have pointed out the fact that the USA is a confederation of relatively independence states, meaning that it would be inappropriate to develop a singular commercial that would be applied uniformly across the country.

Being just one part of civil law (*see* Figure 5.10), commercial law must also follow the protocols that are set out for the law general and for commercial law specifically (Oster, 2021; Paliwala, 2016; Paris & Poorman, 1995; Pellegrino & Sharpe, 1989; Ploughman, 1995; Pogge, 1991; Purdy, 1990). In the USA, the most successful attempt at harmonization was the Uniform Commercial Code. This protocol has been adopted in all the 50 states of the USA. However, there are some modifications that are made by each legislature in the state to suit its own needs. These are powers that are granted by the US constitution and fiercely defended by politicians, especially on the political right.

Commercial is generally dynamic and vibrant since it is subject to regular updates depending on the circumstances (White, 1990; Wicclair, 1991a, b; Wildes, 1997; Wilson, 1994; Woliver, 1990; Wyld & Cappel, 1990). Legislators have shown a willingness to revisit those provisions that seem to create unfairness or an outright form of injustice. A case in point are the concerted efforts to regulate the relationships that exist between employees and customers. Other areas that are reviewed under commercial law include health and safety as well as privacy laws. In the USA, the Occupational Safety and Health Act is a landmark piece of legislation that demonstrates the ways in which commercial is responsive to the needs of people and communities.

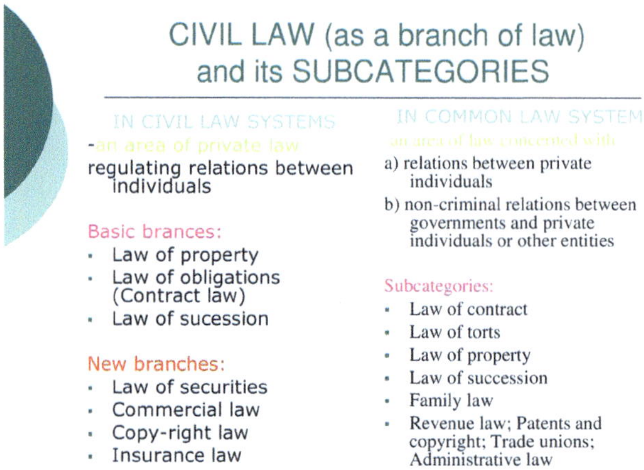

Figure 5.10. Sub-categories of civil law.

Source: Tabitha Lambert (2018) via Slide Player.

Commercial law is a very old form of law based on the transactions between and among human beings (Harris & Holm, 2002; Harvey & Chadwick, 1992; Hasnas, 1995; Hill, 1990, 1991a, b; Hope & Fulford, 1994). Hence, it has had to revolve around the variations in the ways that such transactions are undertaken. That is why the internet has added new elements and considerations that determine the ways in which commercial law is understood and operationalized. For example, a transaction that is completed online using the internet might involve the commercial law regimes of several countries and this might lead to substantial disputes about which of the jurisdictions sets the precedents. Thankfully, there has been broad agreement on some fundamental principles and values of commercial law.

CHAPTER 5 SUMMARY

This chapter has focused on the geopolitics of the law. Specifically, the chapter has shown that the interpretation and implementation of the law can vary significantly across the globe. The variation depends on the needs of local communities as well as the specific legal challenges that they are attempting to address. We have used case studies of human rights, religious law, cultural laws, insolvency, copyright, and commercial law. The next chapter summarizes the subcategories of analytical jurisprudence.

CHAPTER 6

Categories of Analytical Jurisprudence

Contents

In this chapter, we will explore some of the main categories of analytical jurisprudence in existing literature. These include ethical, sociological, traditional, and historical jurisprudence. The chapter will then examine two case studies including Hohfeld's analysis of legal rights and transnational discourse about prison conditions. Overall, this chapter brings together the topics examined under the previous chapters so that they can be analyzed within the existing structures of jurisprudence. The discussion will commence with ethical jurisprudence.

6.1. OVERVIEW OF ETHICAL JURISPRUDENCE

Ethical jurisprudence relates morals and law, even though many reformers have shied away from moralizing the law (Capron, 1990, 1999; Chandler, 1990; Chervenak & McCullough, 1991; Chesterman, 1998; Clark, 2002; Clerkin, 2021). Debates about the relationships between the law and morality have existed since the 19th century. Morals were understood to imply standards of conduct that must be evaluated based on results, ends, and aims. There are four major stages that are involved in the development of morality in law.

The first stage involves undifferentiated ethical customs (Emanuel, 1999; Feinberg, 1991; Fentiman, 1989; Field, 1990, 1991; Figueira-Mcdonough, 1990; Finer, 1991; Fluss & Zeegers, 1990). This is what is known as the pre-legal stage. This is then followed by a strict and codified custom as the second stage. The third stage comprises the infusion of moralities into the law so that it is reshaped. In the fourth and final stage, there is conscious legislation which implies maturity in the law. In that sense, morality and morals are instituted by the legislators while the judge focuses on the law without paying any consideration to moral issues. This is based on the idea that morality will already have been instituted throughout the development processes.

To that end, the conceptualization of ethics can be challenging and problematic because it is contextualized (Okin, 1990; Oster, 2021; Paliwala, 2016; Paris & Poorman, 1995; Pellegrino & Sharpe, 1989; Ploughman, 1995). Ethics are understood to be the essence of human conduct within the confines of a society which sets the standards of ethical behavior. Using a timeframe, it could be argued that ethics comprises how people behaved in the past, how they currently behave, and how they are expected to behave in the future. Ethics are always contextualized and may not translate into a homogenous whole. Nevertheless, there are certain ethics that are virtually universal, e.g., not harming others without legitimate justification. Ethics can be divided into two broad branches (Hamblin & Somerville, 1991; Hardwig, 1991; Harris, 2003; Harris & Holm, 2002; Harvey & Chadwick, 1992; Hasnas, 1995). The first branch comprises an ideal moral code. The second branch comprise a positive moral code. An ideal moral code necessarily deals with natural law which is a system of rights or justice that accrues to all humans by virtue of their humanity rather than through the machinations of any state or earthly authority. Natural law necessarily departs from the rules of society which comprise the second arm of positive moral codes. Natural law is not legislated or man-made but is derived from moral principles that can nevertheless be powerful modifiers of human behavior. For judicial officers, the jurisprudence has significant differences with ethics (*see* Figure 6.1).

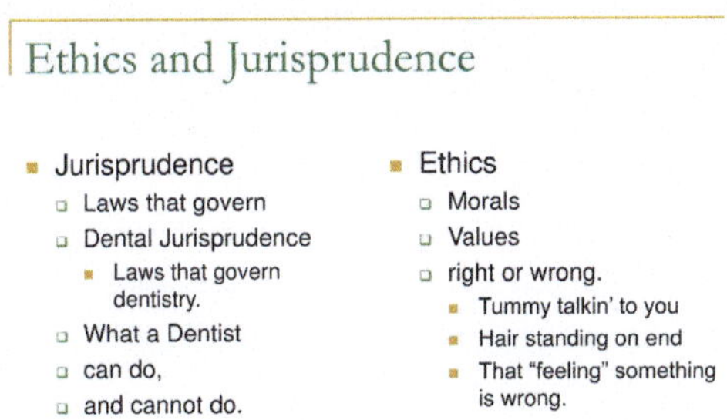

Figure 6.1. Juxtaposing ethics and jurisprudence.

Source: Lee Li (2014) via Slide Serve.

The positive moral code is often given credence because it is made by people that can enforce it (Stacy, 1994; Stauch, 2000; Stein, 1998; Steinbock & McClamrock, 1994; Strauss, 1992; Stroud, 1996; Sullivan & Goldzwig, 1995). Meanwhile, the ideal moral code may be enforced through social pressure but there is no other concrete punishment for failing to adhere to its dictates. Hence, the positive moral code is directed to the way in people behave at specific times and in specific places. Inherent morals are based on public opinion as conceived by a specific society.

Moreover, positive moral codes may change with changes in public opinion (Chervenak & McCullough, 1991; Chesterman, 1998; Clark, 2002; Clerkin, 2021; Coady, 2002; Cohen, 1989; Coughlan, 1989). A case in point is how the law on divorce has changed as attitudes about this end to matrimony have relaxed. A moral code that seeks to return to the morals of the 1910s around marriage is bound to appear anachronistic and hopelessly unenforceable. Jurisprudence then develops a super structure that operates in such a way as to include morals in as far as they are included in the law. Judicial officers are expected to demonstrate ethical behavior as they practice the law. Figure 6.2 represents six ways of demonstrating ethical behavior, although many more exist.

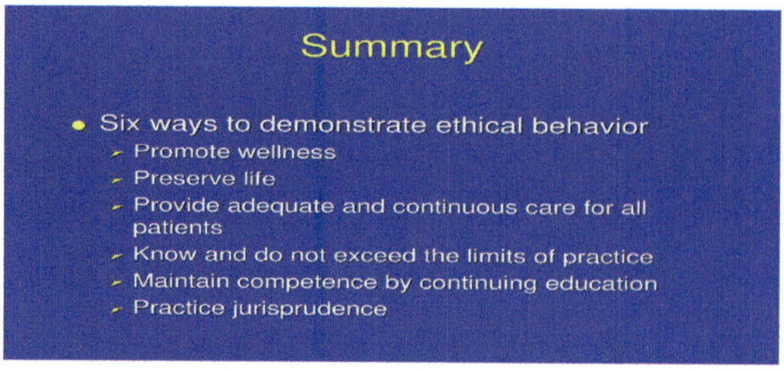

Figure 6.2. Six ways of demonstrating ethics when practicing law.

Source: Byron Atkinson via Slide Player.

The basic conceptualization of jurisprudence is the study of the law and the principles upon which it is founded (McConnell, 1991; McCoy, 1992; Meisel, 1992, 1996; Menzel, 1992; Merrick, 1990; Morreim, 1991; Munzer, 1994). There is a presupposition that the law is a science with all the requisite requirements for defensible evidence. Nevertheless, the law has also been perceived as an art that requires creativity and imagination to execute. Possibly, this explains why law is placed within the humanities in many academic structures despite the fact that it shares much with the social sciences.

Law is also a profession meaning that it requires knowledge to be applied to practical problems (Kadish, 1992; Kahn, 1991; Kalb, 1990; Kamisar, 1993; Kamm, 2001; Kass & Lund, 1996; Kaveny, 1991, 2006). Lawyers and other members of the judicial profession are set apart from the rest of society by virtue of their education, training, and socialization. There are strict standards relating to who can and cannot be a lawyer. Hence, the need for a practicing certificate before one can join the profession.

Jurisprudence is the study of the science of the law and its machinations (Draper, 1993; Dresser, 1995, 2003; Dworkin, 1991, 1992; Dyck, 1992; Eisenstat, 1991; Eldridge, 2021). There are specific reasons why jurisprudence is a necessary part of the development of the law. For example, the research that is inspired by jurisprudence is essential for clarifying various aspects of the law which would otherwise lead to damaging ambiguity. Additionally, jurisprudence allows us to better understand the social impact of the law.

This is a topic that is often neglected by lawyers to their detriment as well as the loss of public confidence in the system. Hence, those that engage in jurisprudence will better understanding the meaning and implications of the laws that they are trying to operationalize. In this instance, the sociological aspects of jurisprudence are important.

6.2. THE TENETS OF SOCIOLOGICAL JURISPRUDENCE

Sociological jurisprudence makes the law more relevant and real for lay people (Alward, 2002; Amaraskekara & Bagaric, 2004; Anderson, 1993; Andrews, 1996; Arinta et al., 2021; Ayres et al., 1993). This is because collective human life is influenced by the law, either directly or indirectly.

In this chapter, Sourav Bhola of RGNUL discusses the sociological school of jurisprudence. The law has been compared to knowledge in being an essential and pervasive aspect of the social condition. Figure 6.3 highlights the sociological aspects of jurisprudence.

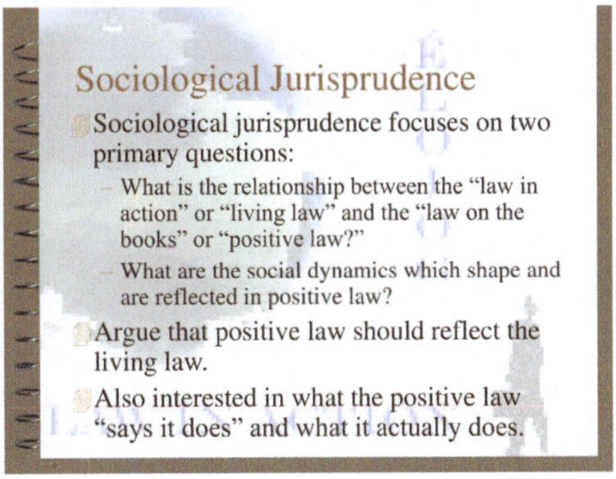

Figure 6.3. The tenets of sociological jurisprudence.

Source: Mia John (2013) via Slide Serve.

The origins of law are rooted in the customs of society in specific times and places (Raymond, 1999; Resnik, 1997; Rich, 1997; Rivard, 1992; Robertson, 1996, 1999; Savulescu, 1994; Schneider, 1992). These laws and rules were designed to govern society under the threat of disorder and dysfunction. Customs typically had nothing more than social sanction. However, the introduction of the King and priests brought in the notion of supremacy and punishment. It would take several revolutions before there was a rebalancing of the relationship between societal welfare and the interests of individuals who form part of that society. Sociology immerses itself in the notions of society and how that society is managed or manages itself (Bonnicksen, 1995; Bradley, 1993; Braithwaite, 1991; Brock, 1991, 1995, 1999; Brody, 1998; Cantor, 2005). Moreover, sociologists pay attention to changes in society and human behavior. Through jurisprudence, we can study the legal aspects of this human life experience. According to the sociological school of jurisprudence, society and the law are inextricably related to each other. Hence, the law is a social phenomenon by virtue of its significant and pervasive impact on society.

One of the important voices in the sociology of the law is August Comte (1798–1857). A notable French philosopher, Comte was the first person to officially use the term sociology. According to his analysis and theory, sociology is the positive science of social facts (Capron, 1999; Chandler, 1990; Chervenak & McCullough, 1991; Chesterman, 1998; Clark, 2002; Clerkin, 2021; Coady, 2002). Comte likened society to an organism which could progress further if guided by scientific principles. Hence, the law is an important tool for maintaining society as well as its desirable progress. Following Comte, several jurists and writers found ways of connecting society to the law so that there would be a legitimate link between the academic disciplines of sociology and law.

The development of the sociological school of jurisprudence was aimed at clarifying and disseminating these relationships (Kaveny, 2006; Khushf, 1994; Knoppers & LeBris, 1991; Kozłowski, 2021; Lane & Grodin, 1997; Mathieu, 1992; May, 1999). Every problem was then perceived through the prism of legality. The same applied to every change in society. This school sought to properly balance the interests of the state and those of the individual so that both are realized in ways that are mutually sustaining. Ehrlich suggested that the centrality of society in legal development supersedes that of juristic decision-making and legislative processes.

According to the sociological school of jurisprudence, every concept or problem has two different aspects (Munzer, 1994; Nelson, 1994; Nobles, 2012; O'Donovan & Gilbar, 2003; Oberman, 1992; Okin, 1990; Oster, 2021; Paliwala, 2016). The first is the sociological view. The other is the legal view. One of the examples that has been cited in existing literature is that of Sati. This was an ancient Indian practice under which the wife would be burned at the funeral pyre of her husband. The legal aspect of this practice includes an abolishment that was enacted in 1798 within Calcutta when the territory was under the jurisdiction of the British Empire.

By 1829, Sati had been banned in other British territories within India. The Prevention of Sati Act (1987) is the current legislation that bans the practice in modern day India. The legislation prohibits anyone from being encouraged or forced into Sati. Additionally, the sociological aspect is demonstrated by the increasing feminism of Indian society and a concern for human rights which means that Sati is considered a ruthless and unacceptable Hindu practice. Together, the legal and sociological aspects ensure that Sati is effectively prohibited in India today.

Such examples can be analyzed under the prism of the sociology of the law (*see* Figure 6.4). The reasons for such analysis have been explored by Podgorecki (Robertson, 1996, 1999; Savulescu, 1994; Schneider, 1992; Schuck, 1994; Sevelin, 2019; Shanley, 1990; Sharpe & Pellegrino, 1997). The first purpose is to identify, understand, and explore how the law works when operationalized. The second function is to provide expertise advise that is especially useful for social engineering. The third purpose is to shape studies about the law so that they are more relevant to the practical needs of society. The final purpose is to ensure that there is harmony when the law struggles to face realities. This can be problematic when juxtaposing traditional and historical jurisprudence.

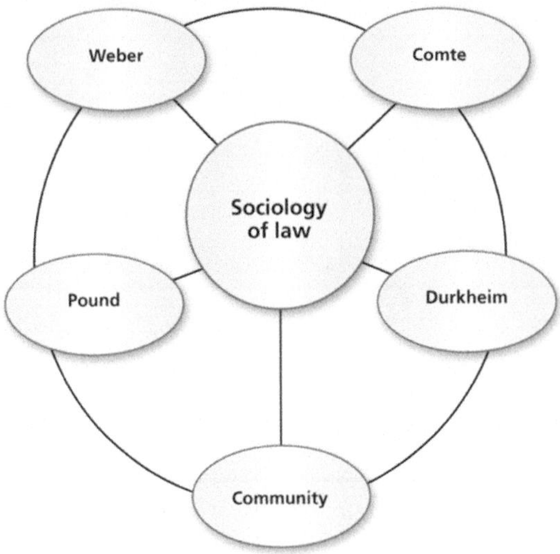

Figure 6.4. The sociology of the law.

Source: Law Explorer.

6.3. TRADITIONAL AND HISTORICAL JURISPRUDENCE

The lines between historical and traditional jurisprudence are blurred by the reality that they co-exist within roughly the same time frame (Rae & DeGiorgio, 1991; Ravven, 2016; Raymond, 1999; Resnik, 1997; Rich, 1997; Rivard, 1992; Robertson, 1996, 1999). One of the key moments in the development of traditional jurisprudence occurred in the 17th century when the Western legal tradition was embedded within a new philosophy of law. This new creation supplemented and complemented two major pre-existing philosophies in terms of legal positivism and natural law theory. These types of seismic changes in the law have continued today. For example, the rise of the virtual legal office (*see* Figure 6.5) has implication for our understanding of jurisprudence and legal practice.

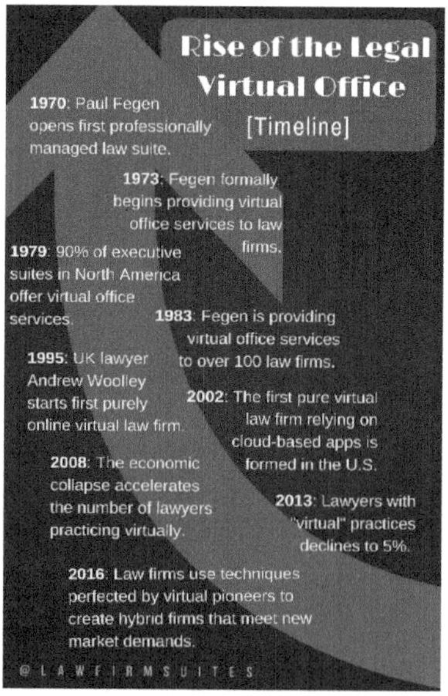

Figure 6.5. The rise of the virtual legal office.

Source: Law Firm Suites.

These changes are born out of necessity and pragmatic acceptance of new realities (Elhauge, 1994; Emanuel, 1999; Feinberg, 1991; Fentiman, 1989; Field, 1990, 1991; Figueira-Mcdonough, 1990; Finer, 1991). The new philosophy that seemingly replaced natural law and positive law was known as historical jurisprudence or the historical school. During the 19th century, the historical school dominated in Europe and USA. Indeed, as late as the earlier part of the 20th century saw this philosophy being referenced by lawyers and judges.

The historical school is specifically pertinent when considering constitutional law (Ploughman, 1995; Pogge, 1991; Purdy, 1990; Quante, 1999; Rae & DeGiorgio, 1991; Ravven, 2016; Raymond, 1999). It is also relevant to those aspects of the law that rely heavily on tradition. A case in point is the application of common law. The historical school is the foundation of the doctrines of precedent which are so prevalent in American and English law. Yet, it is notable that the historical school is open to wide and varied interpretation. Nevertheless, historical jurisprudence has a core meaning in much the same way as positive law and natural law had.

The ways in which these three theories treat the law is instructive about their nature and agenda (Robertson, 1999; Savulescu, 1994; Schneider, 1992; Schuck, 1994; Sevelin, 2019; Shanley, 1990; Sharpe & Pellegrino, 1997; Sheldon & Wilkinson, 1997). For instance, natural law treats the law as an embodiment of concepts and rule or moral principles that emanate from conscience and reason. This contrasts with positivism which perceives law as a coherent body of rules that are laid down or posited and enforced by the sovereign as the ultimate authority responsible for creating law.

Natural law considers the law to be primarily rooted in morality which is reproduced as reason and conscience (Kahn, 1991; Kalb, 1990; Kamisar, 1993; Kamm, 2001; Kass & Lund, 1996; Kaveny, 1991, 2006; Khushf, 1994). It is a contrasting approach from positivism in which law is rooted in politics which is reproduced as the will of the lawmaker. Most thinkers of a positivist persuasion do not deny the moral ends of the law. However, they emphasize the law as a political instrument. Hence, the law comprises rules that manifest the policies that are adopted by political authorities that are legitimately constituted such as parliament.

The positivists argue that the morality of the law can only be explored and even considered after the exact nature of the law has been formally instituted by a legitimate legislative or executive authority (Chandler, 1990; Chervenak & McCullough, 1991; Chesterman, 1998; Clark, 2002; Clerkin, 2021; Coady, 2002; Cohen, 1989). This is diametrically opposed to the position of the naturalists who argue that one cannot know what the law is until they have established what the law ought to be. Legal norms must therefore have moral purposes even when instituted by politicians and other people in authority or power. According to the naturalists, it is only when one has an understanding of moral purpose can one then analyze, interpret, and apply the law.

Based on natural law, there is a denial of any law or rule that contradicts the natural principles of justice (Nobles, 2012; O'Donovan & Gilbar, 2003; Oberman, 1992; Okin, 1990; Oster, 2021; Paliwala, 2016; Paris & Poorman, 1995). This suggests that there is natural and unnatural justice, with the latter being unacceptable in a moral society. Laws that are amoral can therefore be deemed illegitimate and invalid. The challenge of such suppositions is the fact that they encounter the diversities of moral belief and practice that exist in the world.

Seemingly objective issues such as taxation (*see* Figure 6.6 for an illustration of its historical progression in the USA) can be interpreted based on natural or positive law (Walters, 1991, 2012; Waymack, 1991; Weithman, 1999; Whitaker & Edwards, 1990; White, 1990; Wicclair, 1991a). For example, the positivists might argue that taxation is a direct consequence of parliament needing to raise money that can support the state and therefore sustain the society. However, those of a natural law persuasion might reference the need to engage in reciprocity and altruism meaning that those who are better endowed are willing to share their wealthy with the less unfortunate.

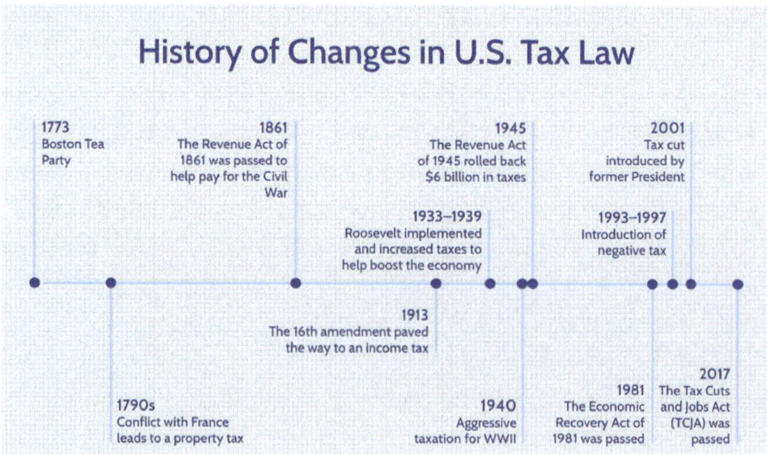

Figure 6.6. Evolution of tax law in the USA.

Source: Investopedia.

The law can evolve along natural and positivist lines simultaneously (Shewmon, 1997; Shultz, 1990; Singleton Jr, 1989; Skene & Parker, 2002; Somerville, 1989; Spurr, 1993; Stacy, 1994). Hence, the reliance on precedent in historical law. Precedent does not necessarily have to be restricted to positivist approaches to the law. It can also include those that are based on natural law. This has been the case when legislating sensitive issues such as marriage, divorce, and inheritance. The authorities that are making the law as well as those that are implementing it must be cognizant of these sensitive considerations.

It is worth mentioning that under natural law, there is a diversity of thought in discerning the natural from the unnatural (Dyck, 1992; Eisenstat, 1991; Eldridge, 2021; Elhauge, 1994; Emanuel, 1999; Feinberg, 1991; Fentiman, 1989). A case in point are the colonial laws that speak of having sexual intercourse the order of nature. Critics of such laws query who decides what is natural or unnatural. However, the same criticism can be laid at the feet of legislators that assume power to regulate behavior when they themselves fall so short of the standards that they have set up. These debates are about legal rights, and this has been the subject of some cases by philosophers including Hohfeld.

6.4. CASE STUDY HOHFELD'S ANALYSIS OF LEGAL RIGHTS

Wesley Newcomb Hohfeld designed a famous project was to clarify juridical relationships between the relevant parties (Coughlan, 1989; Crigger, 1995; Crossley, 1993; Crouch & Elliott, 1999; Daniels & Sabin, 1997; Den Hartogh, 1997; Downie, 1992). Hence, he posits an analytical scheme which splits rights into four different categories. These are in effect jural relationships. Accordingly, exemplifies several analytical distinctions between various legal positions. Figure 6.7 is an example of modelling under this analysis.

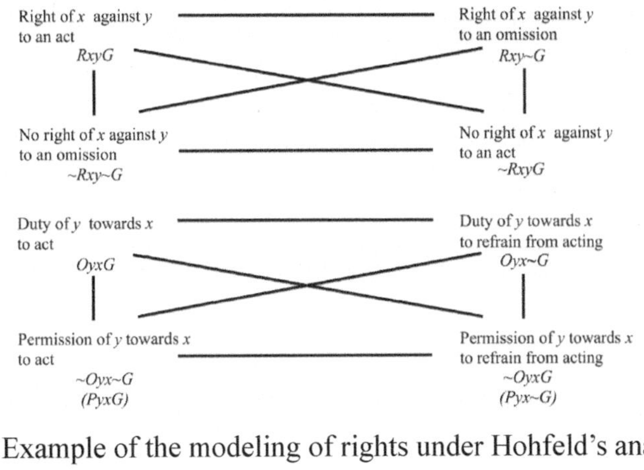

Figure 6.7. Example of the modeling of rights under Hohfeld's analysis.

Source: Cambridge University.

It is notable that Hohfeld's analysis of rights lies in the descriptive exercise of the legal positions (Kass & Lund, 1996; Kaveny, 1991, 2006; Khushf, 1994; Knoppers & LeBris, 1991; Kozłowski, 2021; Lane & Grodin, 1997). These relate to each other by means of logical relations. Those relations have been summarized as of entailment and negation. The process is engaged in an analytical and definitional enterprise. By that token, this process does not concern itself with substantive or empirical enquiry into the concept of a right.

Experts have noted that Hohfeld's ambition was to provide a conceptual understanding for our use of right and duty in practice (Ayres et al., 1993; Bekrycht & Mańko, 2020; Bianchi, 2017; Blair & Kaserman, 1991; Blustein, 1993; Bonnicksen, 1995). This is instrumental in understanding of the nature of our rights. The overall aims shy away from informing us what rights and duties are or should be. Similarly, there is no debate about what their moral foundation is. The analysis does not purport to explore what is necessary for something to count as a right or duty.

The model avoids exploring the justification of rights (Harris & Holm, 2002; Harvey & Chadwick, 1992; Hasnas, 1995; Hill, 1990, 1991a, b; Hope & Fulford, 1994). Hohfeld's instead presents a distinction between four different sets of juridical relationships. These are relationships that have proved instrumental and critical throughout the development of analytical jurisprudence. It is notable that the method of splitting the notion of a right into its constituent elements has many important benefits. Apart from being parsimonious and rather elegant, this approach is fundamental when seeking intelligible and informed assessments of legal positions as parties engage in litigation and prosecution.

At the fundamental level, Hohfeld is analyzing the nature and consequences of rights and duties (Sheldon & Wilkinson, 1998; Shepherd, 1995; Shevory, 1990; Shewmon, 1997; Shultz, 1990; Singleton Jr, 1989). The nature of rights can change with circumstances and lead to differential implications. There are consequences for holding specific Hohfeldian burdens or entitlements. By exposing and analyzing jural relations, Hohfeld helps to untangle the exact nature of jurisprudence as well as legal practices that involve rights. Jurists have nevertheless critiqued the approach suggested by Hohfeld.

To better understand the criticisms of Hohfeld, some analysts have distinguished those that are against his principles and those who do not believe the principles (Chandler, 1990; Chervenak & McCullough, 1991;

Chesterman, 1998; Clark, 2002; Clerkin, 2021; Coady, 2002; Cohen, 1989). This is sometimes expressed as the difference between non-Hohfeldians and anti-Hohfeldians. Hence, some of the critics argue that Hohfeld was wrong in his analysis while others are merely highlighting possible and even better alternatives to Hohfeld. Underpinning these criticisms is the extent to which the analysis can present an accurate and coherent picture of our conception of rights and duties.

One of the strengths of Hohfeld's analysis is that it is clear and coherent, providing exact reasons why certain assumptions and outcomes are included in the analysis while others are excluded (Robertson, 1996, 1999; Savulescu, 1994; Schneider, 1992; Schuck, 1994; Sevelin, 2019; Shanley, 1990; Sharpe & Pellegrino, 1997). In some sense, this is a retort against criticism of judicial analysis of being confusing and semi-detached from the realities of experiencing the legal system at work. As demonstrated in Figure 6.8, there is a counterpart to virtually all the rights and duties that are envisaged under this analysis. This allows us to compare and contrast the consequences of various stances that are adopted in the analysis.

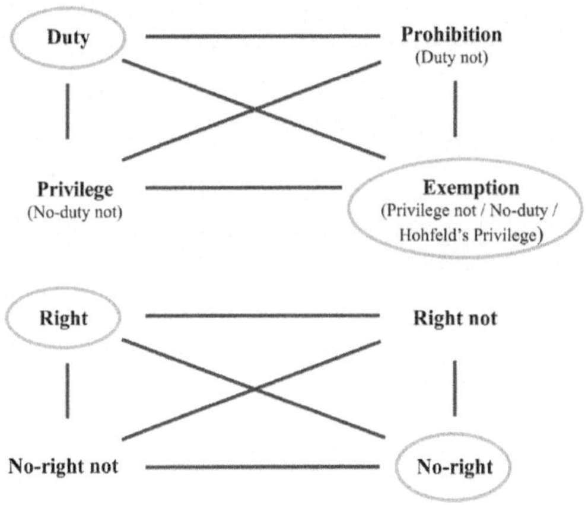

Figure 6.8. Example of a model of rights and responsibilities under Hohfeld's analysis.

Source: Cambridge University.

The definitions that are provided by Hohfeld are demonstrably stipulative rather than being an outcome of empirical inquiry. Hence, the suggestion that they are not susceptible to disproof through moral refutation or empirical research (Sheldon & Wilkinson, 1998; Shepherd, 1995; Shevory, 1990; Shewmon, 1997; Shultz, 1990; Singleton Jr, 1989). That might mean that they are less scientific than certain alternatives that meet this criterion of the scientific method. Others then use this very fact to critique the critics of Hohfeld in as far as they use a scientific method which is not compatible with the ideas and method involved in Hohfeld's analysis.

Some go as far as suggesting that critics who use the scientific method are positing an alternative to Hohfeld rather than criticizing him (Sevelin, 2019; Shanley, 1990; Sharpe & Pellegrino, 1997; Sheldon & Wilkinson, 1997, 1998; Shepherd, 1995). Underpinning this retort is the notion of a plurality of analyses that help develop jurisprudence. In other words, the critiques may not be a rejection of specific analyses but rather the positing of alternatives that could be equally valid. Another issue that attracts diversities of thought is that of prison conditions across the globe.

6.5. CASE STUDY OF TRANSNATIONAL DISCOURSE ABOUT PRISON CONDITIONS

It has been suggested that the humanity of societies is best judged by considering how they treat the least of their members (van Schooten, 2014; Viljoen, 2012; Walters, 1991, 2012; Waymack, 1991; Weithman, 1999; Whitaker & Edwards, 1990). Those that are imprisoned form a vulnerable minority that often does not attract much sympathy, not least because of the sometimes-heinous impacts of the crimes that have been committed. Prisoners of conscience or political prisoners tend to fare better outside the authorities that have imprisoned them. However, there is an overall impression that prison conditions are less than satisfactory. These debates are pertinent to countries like the USA with exponentially rising rates of incarceration (*see* Figure 6.9 for an illustration of this trend).

One of the concerns is the failure to develop an internationally recognized standard of care for those that are incarcerated (Stauch, 2000; Stein, 1998; Steinbock & McClamrock, 1994; Strauss, 1992; Stroud, 1996; Sullivan & Goldzwig, 1995). Perhaps, this can be explained by the competing motivations of those that are responsible for incarcerating humans. Some are focused on retribution and punishment while others are focused on rehabilitation. Then there are those that wish to create a deterrent so that others are not inspired to engage in illegal acts. Then there are those institutions and people that use the threat of imprisonment as a political instrumentality of control.

Because some of these objectives are diametrically opposed to each other, it becomes difficult to harmonize the standards and practices for setting out prison conditions (Hamblin & Somerville, 1991; Hardwig, 1991;

Harris, 2003; Harris & Holm, 2002; Harvey & Chadwick, 1992; Hasnas, 1995). Indeed, some may argue that this is a debate that is secondary to the issues of protecting the public by putting dangerous people out of circulation. Nevertheless, there have been regional and international discussion about the need for consistency and humanity when designing prison conditions where people are incarcerated for a range of reasons.

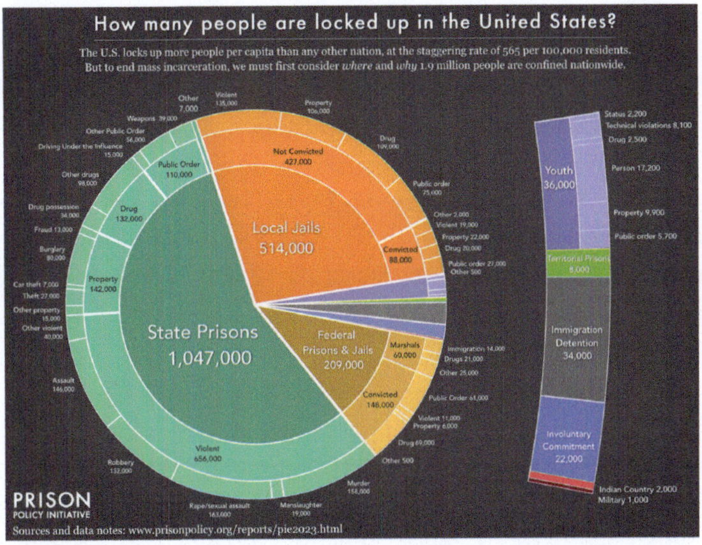

Figure 6.9. High incarceration rates in the USA.

Source: Prison Policy.

The desire for international respectability has meant that the proposals for reform have acquired a legitimacy that they lacked a few decades ago (Paliwala, 2016; Paris & Poorman, 1995; Pellegrino & Sharpe, 1989; Ploughman, 1995; Pogge, 1991; Purdy, 1990; Quante, 1999). That does not mean that there is a wholesale acceptance of prison reform standards that are set at the international level. Indeed, critics have argued that the desire for homogeneity in prison conditions may be more harmful than useful since it fails to account for the unique differences that exist between people and situations.

The state of prison conditions is of international interest since increasingly countries are constructing extradition agreements with each other (Allen, 1992; Alward, 2002; Amaraskekara & Bagaric, 2004; Anderson, 1993; Andrews, 1996; Arinta et al., 2021; Ayres et al., 1993). Domestic law may set out minimum standards for prisons without which judges are restricted in the custodial sentences that they can impose for crimes or other legal infringements. Moreover, some countries are deporting convicted migrants back to home countries which may have worse prison conditions. If there is a risk of significant harm by virtue of such decisions, then the courts may seek to review the relevant policies.

In this debate, it is tempting to speak of a divide between the industrialized nations and the third world with a middling global economy standing in between. The reality is that some of the worst prison conditions exist in some of the most developed countries (Alward, 2002; Amaraskekara & Bagaric, 2004; Anderson, 1993; Andrews, 1996; Arinta et al., 2021; Ayres et al., 1993). A case in point is how long-standing legal traditions were abandoned during the "*War on Terror*" that emerged following the terrorist attacks in New York on the 11th of September 2001. Many young men from Muslim-majority countries or those who were Muslims living in industrialized nations were incarcerated for long periods in harsh conditions without a clear judicial process.

Any attempts to critique these failures based on international law are often rebutted with the primacy of sovereignty (Cantor, 2005; Capron, 1990, 1999; Chandler, 1990; Chervenak & McCullough, 1991; Chesterman, 1998; Clark, 2002). A cynical view might be that countries wish to protect the right to punish and perhaps abuse their own citizens in a manner that they see as fit rather than being subject to the sensibilities of an international community. The notion of transnational legal ordering is often invoked to create space for harmonization.

This then raises the question about the role of jurisprudence in prison conditions. As Figure 6.10 shows, the ways in which judicial officers carry out their functions can either increase or reduce incarceration rates (Blair & Kaserman, 1991; Blustein, 1993; Bonnicksen, 1995; Bradley, 1993; Braithwaite, 1991; Brock, 1991; Brock, 1995). For instance, the failure to deliver justice in time means that many people are languishing on remand in many countries. Besides, an over-reliance on imprisonment might mean that the system is overwhelmed beyond its capacity to function as intended. That is why judicial officers ought to take an interest in the nature and design of prison conditions.

One of the innovations in this area is the development of the topic of transnational legal ordering (Hamblin & Somerville, 1991; Hardwig, 1991; Harris, 2003; Harris & Holm, 2002; Harvey & Chadwick, 1992; Hasnas, 1995). This is a process that is undertaken with consensus, bearing in mind the primacy of issues of sovereignty and the need to address specific localized challenges that may not lend themselves to an overarching homogenous regime. This calls for a better understanding of the interactions that must exist between national, regional, continental, and international legal systems.

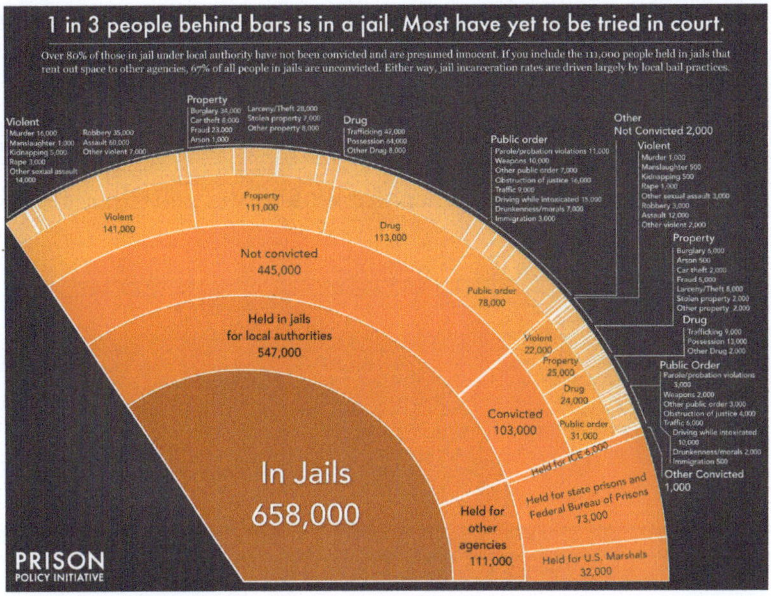

Figure 6.10. High levels of pre-trial incarceration in the USA.

Source: Prison Policy Initiative.

Where there is resistance to internationalization, the reasons for this must be carefully examined because they can tell us a lot about the mindset of communities that ultimately have an interest in deciding the nature of prison conditions (Ayres et al., 1993; Bekrycht & Mańko, 2020; Bianchi, 2017; Blair & Kaserman, 1991; Blustein, 1993; Bonnicksen, 1995). Besides, the progression of humanity means that it is necessary not to create an incarcerated population that is so alienated from mainstream society that it is capable of engaging in some of the worst forms of depravity as a protest. As empirical evidence has shown, the cooperation of the incarcerated is relevant when bringing order to these institutions. Similarly legal officers must pay heed to these conditions as they might be the outcome of judicial decisions.

CHAPTER 6 SUMMARY

This chapter has explored some categories of analytical jurisprudence. Specifically, the chapter has shown that jurisprudence is socially constructed and experienced. Such an assertion holds true regardless of whether the categorization is ethical, sociological, or historical. Hohfeld presents an example of analysis that is multi-faceted, but which is also vulnerable to multiple criticisms. Then the discourses on prison conditions suggest that a homogenous international standard may not always be the most desirable option. The penultimate chapter in this book focuses on the differential and contextualized form of jurisprudence that we know of and experience across the globe.

CHAPTER 7

Differential Application of Contextualized Jurisprudence

Contents

As we come close to the end of this book, it is pertinent to consider how differential forms of jurisprudence can be applied across the globe. This chapter explores a range of issues that might bring this point home. Examples include cultures of corruption in the law, diversities, legal licensing, reform agendas, and the role of local customs. The overall aim of this chapter is therefore to show that the diversities in jurisprudence are pertinent and relevant to the diversities in human experience. A controversial notion such as judicial corruption might start to provide the right contextualization.

7.1. CASE STUDY OF CULTURALLY BOUND NOTIONS OF CORRUPTION AND THE LAW

Despite widespread condemnation, it seems that corruption remains part of the judiciary (Stauch, 2000; Stein, 1998; Steinbock & McClamrock, 1994; Strauss, 1992; Stroud, 1996; Sullivan & Goldzwig, 1995). Some experts speak of a culturally bound institution and norms that support it. For example, language that minimizes the true nature and impact of corruption might be used. A case in point are references to "facilitation" to describe the bribes that are sometimes essential if one is to fully navigate a judicial system that has not come to terms with the realities of corruption. Even single country like the USA will have differential rates of corruption (*see* Figure 7.1) meaning that one size never fits all.

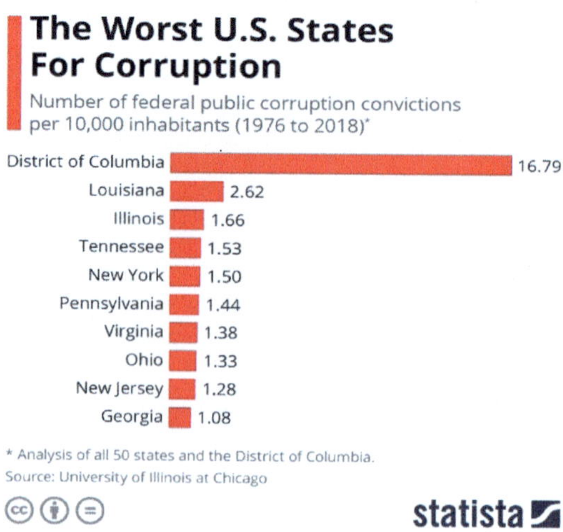

Figure 7.1. The most corrupt states in the USA.

Source: University of Illinois at Chicago via Statista.

Although service users may complain, many of them rely on this corruption to ease their access and avoid long delays (Shultz, 1990; Singleton Jr, 1989; Skene & Parker, 2002; Somerville, 1989; Spurr, 1993; Stacy, 1994; Stauch, 2000). Others may even use it to sway decisions that might have otherwise gone against them. Something that is deemed a form of corruption by one party may be perceived to be administrative pragmatism in another. Indeed, some countries fully expect that poorly paid civil servants might resort to corruption to supplement their meagre wages. In any case, the cultural distaste for corruption can vary widely and this might negatively impact on efforts to tackle this problem.

No matter how ostensibly undesirable it is, corruption is a cultural and social fact in many communities (Robertson, 1996, 1999; Savulescu, 1994; Schneider, 1992; Schuck, 1994; Sevelin, 2019; Shanley, 1990; Sharpe & Pellegrino, 1997). However, critics argue that merely accepting judicial corruption as a social fact is a form of escapism in which the real issues are ignored in favor of hand-wringing platitudes. A highly deterministic and fatalist view of corruption is what is preventing meaningful reform within the judicial system. This is bearing in mind the notion of public confidence in the system and the expectation that judicial officers will be more accountable and principled than lay people.

Some writers have referred to the folk understanding of culturally constructed corruption as a strawman that is formulated in a deterministic way (Rivard, 1992; Robertson, 1996, 1999; Savulescu, 1994; Schneider, 1992; Schuck, 1994; Sevelin, 2019; Shanley, 1990). Interesting euphemisms and colloquialisms have emerged to describe corruption within the legal system. A case in point is the use of the term "*lawruption*." There is a suggestion of inevitability and naturalness about corruption when using these terms. Critics argue that corruption in the judicial system is preventable and manageable with the right tools, values, norms, and values.

This corruption must be tackled in a multidisciplinary fashion, bearing in mind the fact that there are interrelationships between the different arms of the state as well as the complex interactions they have with communities (Nelson, 1994; Nobles, 2012; O'Donovan & Gilbar, 2003; Oberman, 1992; Okin, 1990; Oster, 2021; Paliwala, 2016; Paris & Poorman, 1995). It would therefore be a mistake to assume that only people who are working in the legal profession can tackle its corruption or that it is only outsiders that can effectively address this problem. Rather, there ought to be collaboration and communication among the different interest groups. After all, corruption has far-reaching and peripatetic effects on society. The more conventional views of corruption in the judiciary sometimes normalize this vice (Allen, 1990, 1992; Alward, 2002; Amaraskekara & Bagaric, 2004; Anderson, 1993; Andrews, 1996; Arinta et al., 2021).

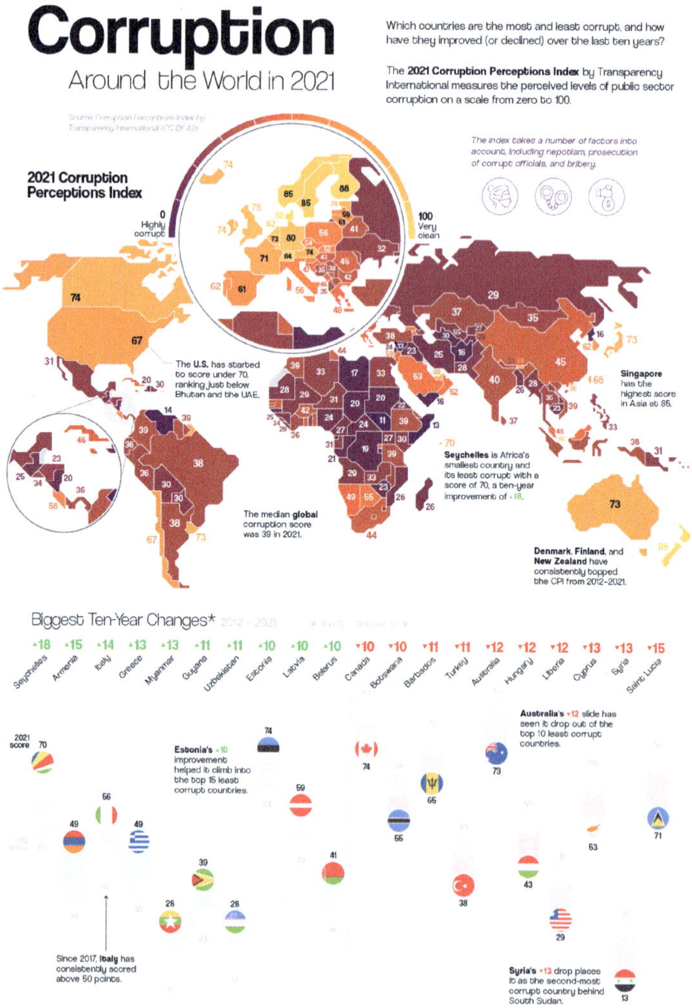

Figure 7.2. Global corruption map.

Source: Visual Capitalist.

By adopting a deterministic and piecemeal approach of getting rid of a few bad apples, this conventional view fails to deal with the systemic causes and effects of judicial corruption. Critics argue that corruption has a special kind of harm that goes beyond that which is caused by theft or fraud. Two major objections have been raised concerning the conventional views of corruption in the judiciary.

The first is known as the triviality objection (Okin, 1990; Oster, 2021; Paliwala, 2016; Paris & Poorman, 1995; Pellegrino & Sharpe, 1989; Ploughman, 1995; Pogge, 1991). Under this objection, there is a notion that everything that humans is necessarily cultural. This means that no substantive efforts are made to fight a vice that is somehow considered human and part of the natural condition. The second objection is that of circularity which suggests that any efforts to explain how and why corruption becomes part of a culture means that corruption becomes a cultural phenomenon. Meanwhile global corruption continues to fester (*see* Figure 7.2).In any case, these objections are mainly raised in political science (Kozłowski, 2021; Lane & Grodin, 1997; Mathieu, 1992; May, 1999; McConnell, 1991; McCoy, 1992; Meisel, 1992). Using circularity and triviality as a prism means that there is an array of concepts surrounding corruption in the judiciary. Some of those concepts may become inoperant in many political contexts. For example, liberal democracies are founded on the notion that government must behave in a responsible manner to make morally defensible policies. Thinking of corruption as a cultural phenomenon also raises issues of diversity in legal practice and education.

7.2. DIVERSITIES IN LEGAL EDUCATION AND PRACTICE

The legal profession is one of the most prestigious and only second to medicine in recent years (Kozłowski, 2021; Lane & Grodin, 1997; Mathieu, 1992; May, 1999; McConnell, 1991; McCoy, 1992; Meisel, 1992). That means that those who enter that profession are necessarily privileged to be admitted. However, stringent entrance criterion means that those who are not already privileged may struggle to get a foothold in the profession (*see* Figure 7.3). The outcome is a profession that starts out being exclusionary and therefore does not reflect the diversity of the communities that it is meant to serve.

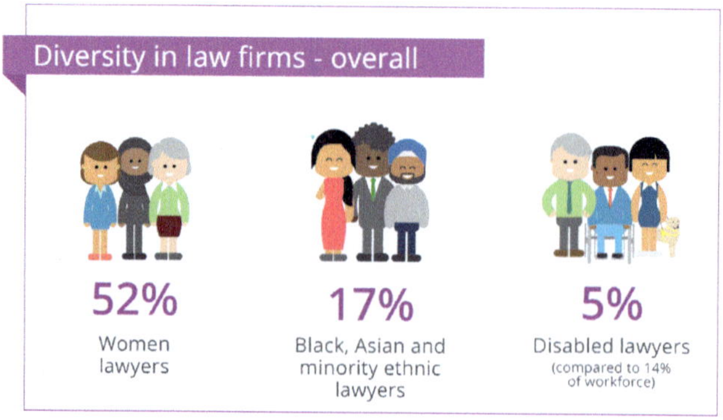

Figure 7.3. Example of diversity issues in law firms.

Source: Solicitor Regulation Authority.

There are arguments for and against diversity depending on one's political view of inclusiveness (Kadish, 1992; Kahn, 1991; Kalb, 1990; Kamisar, 1993; Kamm, 2001; Kass & Lund, 1996; Kaveny, 1991, 2006). For example, some argue that there is nothing wrong with creating an elitist profession if it can deliver the best results. Hence, the stringent entrance requirements mean that only the best can get it. This can be beneficial to the profession in the long run because it is not forced to accept those that are not prepared for the rigors of this work. As an illustrative example, few would want to have their brain operated upon by someone who has been admitted making the quotas rather than by virtue of their brilliance in surgery.

The other side of the coin is the argument that the legal system serves a community that is diverse and must therefore reflect that service (Fentiman, 1989; Field, 1990, 1991; Figueira-Mcdonough, 1990; Finer, 1991; Fluss & Zeegers, 1990; Fortin, 1991; Gelman, 1994). This view rejects the notion of an elevated legal profession that dispenses justices to the great unwashed. According to this argument, the lack of diversity in the profession means that the conduct of its business is necessary exclusionary. Many of the judicial officers may not have any experiences of the real life that people lead such that their decisions are absurd or even harmful.

In the USA for instance, this is an issue that is being tackled incrementally based on a starting point in which the law was demonstrably elitist. The fear is always doing too much too soon such that the legal profession is diluted in terms of standards and community respect (Weithman, 1999; Whitaker & Edwards, 1990; White, 1990; Wicclair, 1991a, b; Wildes,

1997; Wilson, 1994). The 1978 Bakke decision by the Supreme Court was a landmark case in the USA. It set the legal foundation for the integration of selective professional schools and universities. Notably, Justice Lewis Powell delivered the controlling opinion which upheld race-consciousness in admissions.

The underlying principle was that these race-conscious admission decisions would allow the production of a diverse student population which would eventually diversify the profession itself (Rae & DeGiorgio, 1991; Ravven, 2016; Raymond, 1999; Resnik, 1997; Rich, 1997; Rivard, 1992; Robertson, 1996, 1999). Such a diverse profession body would represent a range of experiences and perspectives which would in turn enrich the legal profession. In its immediate implementation, such a policy would open student experiences so that they were more diverse than the previous monolithic experience of white privileged learners.

Those that work in legal academia have sometimes been accused of failing to demonstrate the value and importance of diversity in student experiences (Hill, 1990, 1991a, b; Hope & Fulford, 1994; Hylton, 1990; Kadish, 1992; Kahn, 1991; Kalb, 1990; Kamisar, 1993). Rather, many are more interested in maintaining the status quo because it privileges the profession when compared to the alternatives. Indeed, some institutions have pre-entry examinations which make it even harder for learners from poor backgrounds to make it. Meanwhile, those who oppose corrective measures (such as affirmative action) have been sharpening their arguments and rhetoric.

Due to hostility towards inclusion and diversity, some of the hard-won interventions have been reversed or replaced with seemingly anti-inclusion measures (Harris, 2003; Harris & Holm, 2002; Harvey & Chadwick, 1992; Hasnas, 1995; Hill, 1990, 1991a, b). For instance, a federal appeals court outlawed affirmative action in Texas from 1994. One of the reasons given for this controversial decision was the argument that diversification had not demonstrated any education benefits since its inception. Others argue that these policies disadvantage those who invest in self-improvement. The increasing lawsuits for and against affirmative action suggest that this is not a settled issue, but rather one that is still being contested.

Nevertheless, some of the traditionally conservative states in the USA are making efforts towards highlighting the importance of diversity (Dworkin, 1992; Dyck, 1992; Eisenstat, 1991; Eldridge, 2021; Elhauge, 1994; Emanuel, 1999; Feinberg, 1991; Fentiman, 1989). A case in point are the culturally inclusive practices that are being adopted by the state government in Tennessee (*see* Figure 7.4), a historically problematic state when it comes to race relations in the USA. Some have argued that these controversial issues are based decided through the democratic process such as the organization of referenda on them.

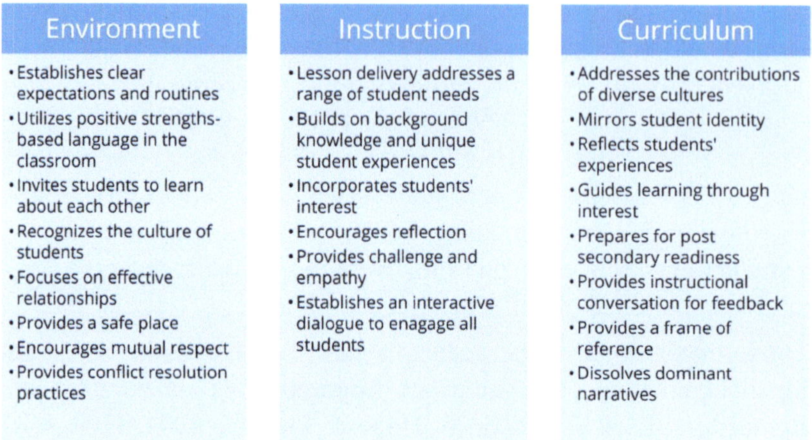

Figure 7.4. Guide to culturally inclusive practices.

Source: Tennessee Government.

Others take the opposite view, arguing that the rights of minorities should not be subjected to a democratic process regardless of how established it is (Kamm, 2001; Kass & Lund, 1996; Kaveny, 1991, 2006; Khushf, 1994; Knoppers & LeBris, 1991; Kozłowski, 2021). This is because majorities are capable of dictatorship and oppression through the ballot box. For example, many Southern states in the USA resented the abolition of slavery and it was entirely possible that referenda on the issue might have returned embarrassing results in which this practice was returned to the states. Rather, the inclusion of minorities is considered by some to be so important that it is beyond the democratic will of the populace.

Then there are those who posit that these arguments are best won through logic and reason (Stacy, 1994; Stauch, 2000; Stein, 1998; Steinbock & McClamrock, 1994; Strauss, 1992; Stroud, 1996; Sullivan & Goldzwig, 1995). If there are pragmatic reasons why the legal profession should be more inclusive, then there is a high chance that those that are in control of decisions will eventually relent and open the right spaces for the right people. To that end, it is necessary to make a practical and business case for the inclusion of minorities even when the structure of society excludes them.

For example, it could be argued that there are many talented lawyers that are being lost to the system because they are born in deprived circumstances. In any case, these interventions improve practice and standards. A similar role is played by the professional licensing system.

7.3. CASE STUDY OF THE LEGAL LICENSING SYSTEM IN THE USA

The licensing process in the USA is meant to ensure that only people that only the most qualified lawyers practice within the jurisdiction (Cantor, 2005; Capron, 1990, 1999; Chandler, 1990; Chervenak & McCullough, 1991; Chesterman, 1998; Clark, 2002). This is also a means of protecting the profession from intruders who would practice without the right qualifications and experience. Because of the unique diversity of regimes by state, the licensing system in the USA is equally differentiated. One is licensed to practice in specific jurisdictions and even in specific fields.

There have been debates about the nature of licensing and its impact on performance (Dworkin, 1992; Dyck, 1992; Eisenstat, 1991; Eldridge, 2021; Elhauge, 1994; Emanuel, 1999; Feinberg, 1991; Fentiman, 1989). For instance, some argue that these are systems which are designed to keep outsiders out. The rationale is that if outsiders are let in then standards will fall. Another argument is that such a prestigious profession should be restricted to responsible citizens rather than allowing anyone to join. Of course, some of these arguments may make the law appear something of a protection racket or a monopoly in which only a few are let in.

Another argument is that the professionalism of law as a practice will be improved through licensing (Kahn, 1991; Kalb, 1990; Kamisar, 1993; Kamm, 2001; Kass & Lund, 1996; Kaveny, 1991, 2006; Khushf, 1994). There are many requirements before one is allowed to practice. The implication is that they act as a sieve to take out those that would be unsuitable by virtue of their poor grades, lack of aptitude, or limited experience. The ultimate beneficiary in these arrangements is the client who knows that if someone is licensed as a lawyer, they meet certain minimum requirements.

Such measures remove the need to engage in stringent background checks and tests before one is hired (Downie & Randall, 1997; Draper, 1993; Dresser, 1995, 2003; Dworkin, 1991, 1992; Dyck, 1992; Eisenstat, 1991). This is particularly important for criminal defendants who may require someone competent at very short notice. If the applicant lawyer is already vetted and licensed, then no further time is wasted in ascertaining their credentials and ability to practice. Besides, the licensing system ensures that lawyers are constantly moderating their behavior and impulses to ensure that they do not lose their license.

Losing the right to practice is one of the most serious professional sanctions that can be levelled against those that have fallen below professional expectations (Hardwig, 1991; Harris, 2003; Harris & Holm, 2002; Harvey & Chadwick, 1992; Hasnas, 1995; Hill, 1990, 1991a, b). It is such a powerful tool that it has proven an effective deterrent against errant lawyers. Moreover, the public is reassured that those who are not fit to practice lose their license and can no longer do harm to the public and profession. However, as Figure 7.5 shows, being unlicensed or under-educated is not an impossible barrier for practicing the law effectively.

Famous Lawyers Who Didn't Go To Law School

Figure	Story
Abraham Lincoln	Before becoming a U.S. President, Lincoln independently studied the law, and passed the Illinois bar exam on his own.
John Adams	The 2nd U.S. President studied as a law apprentice.
Thomas Jefferson	Jefferson – a Lawyer, Founding Father, and principal author of the Declaration of Independence – studied as a law apprentice.
Daniel Webster	Webster, a senator who "shaped several key U.S. Supreme Court cases," studied law in his friend's office.
John Marshall	Marshall, a Chief Justice of the Supreme Court, attended six weeks of lectures at William & Mary before apprenticing instead.
Clarence Darrow	After determining "it would be much more cost effective to work and study in an actual law office," famous lawyer Darrow dropped out of law school and did an independant study.

Figure 7.5. Famous lawyers who did not go to school.

Source: Price Economics.

Critics have argued that the restrictions that are inherent in licensing are meant to protect a club of well-connected people (Sharpe & Pellegrino, 1997; Sheldon & Wilkinson, 1997, 1998; Shepherd, 1995; Shevory, 1990). Anyone that cannot join or maintain that club is prevented from practicing the law. Others argue that if someone has attained an academic qualification and has some experience, then they should be allowed to practice. The additional licensing requirements are problematic because they create burdens that do not always translate into better practice. In that sense, the license to practice is more about exclusivity than protecting the public or raising standards.

Some suggest that a law degree is in effect a license to practice (*see* Figure 7.6). However, that raises questions about the nature of the curriculum (TÄNnsjÖ, 1992; Thomson, 1999; Truog et al., 1991; Turrina et al., 2021; van Delden & Laurie, 2004; Van Der Burg, 1997). Moreover, there are questions about the extent to which the current training and education modalities prepare lawyers for the field. One of the regular complaints concerns people that are qualified but seem unable to practice as expected based on their qualifications. Perhaps a more appropriate response is reforms in the education and training of officers of the courts. The UK is a prime case in point.

Figure 7.6. The US law degree as a business license.

Source: BCG Research.

7.4. CASE STUDY OF LEGAL REFORMS IN THE UK

The legal system in the UK has been under reform on several occasions to reflect the changing needs and proclivities of the society that is subject to these laws and legal systems (Rivard, 1992; Robertson, 1996, 1999; Savulescu, 1994; Schneider, 1992; Schuck, 1994; Sevelin, 2019; Shanley, 1990). The Law Commission regularly reviews the law of England and Wales. There is an implicit requirement to recommend changes where necessary. The Law Commission is independent and was established in 1965 with this independence in mind.

The commission seeks to ensure that the law is fair to all regardless of circumstances (Kalb, 1990; Kamisar, 1993; Kamm, 2001; Kass & Lund, 1996; Kaveny, 1991, 2006; Khushf, 1994; Knoppers & LeBris, 1991). Another aim is to ensure that the law is as simple as possible. Such a requirement is a shift away from previous regimes that created complexities that were beyond the comprehension of lay people. The law commission has a role in ensuring that the judiciary is cost effective.

These complex roles are achieved by conducting research and engaging in extensive consultations with relevant interest groups (Quante, 1999; Rae & DeGiorgio, 1991; Ravven, 2016; Raymond, 1999; Resnik, 1997; Rich, 1997; Rivard, 1992; Robertson, 1996). The commission specializes in certain areas of law. Some of the output from the commission arises when it makes pertinent recommendations to Parliament. This is the supreme legislative authority in the UK, and it is where improvements are made to existing law and practice when needed.

The primary role of parliament in this structure is to implement any changes that have been recommended by the commission (Dresser, 2003; Dworkin, 1991, 1992; Dyck, 1992; Eisenstat, 1991; Eldridge, 2021; Elhauge, 1994; Emanuel, 1999). This is achieved via legislation which is then translated into court practice and decisions. Research indicates that about two thirds of recommendations have been implemented by Parliament. This is a demonstration of the high esteem in which the commission is held. It is also an indicator that the recommendations are often well considered and speak to the needs of the community as well as pertinent issues within the kingdom. There is legislative authority behind this reform agenda in much the same way as other countries deal with issues of reform (Dyck, 1992; Eisenstat, 1991; Eldridge, 2021; Elhauge, 1994; Emanuel, 1999; Feinberg, 1991; Fentiman, 1989). A case in point is the Law Commission Act of 2009. A relevant Protocol came into force in January 2010 to guide this process. One of the main objectives of the protocols was to improve the ratio of recommendations being implemented. Figure 7.7 is an example of some of the reforms that are considered.

Figure 7.7. Suggested reforms in UK charity law.

Source: Law Commission UK.

There are protocols for ensuring follow-up after recommendations are made. Many judicial systems across the globe suffer from the phenomenon of reviews that are not followed up with concrete action (Stauch, 2000; Stein, 1998; Steinbock & McClamrock, 1994; Strauss, 1992; Stroud, 1996; Sullivan & Goldzwig, 1995). The organization of the law commission in the UK is meant to address these gaps. For example, the Lord Chancellor must provide an annual report which sets out the extent to which Parliament has adopted recommendations. The implication is a system of checks and balances which ensures that pertinent issues are not ignored through inertia.

There are many publications that are credited to the law commission. The purpose of these publications is to inform the public about the work that is being done (Meisel, 1992, 1996; Menzel, 1992; Merrick, 1990; Morreim, 1991; Munzer, 1994; Nelson, 1994; Nobles, 2012). They also stimulate public debate which might result in better reforms since the public becomes aware of the issues at stake. For example, the commission produces "*Law under Review*" which is an influential bulletin whose purpose is to outline ongoing projects. Since 1997, this review has been published online.

The Law Commission produces both consultation papers and reports. These are standard contributions to the development of the law and jurisprudence (Hill, 1990, 1991a, b; Hope & Fulford, 1994; Hylton, 1990; Kadish, 1992; Kahn, 1991; Kalb, 1990; Kamisar, 1993). They are also useful instruments for increasing access since they drive transparency in the administration of justice. Readers may find these published as command papers. The relevant literature will also be available within the printed series of Command Papers. These are stored within the Bodleian.

The typical project that is undertaken by the law commission will undergo a specific process that reflects the complexities of the law as well as the various interest groups that may have an interest in its reform (Glass & Speyer-Ofenberg, 1996; Glick, 1992; Gormally, 2002; Gostin, 1995; Greenberg & Kamin, 1993; Grondelski, 1989). These are recommendations that have been adopted across the globe to ensure that reforming the law is a deliberate and transparent process. However, there will be certain differences depending on the jurisdiction. These differences are acceptable reflections of the sovereignty of various states and the need to allow relevant reforms rather than undergoing a wholesale importation of reforms that are fashioned in different jurisdictions.

The starting point is the law commission reviewing an area of the law to ascertain what is working and what could work better. This is the stage at which some of the abuses and gaps are identified (Agich & Spielman, 1997; Allen, 1990, 1992; Alward, 2002; Amaraskekara & Bagaric, 2004; Anderson, 1993; Andrews, 1996). It is important that the remit of the project is decided so that it does not go beyond specific boundaries. This also helps to ensure that time and other resources are well spent rather than investigating every minute problem that could arise in the judiciary. The relevant government department will sanction the remit of the commission in this area.

A detailed study of the law then follows with the assistance of experts. One of the techniques used in these reviews is to ascertain how different systems deal with the same problem with differential or identical results (Figueira-McDonough, 1990; Finer, 1991; Fluss & Zeegers, 1990; Fortin, 1991; Gelman, 1994; Glass & Speyer-Ofenberg, 1996; Glick, 1992; Gormally, 2002). The investigation may also consider other jurisdictions especially the ones that are in similar circumstances to the UK. The overriding principle is to learn from mistakes and create the foundation for improvements in the future. This is an onerous task, bearing in mind the complexities of UK law (*see* Figure 7.8).

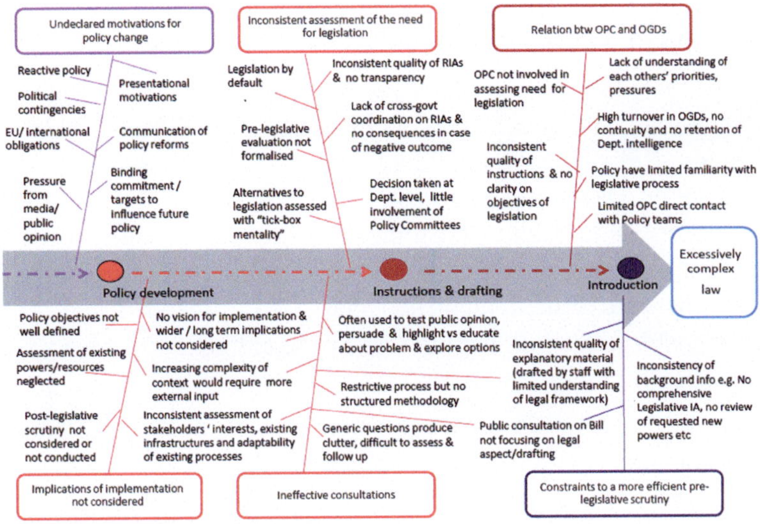

Figure 7.8. The complexities of UK laws.

Source: UK Government.

Having closely examined the law and identified any defects, the commission will then prepare a consultation paper. This paper is like the ones used in other jurisdictions in as far as it sets out the law and the defects that have been identified (Clerkin, 2021; Coady, 2002; Cohen, 1989; Coughlan, 1989; Crigger, 1995; Crossley, 1993; Crouch & Elliott, 1999; Daniels & Sabin, 1997). Various solutions are presented with the advantages and disadvantages of each solution discussed. The consultation paper invites commentary from interested parties. The parties may include those that are in the legal profession, members of the public, and the media.

The commission actively encourages feedback from the public who are primary interest holders within the structure (Oster, 2021; Paliwala, 2016; Paris & Poorman, 1995; Pellegrino & Sharpe, 1989; Ploughman, 1995; Pogge, 1991; Purdy, 1990). The commentaries may go beyond the initial report and highlight areas that have not yet been fully investigated by the commission. Having reviewed and incorporated these comments, the commission will submit a report to the Minister of Justice and Lord

Chancellor. That report will include the final recommendations from the commission with justification and rationale. A draft bill may be included to demonstrate how the recommendations could be given effect. Other countries may include local customs in their reviews and resultant improvements.

7.5. IMPACT OF LOCAL CUSTOMS ON THE LAW

Local customs have a critical role to play in the development and implementation of the law as well as jurisprudence (Clerkin, 2021; Coady, 2002; Cohen, 1989; Coughlan, 1989; Crigger, 1995; Crossley, 1993; Crouch & Elliott, 1999; Daniels & Sabin, 1997). There will be certain difficulties that are observed in adding customs into law, not least because of the diversity and complexity of customs. One must have a clear picture of how these customs were formed, identified, classified, embedded, and continued. Hence, that exploration will begin to reveal the culture of people in a specific place at a specific time.

As Figure 7.9 demonstrates, customers may be claims to certain rights that are not universally recognized (Emanuel, 1999; Feinberg, 1991; Fentiman, 1989; Field, 1990, 1991; Figueira-McDonough, 1990; Finer, 1991; Fluss & Zeegers, 1990). The case of Sati discussed elsewhere in this book (burning widows at the funeral pyres of their deceased husbands in India), one's claims might seriously infringe on the rights of others. They may even disrupt the sensibilities of societies that consider themselves civilized. Besides, there is an expectation that customs will change with time and place. Hence, there can be no rigid adherence to some infallible form of custom law.

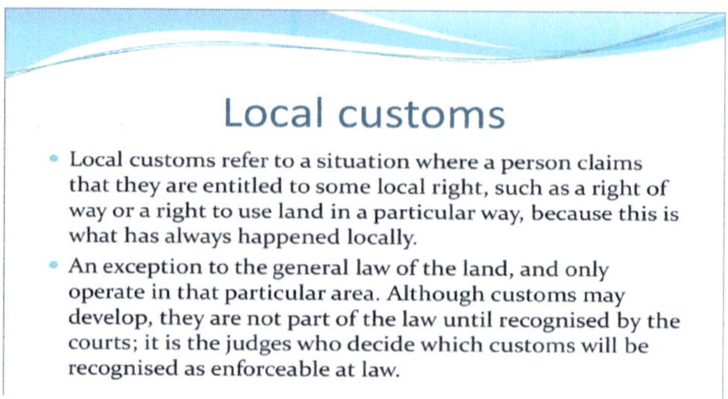

Figure 7.9. Local customs under UK law.

Source: George Allen via Slide Player.

There exists some interaction of different sources of law (Allen, 1990, 1992; Alward, 2002; Amaraskekara & Bagaric, 2004; Anderson, 1993; Andrews, 1996; Arinta et al., 2021). A case in point is international law which is derived from a combination of treaty laws and general customary practice. Local customs will represent certain cultural dynamics including specific features and faces. However, that can be problematic since it is challenging to distinguish treaty laws and customary practice when the final legislation has been put into practice.

Researchers have struggled to crystallize the meaning of custom logic when faced with a fast-changing world that demands change (Shewmon, 1997; Shultz, 1990; Singleton Jr, 1989; Skene & Parker, 2002; Somerville, 1989; Spurr, 1993; Stacy, 1994). Whereas the traditionalists would rather retreat into custom, some reformers are questioning the very basis of some of these laws. Moreover, there are other areas of conflict between localized and generalized customs. For instance, some countries comprise many communities and tribes with their own customs. It then becomes a complicated task to harmonize these customs into a national law that is acceptable to the populace.

Two major categories of logic may be competing when establishing and maintaining laws (Crossley, 1993; Crouch & Elliott, 1999; Daniels & Sabin, 1997; Den Hartogh, 1997; Downie, 1992; Downie & Randall, 1997). Custom logic will rely on tradition, practice, and culture to form and identify local laws as well as international laws. These are derived from the same ingredients which could either be in the form of "*opinio juris*" or common practice. The continuity of an existing customary rule will call for a different approach. For example, states may question the continuity of customs which operate as a treaty in cases of State succession to international law. The latter will follow a treaty logic rather than a custom logic.

International law has traditionally paid heed to customs which provide the basis for many of the ideas that it posits (Skene & Parker, 2002; Somerville, 1989; Spurr, 1993; Stacy, 1994; Stauch, 2000; Stein, 1998; Steinbock & McClamrock, 1994). This belies the caricature of international law as a collection of complex rules that are designed by an unaccountable technocracy which has little connection to the communities that are impacted by this international law in one way or another. Indeed, research has shown that customs are a major source of international law in areas such as the protection of vulnerable communities. Contrary to the assertions by its critics, international law does not seek to devastate local customs and culture (Allen, 1992; Alward, 2002; Amaraskekara & Bagaric, 2004; Anderson, 1993; Andrews, 1996; Arinta et al., 2021; Ayres et al., 1993). Rather, international law seeks to amalgamate the diversities of customs across the globe into a coherent whole which can improve world peace and prosperity. Indeed, one of the reasons that international law may be slow to react to the need for legislation is because of a consultative process that seeks to ensure that no nation is left behind when deciding such protections.

The major problems arise when there is an ongoing customary practice that is effectively banned or made obsolete by international legislation (Crossley, 1993; Crouch & Elliott, 1999; Daniels & Sabin, 1997; Den Hartogh, 1997; Downie, 1992; Downie & Randall, 1997). This is when local people may complain about their excluded or some level of cultural hegemony. It is at this point that there is a fierce debate between following custom logic or treaty logic. Besides, things become significantly more problematic when some of the most powerful nations on earth such as the USA are calling for specific international law but then refusing to follow that law based on sovereignty.

Overall, the sources of law can be complex, and custom is just one of many options that are considered (Van Der Burg, 1997; Van der Burg & Brom, 2000; van Schooten, 2014; Viljoen, 2012; Walters, 1991, 2012). Figure 7.10 is a case in point with the multi-faceted development of the law in the UK. The need to assimilate a range of customs in a singular international law is often at the heart of many of the disputes surrounding sovereignty versus the global community. There are specific agreements and protocols that are referenced when embedding international law in domestic or local customs. Some of these include estoppel, acquiescence, and tacit agreements.

Whereas consensus is desirable, it is not always clear that this is achieved as a prerequisite for the institution of international law (Shewmon, 1997; Shultz, 1990; Singleton Jr, 1989; Skene & Parker, 2002; Somerville, 1989; Spurr, 1993; Stacy, 1994). For instance, some of the smaller states have complained about being bulldozed by the larger states to accept laws that are demonstrably against their own interests. Then there are those who have influence that is sufficient to withstand this pressure but are then turned into international pariahs because they refuse to acquiesce to laws that have been fashioned by other hegemonic powers.

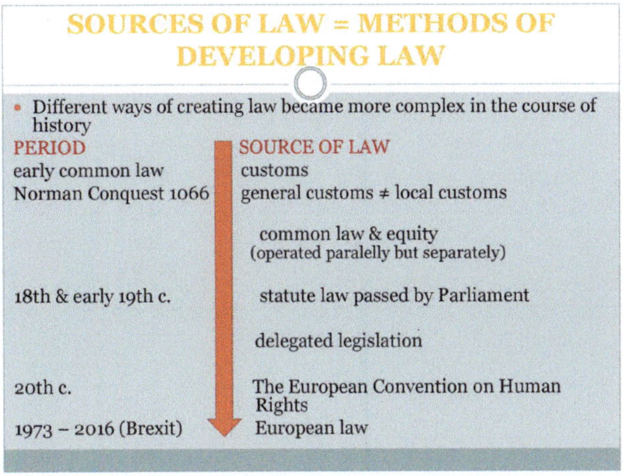

Figure 7.10. The development of the law in the UK.

Source: Andrés Ferreyra Campos via Slide Player.

Sometimes, the misunderstanding emanates from a lack of understanding of local customs and their instrumentality (Ploughman, 1995; Pogge, 1991; Purdy, 1990; Quante, 1999; Rae & DeGiorgio, 1991; Ravven, 2016; Raymond, 1999). Reforming international law or even local customs ought to be a deliberative process that involves extensive consultation. Unfortunately, the desire to resolve problems that emanate means that some of this deliberation is eschewed in favor of quick solutions that seem to work but are not sustainable in the long run. Custom has a role to play in local and international law. The nature and extent of that role is subject to this deliberate process of reform.

CHAPTER 7 SUMMARY

This penultimate chapter in the book has considered the differential application of contextualized jurisprudence. For instance, the chapter has shown that corruption is not an inevitable or culturally essential part of society. Rather, this chapter highlights the possibilities of real reform and change in terms of diversity and the incorporation of local customs. The final chapter in the book will consider the current trends in jurisprudence and what they portend for the future of this aspect of the law.

CHAPTER 8

Critique of Current Jurisprudence and Prospects

Contents

As we close this book, it is pertinent to consider the current trends in jurisprudence and their implications for the entirety of legal practice. The chapter opens with a critique of populism in law. The second section considers the extent of judicial independence and interdependence. The third section revisits the efficiency of the justice systems bearing in mind the risks of corrupt practices. In the fourth section, we posit ways of bringing jurisprudence and justice closer to the people. The final chapter then closes with an emphasis on the benefit of diversifying the legal profession. Ironically, some have argued that this diversification is populist in nature. Hence, the appropriateness of making it a starting point for this final chapter in the book.

8.1. RESPONDING TO POPULIST DEMANDS OF THE LAW

The topic of law-and-order populism or penal populism has proved to be lucrative for politicians who wish to get into power by demonizing less sympathetic minorities such as prisoners and migrants (Ayres et al., 1993; Bekrycht & Mańko, 2020; Bianchi, 2017; Blair & Kaserman, 1991; Blustein, 1993; Bonnicksen, 1995). As is often the case in these instances, there is no coherent philosophical positioning to justify some of the harshest rhetoric that is relied on by politicians to raise temperatures and distract from other significant failings within the political class.

This populism has been demonstrated in various ways including enacting harsh penalties for previously simple crimes and generally competing to wear the label of "*toughest on crime*" (Schneider, 1992; Schuck, 1994; Sevelin, 2019; Shanley, 1990; Sharpe & Pellegrino, 1997; Sheldon & Wilkinson, 1997, 1998). Populism is inspired by public perceptions that crime is out of control and that politicians are not doing enough to deal with the problem. Both these assumptions may be erroneous, but they drive electoral politics and might dissuade those that are looking for a more moderate approach.

Consequently, it is the most reactionary voices on the debates about crime which get most attention from the media (Dworkin, 1992; Dyck, 1992; Eisenstat, 1991; Eldridge, 2021; Elhauge, 1994; Emanuel, 1999; Feinberg, 1991; Fentiman, 1989). Some politicians may not be included to engage in penal populism but are forced to do so when attacked by opponents for being "*soft on crime*." The media will play its part by sensationalizing any part of the criminal justice system, especially if it involves immigrants or people from ethnic minorities. The public interest is redefined as a competition to see who is more oppressive. The effects of penal populism can be dire for those who are incarcerated (Den Hartogh, 1997; Downie, 1992; Downie & Randall, 1997; Draper, 1993; Dresser, 1995, 2003; Dworkin, 1991, 1992). When these policies are followed, there is an explosion who are imprisoned for a long time. The outcomes of these policies are extensive and even impact on the ways in which the judiciary carries out its work. For example, minimum sentencing and three-strike rules given that defendants can be imprisoned for decades when the current judge would normally merit no more than 5 years in prison.

Politicians tend to respond to populist demands because they perceive them to be a fast way of achieving popularity especially if there are other potentially distracting challenges (Stroud, 1996; Sullivan & Goldzwig, 1995; Sulmasy, 1989; TÄNnsjÖ, 1992; Thomson, 1999; Truog et al., 1991; Turrina et al., 2021). A case in point is when dictatorial regimes in the developing world respond to complaints about human rights by demanding that offenders (including political prisoners) are automatically placed on remand without bail. This gives the impression of tackling crime whilst creating opportunities for the mass incarceration of political opponents under the guise of lawful arrest.

The effects of populism on democracy are well documented (*see* Figure 8.1 for an example). However, the effects on the judicial system are yet to be philosophically and analytically clarified (Coady, 2002; Cohen, 1989; Coughlan, 1989; Crigger, 1995; Crossley, 1993; Crouch & Elliott, 1999; Daniels & Sabin, 1997).

	Threat	Corrective
Responsiveness: popular control and decision-making (participation, representation, government capability)	Negative: control over institutions, hollowing out the representative process HYPOTHESIS 1: Populist parties harm the quality of democracy, affecting all its functions.	Positive: re-emphasis on responsiveness. HYPOTHESIS 2: Populist parties improve participation, representation, civil society and the public sphere.
Responsibility: Liberal protections (checks and balances, rule of law, individual liberties)	Negative: dismantling institutions (Hypothesis 1)	Negative: populists emphasize vertical over horizontal control. HYPOTHESIS 3: Populists parties harm liberal protections (checks and balances, the rule of law, as well as individual liberties)
Intermediaries between politics and society (public sphere, civil society, transparency)	Negative: populists as the only true voice of the people, denying pluralism (Hypothesis 1)	No effect

Figure 8.1. Effects of populism on democracy.

Source: Cambridge University.

For a profession that prides itself on impartiality, lawyers, and judges may be challenged by ethical dilemmas when implementing populist policies that are contrary to their own values or perceptions of the law. For example, the automatic denial of bail might contradict the notion of Habeus Corpus and hence make such decisions very problematic for judicial officers.

Some sociologists have argued that populism arises when there is disaffection by a segment of society (Fortin, 1991; Gelman, 1994; Glass & Speyer-Ofenberg, 1996; Glick, 1992; Gormally, 2002; Gostin, 1995). For instance, the perpetual victims of crime who have not received the redress that they are looking for may turn to populism as a potential solution. Others may blame the judiciary for not doing its work of imprisoning dangerous offenders meaning that they go on to commit even worse crimes. Some of the harrowing examples is where a future serial offender is given light sentences until they commit a major crime whose effects cannot be reversed. The same can be seen where foreigners commit crime, and the local populace argues that a strong immigration system may have prevented such criminality by keeping out the criminals.

Unsurprisingly, populism can be very unpopular with the intellectual class who consider it to be a base form of politicking (Glass & Speyer-Ofenberg, 1996; Glick, 1992; Gormally, 2002; Gostin, 1995; Greenberg & Kamin, 1993; Grondelski, 1989). Others posit that populism can be fought by tackling corruption (*see* Figure 8.2 for a demonstration of this argument). Then there are those who suggest that the best response to penal populism is to ensure that justice is done and be seen to be done. A case in point is the use of open sentencing so that the public understands how and why someone has been convicted before that person is given an appropriate sentence. Indeed, the UK has even given victims and members of the public the right to contest sentences that are considered lenient.

The problem with such open justice mechanisms and programs is the fact that the administration of justice becomes nothing more than a reality show (Eisenstat, 1991; Eldridge, 2021; Elhauge, 1994; Emanuel, 1999; Feinberg, 1991; Fentiman, 1989; Field, 1990, 1991). Judges may start playing to the gallery to acquire a reputation for being tough. Besides, it is worth noting that incarceration is one of the most expensive forms of punishment. Hence, incarcerating large numbers of people is going to make the system less efficient and may inadvertently increase crime but not allowing offenders to reform. The USA, which has experimented with open justice systems, has not always produced the best outcomes. For instance, trial by public opinion might mean that people who are innocent are convicted and punished. Underpinning some of these debates is the search for judicial independence.

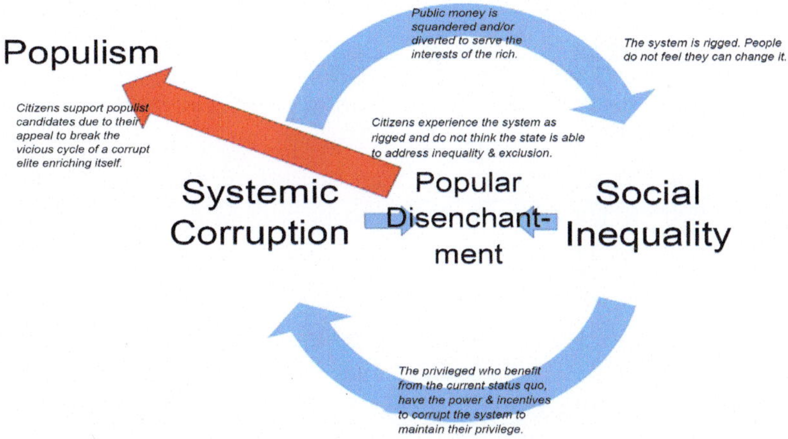

Figure 8.2. The link between populism and corruption.

Source: Global Anti-Corruption Blog.

8.2. JUDICIAL INDEPENDENCE AND INTERDEPENDENCE

Although the judiciary is part of the government, it must remain independent and seemingly impartial to maintain public confidence in its work (Robertson, 1999; Savulescu, 1994; Schneider, 1992; Schuck, 1994; Sevelin, 2019; Shanley, 1990; Sharpe & Pellegrino, 1997; Sheldon & Wilkinson, 1997). Judicial independence requires that the judiciary should be independent from the other branches of government. More specifically, courts should not be subject to improper influence from the other branches of government. Similarly, the courts should be free from private or partisan interests which corrupt their work and mandate.

Judicial independence is important to the idea of separation of powers (O'Donovan & Gilbar, 2003; Oberman, 1992; Okin, 1990; Oster, 2021; Paliwala, 2016; Paris & Poorman, 1995; Pellegrino & Sharpe, 1989). This is an important political science concept that is responsible for good governance in democracies. Many countries achieve judicial independence through different means of judicial selection. The implication is that choosing judges must guarantee their independence. This starts with the decision maker who must either be impartial or have such significant restrictions that they cannot engage in partisan behavior. However, the fact that a politician makes the decision can overturn this goal.

One way to promote judicial independence is by granting life tenure or long tenure for judges (Clark, 2002; Clerkin, 2021; Coady, 2002; Cohen, 1989; Coughlan, 1989; Crigger, 1995; Crossley, 1993; Crouch & Elliott, 1999). The rationale is that these judges are no longer beholden to anybody since they do not fear losing their jobs. This approach ideally frees judicial officers to decide cases and make rulings according to the rule of law and judicial discretion. The alternative would be judges that are continuously making calculations about their tenure and ruling accordingly.

Ideally, independent judges are not afraid to make their rulings on law even if those decisions are politically unpopular or opposed by powerful interests (Anderson, 1993; Andrews, 1996; Arinta et al., 2021; Ayres et al., 1993; Bekrycht & Mańko, 2020; Bianchi, 2017; Blair & Kaserman, 1991). This concept can be traced back to 18th-century England. At the time, judges were appointed by the king at the behest of powerful politicians. The idea was that these were the servants of the sovereign and government to the extent that they could not reasonably make rulings that were contrary to government policy.

That model has been adopted by many nations where the judges are appointed by the head of government or head of state (Nobles, 2012; O'Donovan & Gilbar, 2003; Oberman, 1992; Okin, 1990; Oster, 2021; Paliwala, 2016; Paris & Poorman, 1995). Except for certain cases, the likelihood is that the politician will appoint those judges who are politically aligned with them. Meanwhile, those that express opposing views or are suspected of being contrary to the prevailing belief system are not given the chance to join the courts. The result are decisions tinged with political influence.

The idea of a completely impartial court has been critiqued as being impractical and not fully achievable (Cantor, 2005; Capron, 1990, 1999; Chandler, 1990; Chervenak & McCullough, 1991; Chesterman, 1998; Clark, 2002). For example, Figure 8.3 shows that there are heroes and villains in these discussions. The ability of the judiciary to check the legislature is enhanced by the power of judicial review in some jurisdictions. This power can be used in mandating certain action when the judiciary perceives that a branch of government is refusing to perform a constitutional duty.

Figure 8.3. The heroes and villains of judicial independence.

Source: Proteus Fund.

Another mechanism that is deployed by the courts is by declaring laws passed by the legislature unconstitutional (Hamblin & Somerville, 1991; Hardwig, 1991; Harris, 2003; Harris & Holm, 2002; Harvey & Chadwick, 1992; Hasnas, 1995). These can be controversial because some might argue that the courts should always be subject to the politicians who are representatives of the people. Ruling a country through judges is deemed dangerous by some people because it may represent an erosion of the sovereignty of the people.

Others suggest that judges are already prejudiced by their training and socialization so that they think and behave in specific ways (Fentiman, 1989; Field, 1990, 1991; Figueira-McDonough, 1990; Finer, 1991; Fluss & Zeegers, 1990; Fortin, 1991; Gelman, 1994). Therefore, it would be unrealistic to consider judicial independence as the only means of ensuring that rulings are made in an impartial manner. Judicial independence serves as a safeguard for the rights and privileges provided by a limited constitution. Hence, the need to protect it in the design of the judiciary and government.

For instance, judicial independence prevents executive and legislative encroachment upon those rights that are held dear by societies (Raymond, 1999; Resnik, 1997; Rich, 1997; Rivard, 1992; Robertson, 1996, 1999; Savulescu, 1994; Schneider, 1992). A case in point is the right to a fair trial. This independence serves as a foundation for the rule of law and democracy. Indeed, many countries pride themselves on an independent judiciary as a key indicator of their democratic credentials. Politicians may be unseated when they interfere with this independence. Indeed, the international community ostracizes countries which do not guarantee judicial independence.

The rule of law means that all authority and power must come from an ultimate source of law (Steinbock & McClamrock, 1994; Strauss, 1992; Stroud, 1996; Sullivan & Goldzwig, 1995; Sulmasy, 1989; TÄNnsjÖ, 1992). Under an independent judicial system these sources are respected and protected. The implication is that the courts and its officers are free from inappropriate intervention in the judiciary's affairs. This holds true even if the interference is allegedly on national security grounds. With this independence, the judiciary can safeguard people's rights and freedoms. Moreover, an independent judiciary can ensure equal protection for all regardless of circumstances.

The effectiveness of the law is sometimes conditioned on judicial independence (Lane & Grodin, 1997; Mathieu, 1992; May, 1999; McConnell, 1991; McCoy, 1992; Meisel, 1992, 1996; Menzel, 1992). The same can be said of the respect that people have for the law. Where there is respect for judicial independence, the government which enacts law is dependent upon the judiciary's independence to operationalize fair decisions. This approach is a pillar of economic growth. The rationale is that multinational businesses and investors have confidence to invest in the economy of a nation who has a strong and stable judiciary that is independent of interference. This can be critical when protecting the right to private property.

The judiciary's role in deciding the validity of presidential and parliamentary elections also necessitates independence of the judiciary (Van Der Burg, 1997; Van der Burg & Brom, 2000; van Schooten, 2014; Viljoen, 2012; Walters, 1991, 2012). Nevertheless, there are some demerits that are associated with judicial independence. For example, there is a possible abuse of power by judges. A case in point is where judges create laws and obstacles that were never envisioned by parliament or the government.

Another potential risk in judicial independence is the leeway given to self-interest (Shewmon, 1997; Shultz, 1990; Singleton Jr, 1989; Skene & Parker, 2002; Somerville, 1989; Spurr, 1993; Stacy, 1994). Here, the judges will do everything in their power to protect and maintain their power. That means that the administration of justice takes a secondary position. Truly independent judges have been accused of ideological dedication which is contrary to the needs and aspirations of the state. Others suggest that excessive judicial independence can create fertile grounds for corruption. The Portuguese system (*see* Figure 8.4) is an example of the potential risks that must be mitigated through checks and balances (Allen, 1992; Alward, 2002; Amaraskekara & Bagaric, 2004; Anderson, 1993; Andrews, 1996; Arinta et al., 2021; Ayres et al., 1993). Those who raised the idea of divided government did not intend that the judiciary, or indeed any arm of government, would be completely independent without any oversight. Rather, the expectation was a series of complex interdependences and independences which would counteract the worst excesses of each system.

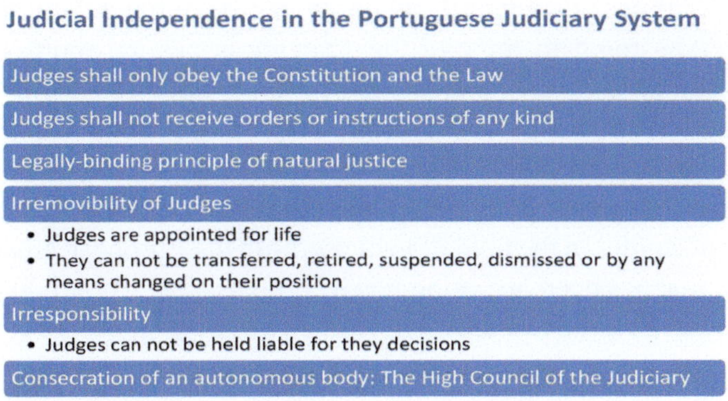

Figure 8.4. Judicial independence under the Portuguese system.

Source: Sophia Stewart via Slide Player.

Any power that is unfettered is bound to inspire some to exploit it. Unfortunately, there have been cases of judges and the judiciary acting in ways that are contrary to the public interest (Kamm, 2001; Kass & Lund, 1996; Kaveny, 1991, 2006; Khushf, 1994; Knoppers & LeBris, 1991; Kozłowski, 2021). The respect that is typically afforded to judges can be abused in the knowledge that very few would question the decisions made by the highest courts in the land. However, we must remember that it is the US Supreme Court that once legalized slavery and treated non-white people as a fraction of a human. Therefore, it always makes sense to have some control over the activities of the judiciary. This bears in mind the fact that judicial corruption does exist and is a real problem in some jurisdictions.

8.3. THE COUNCIL OF EUROPE AND JUDICIAL EFFICIENCY

There are many ways in which the judiciary can be corrupt or inefficient (Figueira-McDonough, 1990; Finer, 1991; Fluss & Zeegers, 1990; Fortin,

1991; Gelman, 1994; Glass & Speyer-Ofenberg, 1996; Glick, 1992; Gormally, 2002). In other words, this is not an infallible institution that must always be taken at its word. It is assumed that a corrupt judicial system is also necessarily inefficient. Therefore, efforts are made to create certain checks and balances that reduce these risks. A reform agenda may be put in place if corruption is endemic or if there is reluctance on the part of the judiciary to engage in a process of self-examination.

At other times, a supranational entity can be granted the task or power to oversee and regulate some of the strategic issues impacting on local or national judiciaries (Turrina et al., 2021; van Delden & Laurie, 2004; Van Der Burg, 1997; Van der Burg & Brom, 2000; van Schooten, 2014; Viljoen, 2012). A case in point is the Council of Europe and its role in the protection or promotion of human rights. The Council of Europe is a widely recognized as a reference point in the field of justice within the European area. This is an institution that has been operating for over 60 decades, even though its remit is not without its controversies.

There are 47 member states that follow the protocols that are set by the Council of Europe. These are more in the form of common standards than dictates (Hope & Fulford, 1994; Hylton, 1990; Kadish, 1992; Kahn, 1991; Kalb, 1990; Kamisar, 1993; Kamm, 2001; Kass & Lund, 1996). The standards include the efficiency of delivering justice, the independence of the judiciary, and the quality of decisions that are handed down. The European Union has recognized many of the recommendations made by the Council of Europe, especially with regards to the independence of the judiciary.

Monitoring and evaluation are critical components of the work that is assigned to the Council of Europe (Shevory, 1990; Shewmon, 1997; Shultz, 1990; Singleton Jr, 1989; Skene & Parker, 2002; Somerville, 1989; Spurr, 1993). For instance, the council monitors the work of European judicial systems. This is done under the auspices of the European Commission for the Efficiency of Justice (CEPEJ). Where needed, the council will provide ongoing support to members who wish to improve the functionality of their judicial systems. Some of the potential improvements are meant to ensure that member states are compliant with the recommendations that have been given to them.

The creation of the Council of Europe was inspired by the need to develop a community that would remain a beacon for huma rights (Whitaker & Edwards, 1990; White, 1990; Wicclair, 1991a, b; Wildes, 1997; Wilson, 1994; Woliver, 1990). This is done by promoting the rule of law. All member states are expected to uphold the highest standards of democracy and good governance. The statue that sets out the Council of Europe details the obligations of states under this arrangement. The council will offer expertise and guidance on the practical and substantive implications of the principle of judicial independence and efficiency. As Figure 8.5 shows, there has been a marked improvement in efficiencies among the member state judicial systems.

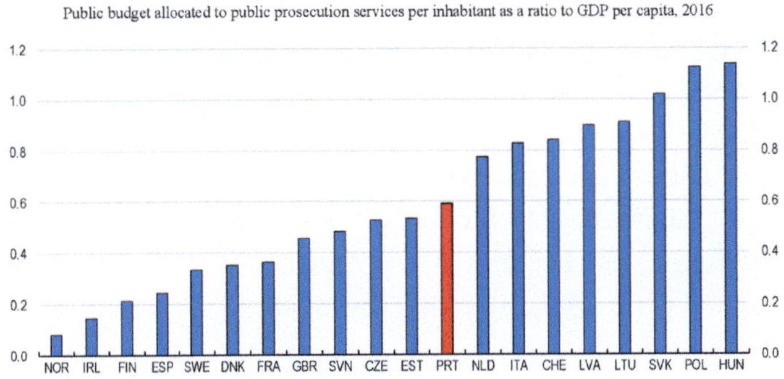

Note: The numbers are multiplied by 1000.
Source: European Commission for the Efficiency of Justice (CEPEJ).

Recommendations to enhance judicial efficiency

Institutional settings of the judicial courts

Key recommendations

- Increase the managerial autonomy of the courts so that they can effectively allocate resources such as judges, other judiciary staff and budgets.
- Fully analyse the data collected from the information system on court proceedings (CITIUS) so that it allows the courts to identify problematic cases and those that should be prioritised.

Other recommendations

- Improve the CITIUS information system by extending on-going efforts on digitalisation.
- Review the overall system of performance evaluation of judges with a view to ensuring its full objectivity.
- Provide access to detailed data on court decisions to allow the quality of court decisions, case complexity and related costs to be identified in order to assess court performance and the effects of past reforms.
- Strengthen legal assistance to judges by increasing the specialisation of clerks and ensuring the organisation of clerks is flexible.
- Consider introducing assistant judges in lower level courts.

Figure 8.5. Comparative analysis of budgetary expenditures on prosecutions.

Source: García & Jin (2019) via Semantic Scholar.

Some of the outcomes of the efforts by the Council of Europe include an improvement in the legislative processes of member states (Fentiman,

1989; Field, 1990, 1991; Figueira-McDonough, 1990; Finer, 1991; Fluss & Zeegers, 1990; Fortin, 1991; Gelman, 1994). Recently, there has been an interest in focusing on the needs of service users rather than trying to maintain a status quo that favors those that are already entrenched within the judicial system. Whereas specific countries may be worried about the infringement on their national sovereignty, there are also comparative advantages of being a member of the Council of Europe.

Research has shown that members of this organization tend to have better indicators in terms of independence, quality, and efficiency when compared to the rest of the world (Kamm, 2001; Kass & Lund, 1996; Kaveny, 1991, 2006; Khushf, 1994; Knoppers & LeBris, 1991; Kozłowski, 2021). For instance, this is the only European organization that provides a full cycle of support to members through creating reference standards as well as capacity building tools. The monitoring function of the council ensures that no member state completely loses the responsibility to safeguard the human rights of its citizenry.

The success of the organization has been so significant that it has acted as a reference point in many instances across the globe (Shepherd, 1995; Shevory, 1990; Shewmon, 1997; Shultz, 1990; Singleton Jr, 1989; Skene & Parker, 2002; Somerville, 1989). Some of the key bodies that are created and supported by the council are referenced in other jurisdictions. For example, the European Court of Human Rights has been listed as upholding a high level of respect for the rights of people and communities. There is a wealth of case law that provides precedents and guidance to other parts of the world which are seeking to improve their own judicial systems.

The council helped create the conditions under which the European Court of Human Rights interpreted and developed the requirements of a fair trial (Elhauge, 1994; Emanuel, 1999; Feinberg, 1991; Fentiman, 1989; Field, 1990, 1991; Figueira-McDonough, 1990; Finer, 1991). These are enshrined in Article 6 of the European Convention on Human Rights (ECHR). That is a binding treaty for members of the Council of Europe. Other substantive guidance is provided by the likes of Consultative Council of European, European Commission for Democracy through Law, Consultative Council of European Judges, and the Venice Commission. These bodies invariably focus on issues such as the organization of judicial systems.

In doing so, the bodies promote the independence of the judiciary (Fluss & Zeegers, 1990; Fortin, 1991; Gelman, 1994; Glass & Speyer-Ofenberg, 1996; Glick, 1992; Gormally, 2002). They are also interested in the ethics and liability of judges who operate in these systems. A case in point are the comments on the funding and management of courts. Another area of interest is the training of judges as well as the function of the prosecution. The council will explore the relations that the prosecutors have with the judiciary in a democratic society. Besides, it may provide commentary on the role of the prosecution outside the criminal law field.

The Council of Europe acts as an evaluator of the day-to-day functioning of European court systems (Knoppers & LeBris, 1991; Kozłowski, 2021; Lane & Grodin, 1997; Mathieu, 1992; May, 1999; McConnell, 1991; McCoy, 1992). Such a function is undertaken through the CEPEJ which comprises qualified experts from member states. This institution was set up to assess and improve the efficiency of judicial systems. Such a goal would be achieved by means of practical tools and measures that could be deployed among the member states. Thus, every 24 months the CEPEJ publishes a report. Its contents are based on a proven scientific process. Indeed, the protocol for this report is widely validated by the scientific and judicial community in Europe and the globe.

During the process of preparation of the report, the council curates data related to key indicators for the function of judicial systems (Grondelski, 1989; Hamblin & Somerville, 1991; Hardwig, 1991; Harris, 2003; Harris & Holm, 2002; Harvey & Chadwick, 1992). The underlying data sets are collected from member states. These are then verified before being included in a database made up of more than 3 million entries. The report then provides a detailed picture of the situation of European judicial systems. These trends and information can then be utilized to improve the operations of judicial systems elsewhere.

Many experts have commended its role as an important comparative tool (Dyck, 1992; Eisenstat, 1991; Eldridge, 2021; Elhauge, 1994; Emanuel, 1999; Feinberg, 1991; Fentiman, 1989; Field, 1990). The presentation of information (e.g., graphs, tables, illustrations, and comments) helps observers in understanding the day-to-day function of courts. The information contained in the reports also underlines the main trends in judicial systems. Moreover, the report is useful in identifying the key issues to be addressed. These then can become action points for improving the operations of the judiciary in a range of relevant areas.

The report produced by the council is an important tool for policy makers (Kamisar, 1993; Kamm, 2001; Kass & Lund, 1996; Kaveny, 1991, 2006; Khushf, 1994; Knoppers & LeBris, 1991). It has also been referenced by legal professionals as well as academic researchers. The contents of this report can guide all these experts in their judicial reform endeavors. For instance, CEPEJ has developed specific tools aimed at addressing the excessive length of judicial proceedings. This was presented in the form of the SATURN Guidelines. It also includes the checklist for judicial time management. Other tools focus on developing user-oriented policies in the field of justice. A case in point is the checklist for promoting the quality of justice in courts.

All these tools have been applied in several courts throughout Europe (Viljoen, 2012; Walters, 1991, 2012; Waymack, 1991; Weithman, 1999; Whitaker & Edwards, 1990; White, 1990). They are designed with a view to speeding up judicial proceedings. Another overarching goal is increasing users' satisfaction with justice services. The CEPEJ efforts have been specifically mentioned as a European reference point. This was done within the framework of the EC Forum for Justice. Specifically, this was part of the EC Communication released on the 4th of February 2008. Another specific project is the Stockholm Program. The CEPEJ co-operates closely with the European Commission. It is a close partner of the Council of the European Union as well as the European Parliament. Hence, it is often requested to avail these bodies of its expertise beyond European borders.

Notably, the Council of Europe has a track record in the implementation of capacity building projects (Dresser, 2003; Dworkin, 1991, 1992; Dyck, 1992; Eisenstat, 1991; Eldridge, 2021; Elhauge, 1994; Emanuel, 1999). These are initiatives which draw on the organization's longstanding experience in cooperation activities. The council has specifically supported member states in the implementation of European standards on an independent and efficient judiciary. The Council of Europe addresses pertinent issues such as the role and responsibilities of judicial self-governing bodies. Moreover, it has provided advice on the embedding of training institutions. Others have benefitted from its recommendations on improving court management in line with European standards. This is a reference institution for generally ensuring a better functioning judicial system.

The council recruits a network of practitioners, experts, researchers, academics, and members of specialized monitoring bodies (Wilson, 1994; Woliver, 1990; Wyld & Cappel, 1990; Yamada, 2019; Zohar, 1991; Zomerski, 2020). These professionals make available their expertise to member states on these different aspects of judicial reform. Membership of the Council of Europe obliges member states to apply the standards that are routinely developed by the organization. These are particularly relevant to the requirements relating to the judiciary as well as human rights. The institution remains invested in fostering best practices in the democratic processes of the member states. These standards are also part of the European Union acquis. The implication is that their fulfilment is crucial in the accession path of certain countries to the European Union.

Framing projects within the context of cooperation with the Council of Europe offers additional guarantees (Shevory, 1990; Shewmon, 1997; Shultz, 1990; Singleton Jr, 1989; Skene & Parker, 2002; Somerville, 1989; Spurr, 1993). This is pertinent to the desired alignment of member states' justice systems with European standards. It also addresses critical issues of sustainability. The Council of Europe intervenes in all its member states. Several European Union and Council of Europe Joint Programs (JP) have been designed in this way. Additionally, there is a scheme for voluntary contributions (VC) which have been implemented in Central, Southern, and Eastern Europe.

Recent examples include the increased transparency, independence, and efficiency of the justice system of the Republic of Moldova. The underlying principle is that improving justice systems in one part of the content will have overall benefits for all other parts of the continent (Whitaker & Edwards, 1990; White, 1990; Wicclair, 1991a, b; Wildes, 1997; Wilson, 1994; Woliver, 1990). The project aimed to improve the management of the justice system whilst simultaneously guaranteeing fairer access to justice for all citizens regardless of their situation. Hence, the project focused on the professions contributing to the administration of justice. Examples of these professions and occupations include prosecutors, judges, lawyers, public defenders, and auxiliary staff. Consequently, an updated database on Moldovan legislation was put in place to facilitate the sharing of information and knowledge. The National Institute of Justice appropriately provides training to judges and court staff. It was set up and supported in its initial stages of operation.

Recommendations were made to bring lawyers' activities in line with European standards (Fentiman, 1989; Field, 1990, 1991; Figueira-McDonough, 1990; Finer, 1991; Fluss & Zeegers, 1990; Fortin, 1991; Gelman, 1994). This focused on spreading best practice and learning from past mistakes. Expertise was also provided about the creation of a private system of enforcement of domestic courts decisions despite challenges and pockets of resistance. Additionally, there was targeted support to the reform of the judiciary in Serbia in the light of Council of Europe standards. The project was funded by the World Bank. It was developed to support the on-going process of reform of the judiciary outlined in the 2006 National Judicial Reform Strategy (NJRS).

This project comprised a comprehensive stock-take of the reforms and their results (Kamm, 2001; Kass & Lund, 1996; Kaveny, 1991, 2006; Khushf, 1994; Knoppers & LeBris, 1991; Kozłowski, 2021). This was designed to identify the obstacles hindering judiciary reform in Serbia. A comprehensive expert report was drawn up. This document set out specific recommendations for improving the independence of the judiciary as well as achieving transparency and accountability in the system. The goal was achieving optimum efficiency of the Serbian justice system. This was accompanied by a roadmap for implementation of the recommendations.

Transparency and Efficiency of the Judicial System of Ukraine (TEJSU) was another important goal that has been pursued over time (Shepherd, 1995; Shevory, 1990; Shewmon, 1997; Shultz, 1990; Singleton Jr, 1989; Skene & Parker, 2002; Somerville, 1989). The JP contributed to strengthening the efficiency and independence of the judicial system in Ukraine. This was in line with European standards in much the same way as other member states had benefitted. A specific innovation was the continuous development of legal reforms. The project aimed for institutional support and capacity building within this justice system. The project worked in close co-operation with all the Ukrainian decision-makers. One of the modalities was working with change champions in the form of reforming prosecutors, judges, advocates, lawyers, and court clerks. The project also targeted administrative teaching staff of judges' and prosecutors' training structures.

Based on an evaluation of the project achievements, all partners and beneficiaries received the necessary tools for the development and the establishment of a transparent and efficient judiciary system at different levels in Ukraine (Elhauge, 1994; Emanuel, 1999; Feinberg, 1991; Fentiman, 1989; Field, 1990, 1991; Figueira-McDonough, 1990; Finer, 1991). The project outcomes were achieved by providing detailed advice and recommendations. Hence, the JP helped the Ukrainian authorities increase the compliance of a number of key laws with European standards. One of the key target areas was the Law on the Judiciary and the Status of Judges. Another target was the Law amending certain legislative Acts of Ukraine in relation to the prevention of abuse of the right to appeal. Additionally, attention was paid to the law on Free Legal Aid. Some of the tangible outcomes included improvements in the regulation on an automatic case-management system in Ukrainian courts. Experts argue that the biggest achievement was the reform of the Criminal Procedure Code.

Capacity building with the main beneficiaries was at the heart of the anticipated outputs (Fluss & Zeegers, 1990; Fortin, 1991; Gelman, 1994; Glass & Speyer-Ofenberg, 1996; Glick, 1992; Gormally, 2002). Key professional groups became acquainted with legal topics which had hitherto been shrouded in mystery or even ignorance. A case in point was the training provided on the methodology of the interpretation of legal acts. The project enhanced the application of legislation against corruption. Even more sensitive was the application of the law against racism and intolerance.

These had been major complaints that had not been satisfactorily addressed before (Knoppers & LeBris, 1991; Kozłowski, 2021; Lane & Grodin, 1997; Mathieu, 1992; May, 1999; McConnell, 1991; McCoy, 1992). By tackling issues of legal aid, the project ensured that financial distress was not as much of a barrier to justice as it once was. The project implemented a system for monitoring network devices and applications within the ECHR and the case law of the ECtHR. Many benefitted from the new case management system for general courts. The project also supported judicial education. Indeed, one of the tangible outcomes was the implementation of the new case management system in general courts.

Alternative dispute resolution (ADR) put mediation as a tool on the map for Ukrainian citizens and the authorities thanks to the organization of a Mediation Week and the setting up of four pilot courts around the country devoted to mediation as a means towards decreasing the number of cases dealt with by courts and strengthening the efficiency of courts. The Project Team assisted all beneficiaries through institutional support to overcome differences and facilitate dialogue between them.

This support promoted the signature of mutual co-operation agreements between the different institutions (Grondelski, 1989; Hamblin & Somerville, 1991; Hardwig, 1991; Harris, 2003; Harris & Holm, 2002; Harvey & Chadwick, 1992). Under such arrangements, these institutions committed themselves to working together in a certain number of common areas. Moreover, the institutions agreed to enhanced networking and exchange of information. The project gathered under the same umbrella. This was a major milestone since it was for the first time ever. The union involved two key stakeholders including the Academy of Judges and the Academy of Prosecutors. This initiative enhanced the dialogue between the two institutions.

The dissemination of European standards and the awareness of the work of the CoE was instrumental in raising awareness about expectations as well as highlighting any limitations that needed to be addressed (Dyck, 1992; Eisenstat, 1991; Eldridge, 2021; Elhauge, 1994; Emanuel, 1999; Feinberg, 1991; Fentiman, 1989; Field, 1990). The sharing of knowledge was achieved through a range of activities which were organized during the whole implementation period of the project. This was done along with a series of publications on human rights.

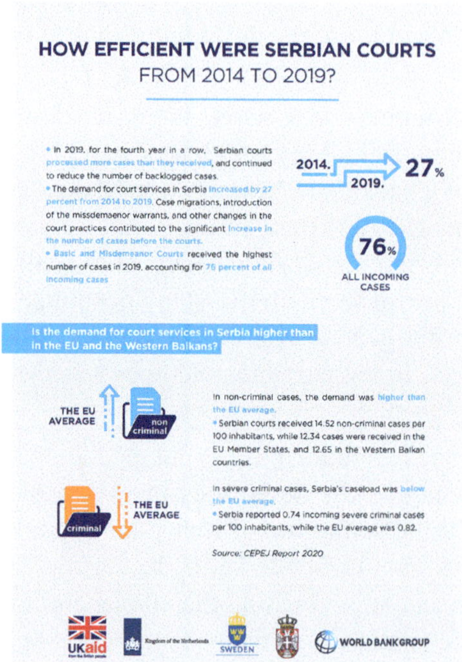

Figure 8.6. Evaluating the efficiency of Serbian courts.

Source: Multi Donor Trust Fund for Justice.

The work that is undertaken by the council and its subsidiaries is meant to address longstanding issues that prevent judicial excellence (Kamisar, 1993; Kamm, 2001; Kass & Lund, 1996; Kaveny, 1991, 2006; Khushf, 1994; Knoppers & LeBris, 1991). The case of the Serbian courts (*see* Figure 8.6) shows that being in Europe is no guarantee of democratic credentials or court efficiency. Part of the remit of the council is therefore to proactively ensure that even non-EU members are included in the reforms.

Technical support was provided to national stakeholders within Ukraine under this project (Viljoen, 2012; Walters, 1991, 2012; Waymack, 1991; Weithman, 1999; Whitaker & Edwards, 1990; White, 1990). For instance, the project allowed for the installation of computer workstations for the regional branches of the National School of Judges. Consequently, all 737 Ukrainian courts were connected to VPN hardware and software. The network was equipped with LAN. Additionally, all the general courts of Chernivtsi region were computerized. Moreover, the High Council of Justice was provided with IT equipment.

Another important project was promoting access to justice in Armenia (Dresser, 2003; Dworkin, 1991, 1992; Dyck, 1992; Eisenstat, 1991; Eldridge, 2021; Elhauge, 1994; Emanuel, 1999). The JP is on-going and facing certain challenges because of the low-base starting point. The project supports the judicial reforms undertaken by the Armenian government. This is achieved through the promotion of the rule of law and human rights. Additionally, the project aims for the improvement of the efficiency of the judiciary and access to justice. It has been notably supporting the Chamber of Advocates as well as improving training and education of judges and court personnel. The project was credited with facilitating access to justice and transparency of the judiciary.

Following these interventions, a new Law establishing the School of Advocates was adopted. Moreover, all the regulatory and teaching tools needed for the school to function effectively were adopted. A new curriculum for initial training of judges is being drawn up and is part of the long-term plan of improving legal education in Europe and across the globe (Wilson, 1994; Woliver, 1990; Wyld & Cappel, 1990; Yamada, 2019; Zohar, 1991; Zomerski, 2020). The Project supports the development of an e-notary system which will contribute to strengthening the security of transactions and legal acts.

More recently, the council has participated in enhancing the role of the supreme judicial authorities in respect of European standards within Turkey (Fentiman, 1989; Field, 1990, 1991; Figueira-McDonough, 1990; Finer, 1991; Fluss & Zeegers, 1990; Fortin, 1991; Gelman, 1994). The purpose of this on-going project is to enhance the roles of the Higher Courts in the judicial system within a country that has demonstrated ambitions to join the European Union. These goals are achieved by reinforcing their awareness of the acquis. These are the rights and freedoms guaranteed by the European Court of Human Rights. The project also addresses the implementation and embedding of the provisions of the European Social Charter as well as other pertinent European standards. There is an overarching goal to enhance co-operation and exchange of good practice with European peer institutions.

The peer-to-peer exchange of experience with equivalent European institutions is of paramount importance during the reform process (Pogge, 1991; Purdy, 1990; Quante, 1999; Rae & DeGiorgio, 1991; Ravven, 2016; Raymond, 1999; Resnik, 1997). Indeed, this has been significantly reinforced through developing sustainable contacts between the Turkish High Courts and European institutions have been established. One of the notable benefits is an enhanced level of direct cooperation even at the highest levels the institutional structures.

The project has organized different visits mainly to the European Court of Justice in Luxembourg and the European Court of Human Rights in Strasbourg. These visits allow different actors to gain insight into the management of the judicial system within a modern European state. Other fact-finding missions have been to the European institutions in Brussels and The Hague. Consequently, the highest judicial authorities in Turkey have been able to reinforce their skills on the domestic application of European standards. This is an instrument step in enhancing their capacity to develop the regulatory frameworks (Coady, 2002; Cohen, 1989; Coughlan, 1989; Crigger, 1995; Crossley, 1993; Crouch & Elliott, 1999; Daniels & Sabin, 1997).

Another important contact modality is a range of conferences and roundtables (Hasnas, 1995; Hill, 1990, 1991a, b; Hope & Fulford, 1994; Hylton, 1990; Kadish, 1992; Kahn, 1991). These are organized to touch on various topics that are of relevance to the stakeholders. Indeed, the contact points include established international platforms for the partner institutions to articulate and discuss various internal difficulties. The discussions led to a good understanding of the case law. It also created the basis for a better implementation of the ECHR at the national level. As part of the cooperation efforts, the project places groups of Turkish judges at the Registry of the ECtHR. The placements last half a year and allow the officers to undergo on-the-job training by experienced lawyers from the Registry of the ECtHR.

It is expected that the trained judges will have an increased knowledge of the ECtHR. This is valuable information which they will subsequently share with their peers in Turkey (Bradley, 1993; Braithwaite, 1991; Brock, 1991, 1995, 1999; Brody, 1998; Cantor, 2005; Capron, 1990). The JP supports the Turkish Constitutional Court. One of the key joint projects involves establishing a system for the review of individual constitutional complaints. This is a fundamental right for Turkish citizens after the referendum in September 2012. This is being pursued through capacity-building of representatives of the Registry of the Constitutional Court. It is also emphasized through exchanges of experience and good practice with other European Constitutional Courts.

Promotion of judicial reform involves addressing human and minority rights (Van der Burg & Brom, 2000; van Schooten, 2014; Viljoen, 2012; Walters, 1991, 2012; Waymack, 1991; Weithman, 1999). A case in point is the project that is being undertaken by the council in Georgia. This is in accordance with Council of Europe standards The Project. The project was funded by Denmark. Overall, this project pursues two main objectives. The first involves improving the judicial and correctional system. The second objective involves strengthening the capacity of the Public Defender's Office.

These are considerations which have proved important in the reform of other judicial systems across the globe (Glass & Speyer-Ofenberg, 1996; Glick, 1992; Gormally, 2002; Gostin, 1995; Greenberg & Kamin, 1993; Grondelski, 1989). The Project focuses on training. This is essentially prioritizing the training of judges in the human rights field. The project is pertinent in the light of the requirements of the ECHR. The development comes in the wake of the implementation of a new Code of imprisonment in 2010. To that end, the staff of penitentiary institutions has also been trained in order to help ensure respect for human rights and the full implementation of Council of Europe standards.

Technology remains an important component of judicial efficiency and management (Braithwaite, 1991; Brock, 1991, 1995, 1999; Brody, 1998; Cantor, 2005; Capron, 1990, 1999). One pertinent project that was undertaken by the council involved the strengthening of the court management system in Turkey. The project aims to improve the function and efficiency of the Turkish judiciary according to European standards. This requirement is provided in the EU Accession Partnership and the National Program for the Adoption of the acquis.

The JP focuses on the reform of the Turkish court management system. This is done to make it more professional. The effective use of technologies improves the judicial system by making it more effective and efficient (Nobles, 2012; O'Donovan & Gilbar, 2003; Oberman, 1992; Okin, 1990; Oster, 2021; Paliwala, 2016; Paris & Poorman, 1995). Turkey already expressed an interest in improving its use of modern technologies within the judicial system. It follows up a previous pilot project aimed at introducing a new court management system in Turkey. This initial project targeted five pilot courts. Its success inspired even more investment in similar projects.

The current project aims to strengthen the new court management system by facilitating the adoption of legislation and continuing the implementation of court management practices tested in the previous project (Agich & Spielman, 1997; Allen, 1990, 1992; Alward, 2002; Amaraskekara & Bagaric, 2004; Anderson, 1993; Andrews, 1996). These practices concern the setting up of information and front office desks. Such facilities have proved instrumental in the proper functioning of other judicial systems. The project involved the appointment and training of judicial assistants. Further facilitation was provided to court managers and media spokespersons. Overall, there was an increased application of quality and external relations policies. Hence, the process made it easier to explore methods of ADR.

The successful application of these new practices will allow for the dissemination of the new court management system throughout Turkey and other parts of Europe (Alward, 2002; Amaraskekara & Bagaric, 2004; Anderson, 1993; Andrews, 1996; Arinta et al., 2021; Ayres et al., 1993). The Council of Europe implements regional and multilateral programs in justice. The European Union or Council of Europe JP on "*Enhancing judicial reform in Eastern Partnership countries*" is a case in point. The Project supports the on-going process of judiciary reform in Azerbaijan, Armenia, Moldova, Georgia, and Ukraine. This is a multilateral forum for identifying and discussing obstacles to the implementation of European standards.

Three comprehensive reports have been drawn up under the Project. Research remains a critical component of reforming the judicial system in any part of the world (Hill, 1990, 1991a, b; Hope & Fulford, 1994; Hylton, 1990; Kadish, 1992; Kahn, 1991; Kalb, 1990; Kamisar, 1993). The projects that were sponsored by the Council of Europe aimed at analyzing the legislation and practice of each beneficiary in the light of relevant European standards and then setting out recommendations. The themes of the reports are judicial self-governing and the career of judges. They also address issues pertaining to the lawyers' professions as well as the training of judges. The reports have been discussed in-depth with the national authorities during several bilateral meetings. There is always an underlying objective to bring the justice system closer to the people that it is meant to be serving.

8.4. BRINGING JURISPRUDENCE CLOSER TO THE PEOPLE

Inaccessibility to justice is a major issue internationally (Field, 1991; Figueira-McDonough, 1990; Finer, 1991; Fluss & Zeegers, 1990; Fortin, 1991; Gelman, 1994; Glass & Speyer-Ofenberg, 1996; Glick, 1992). Unfortunately, research has shown that in some countries access to justice has decreased in recent years. A case in point is how the growth of inequality and decline of state support have left access to justice in a sorry state even among the most advanced liberal democracies. This calls for concerted efforts to protect peoples' rights. Figure 8.7 highlights some of the pertinent issues when ensuring better access to justice across the globe.

Figure 8.7. Increasing access to justice.

Source: Adopted from: Open Law Lab.

Many of the changes that are posited by experts start with the grassroots (Meisel, 1996; Menzel, 1992; Merrick, 1990; Morreim, 1991; Munzer, 1994; Nelson, 1994; Nobles, 2012; O'Donovan & Gilbar, 2003). That is based on the notion that the justice system impacts those at the bottom of the social rudders in much more profound ways than it would affect those that are within the higher echelons. The importance of community-based solutions cannot be under-estimated since this is where injustice is experienced, and it is therefore the best place to create the space for workable solutions.

One of the solutions posited and partially implemented in several states is to make the justice system more representative of the communities that it serves (Pellegrino & Sharpe, 1989; Ploughman, 1995; Pogge, 1991; Purdy, 1990; Quante, 1999; Rae & DeGiorgio, 1991; Ravven, 2016). That means bringing in marginalized communities that have traditionally been excluded from this profession. This type of reform has not been without its challenge since some argue that it represents a slippery slope towards falling standards. One of the areas that has been vociferously attacked is the notion of using affirmative action to include minorities. Those that advocate for a more traditional approach suggest that the recruitment criterion must never be watered down even if it means that certain minorities are effectively excluded.

Another important contributor to improved access to justice is promotion of pro bono (Figueira-McDonough, 1990; Finer, 1991; Fluss & Zeegers, 1990; Fortin, 1991; Gelman, 1994; Glass & Speyer-Ofenberg, 1996; Glick, 1992; Gormally, 2002). This is effectively free-of-charge work by all lawyers and law organizations at their own initiative. The underlying rationale is that poor people should not be denied access to justice. Whereas the provision of pro bono work has always been encouraged in the professions, it is mainly on a voluntary basis. Any attempt to coerce people into providing free support would be counterproductive. For example, the quality of services may be reduced drastically if someone knows that they are not going to be paid for their efforts. Indeed, we have already seen the bad reputation that public defenders have because they are not paid as highly as their counterparts in private practice.

The education of lawyers and legal officers must reflect the needs of society and the changing nature of the law (Dworkin, 1992; Dyck, 1992; Eisenstat, 1991; Eldridge, 2021; Elhauge, 1994; Emanuel, 1999; Feinberg, 1991; Fentiman, 1989). However, it seems that existing training programs are stuck in a traditional mindset that seeks to separate the profession from the rest of society. The reasons for this separation are more to do with prestige than the need to deliver better services to the populace. A curriculum process that includes pertinent topics may be appropriate for a field that seeks to remain relevant to people who are living in the 21st century.

Yet, the very foundation of the reform agenda has been contested (Bekrycht & Mańko, 2020; Bianchi, 2017; Blair & Kaserman, 1991; Blustein, 1993; Bonnicksen, 1995; Bradley, 1993). Some critics argue that there is nothing fundamentally wrong with the system as it stands.

Therefore, attempts to change it for the sake of change may not yield the results that are anticipated. If anything, such reforms may undo some of the achievements that have organically emerged in the legal system. Others call for incremental changes rather than a radical change that is bound to destabilize the legal profession.

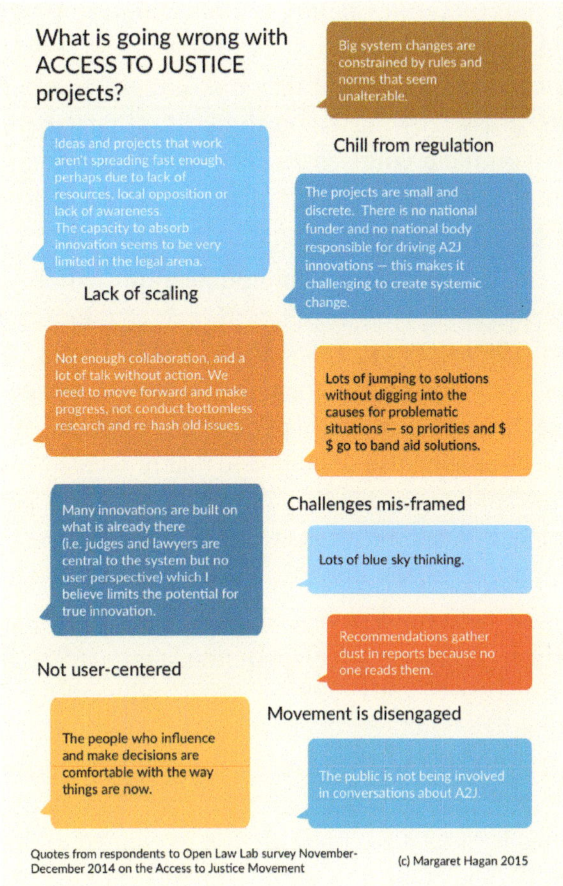

Figure 8.8. The reform agenda in justice.

Source: Margaret Hagan (2015) via Open Law Lab.

In any case, all the reforms should be localized since it is the local community that best understands its needs (Bonnicksen, 1995; Bradley, 1993; Braithwaite, 1991; Brock, 1991, 1995, 1999; Brody, 1998; Cantor, 2005). Certainly, the change agenda should not be imported from other parts of the world that consider themselves to be more enlightened. Indeed, the decolonization of the judicial system is taking root in some of the old colonies that were forced to accept imported solutions to problems that were also imported from abroad. Figure 8.8 is an example of an authentic reform agenda that is locally inspired.

The feedback that is provided by those that interact with the legal systems is that they are not getting the level of support that they anticipate (Stein, 1998; Steinbock & McClamrock, 1994; Strauss, 1992; Stroud, 1996; Sullivan & Goldzwig, 1995; Sulmasy, 1989; TÄNnsjÖ, 1992). For example, there are complaints about delays that discourage people from reporting cases. Others are stressed by the tedious processes that they must go through before they can complete court cases. The language and systems that are used in a contemporary court are often of another age and do not make sense to the lay people that are seeking redress.

The issue of language and communication has been particularly problematic (Purdy, 1990; Quante, 1999; Rae & DeGiorgio, 1991; Ravven, 2016; Raymond, 1999; Resnik, 1997; Rich, 1997; Rivard, 1992). Lawyers are notorious for being opaque and for using flowery language. Some see it as a sign of prestige that means ordinary people are respectful of the profession. Others see it as a confusing use of language that prevents people from really understanding the challenges that they are facing. Legal documents are long and hard to decipher. When reforms are made, the traditionalists argue that this is a dilution of the respect that the judiciary has earned in society.

The separation between lawyers and ordinary people is real and can have consequences (Blustein, 1993; Bonnicksen, 1995; Bradley, 1993; Braithwaite, 1991; Brock, 1991, 1995, 1999; Brody, 1998). This starts with the dress code that is often used in courts. Judges are often dressed in wigs and elaborate gowns. Once again, there is a struggle between tradition and the realities of a modern audience that expects better. At other times, perfectly valid explanations for this dress code are not explained to the public so that it is left to speculate and come up with its own rationale for why judges dress in specific ways. For instance, the use of wigs has created anonymity for the judges so that they cannot be recognized by defendants when in normal dress. However, those explanations are rarely shared with the public which perceives judicial officers to be opaque and esoteric.

In the developing world, judges are facing undue political pressure from the state which wishes that they make decisions which are in line with an authoritarian stance (Cantor, 2005; Capron, 1990, 1999; Chandler, 1990; Chervenak & McCullough, 1991; Chesterman, 1998; Clark, 2002). Besides, the decisions that are given by the courts are sometimes ignored by security agencies on the grounds that the greater public good calls for such decisions to be cast aside. For the ordinary people, this corruption of the justice system erodes confidence. For example, many people in the developing world are placed on remand for political reasons and then released without charge or compensation after spending months in prison. Others are immediately re-arrested by security agents when offered bail by the courts.

Another challenge that courts are facing in the developing world is poor resourcing (Robertson, 1999; Savulescu, 1994; Schneider, 1992; Schuck, 1994; Sevelin, 2019; Shanley, 1990; Sharpe & Pellegrino, 1997; Sheldon & Wilkinson, 1997). Although budgets for the criminal justice department may easily pass, they are often targeted towards incarceration rather than crime prevention. Indeed, some officers complain of limited opportunities for professional development. The implication is that the justice system remains stagnant. At other times, funding is provided by donor agencies from the developed world. However, that raises the pertinent question of latent colonialization. In the Western or industrialized world, they have slightly different problems which often stem from the lack of diversity in the legal profession.

8.5. DIVERSIFICATION OF THE LEGAL PROFESSION

The legal profession remains an exclusive one for one reason or another (Rich, 1997; Rivard, 1992; Robertson, 1996, 1999; Savulescu, 1994; Schneider, 1992; Schuck, 1994; Sevelin, 2019). It is an elitist undertaking that requires extensive training and education which is beyond the capabilities of people from working class backgrounds. Moreover, there are specific countries with localized injustices such as the racial injustice that exists in the USA. If the profession is dominated by white privileged males, then it is unlikely to provide an adequate response to those that are on the margins but would like to join the profession. This is not just a problem for the profession but reports society-wide challenges such as the difficulty in reporting and resolving discrimination (*see* Figure 8.9).

The reform of the judiciary is not just about adding minority people into positions of influence (Glick, 1992; Gormally, 2002; Gostin, 1995; Greenberg & Kamin, 1993; Grondelski, 1989; Hamblin & Somerville, 1991). This is an important step, but it does not complete the process of cultural transformation. Education, training, and sensitization are equally important tools in creating institutions that are inclusive and respectful of diversities. Moreover, it is important to note that this is not just a case of one type of diversity. Rather, it is an acknowledgement that the judicial system should be welcoming to the community.

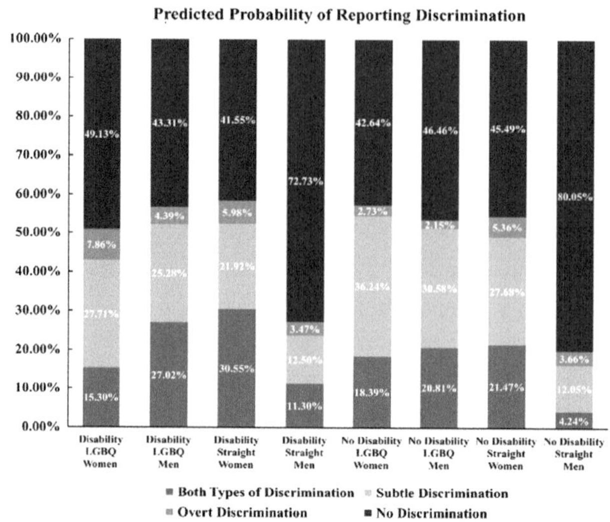

Figure 8.9. Predicators of likelihood of reporting discrimination.

Source: Cambridge University.

There will be many options that could potentially be explored for encouraging diversity (Skene & Parker, 2002; Somerville, 1989; Spurr, 1993; Stacy, 1994; Stauch, 2000; Stein, 1998; Steinbock & McClamrock, 1994). Figure 8.10 highlights some of the inclusion practices that may be considered by practitioners and institutions that are embedded within the legal system. It is also important to recognize the possibilities and limitations of inclusion. For example, the mere fact that the judiciary is inclusive will not detract from some of its failings including the inability to deliver justice in an accessible way.

Besides, one evil must not be replaced by another evil. A case in point is where the diversification schemes have become so dogmatic that they are excluding otherwise competent practitioners (Rich, 1997; Rivard, 1992; Robertson, 1996, 1999; Savulescu, 1994; Schneider, 1992; Schuck, 1994; Sevelin, 2019). The overall goal should be to ensure that anyone who is capable and willing to practice in the profession is given a fair chance to join it. That means building on some of the achievements that are already existent rather than trying to destroy everything for purposes of building from scratch.

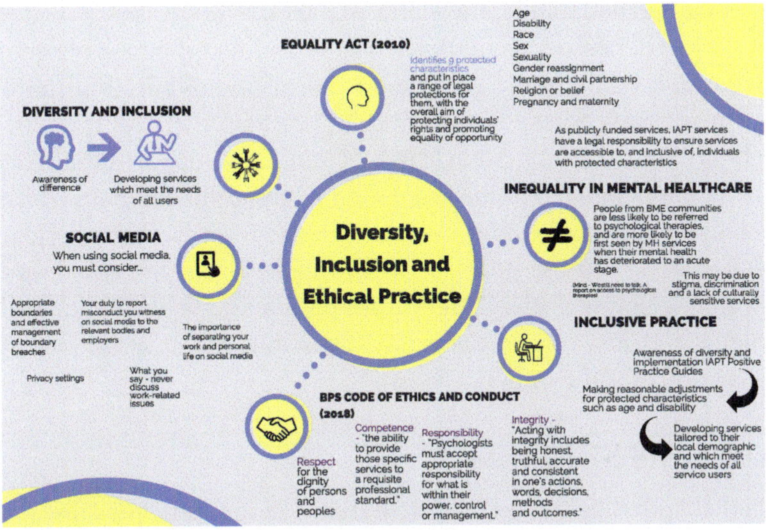

Figure 8.10. Examples of diversity and inclusion practices.

Source: University of Reading.

Changing tradition often ruffles feathers and is likely to elicit some form of resistance (Wilson, 1994; Woliver, 1990; Wyld & Cappel, 1990; Yamada, 2019; Zohar, 1991; Zomerski, 2020). There are many people who have been brought up in a judicial tradition that they consider sacrosanct. To them, any notion of change is akin to sacrilege. Yet, these are the very same people that are interested in ensuring that the judicial process remains intact and an integral part of our community life. The challenge for reformers is in persuading those that are conservative in their perspectives that it is beneficial and pertinent to engage in a process of reform. That is why one of the options considered is that of incremental change which does not cause as much disruption as would be the case if there were abrupt changes in the judiciary. At the same time, we must recognize the fact that there are people who are legitimately interested in change because they have been oppressed by an ineffective judicial system for a long time (Paris & Poorman, 1995; Pellegrino & Sharpe, 1989; Ploughman, 1995; Pogge, 1991; Purdy, 1990; Quante, 1999; Rae & DeGiorgio, 1991). These are the people that are wrongly incarcerated or denied their civil rights. Then there are those that lose money and property because of judicial corruption. To these people, any suggestion of incrementalism seems like a betrayal and a denigration of their legitimate interests or demands. Nevertheless, the places where judicial reform has successfully occurred are the ones that are willing to adopt a more pragmatic approach that considers the long-term impact of the decisions made today. Despites its weaknesses, the judicial system and its officers have continued to manage one of the most complex areas of community and public life (Singleton Jr, 1989; Skene & Parker, 2002; Somerville, 1989; Spurr, 1993; Stacy, 1994; Stauch, 2000; Stein, 1998). Credit and support should be given to those that are engaged in the process of making the judicial system more efficient and effective. Besides, virtually all the reforms that are posited require investment and the political will to make decisions which are challenging and sometimes attract significant resistance. The study of analytical jurisprudence is just one of the many steps that are necessary to achieve these ambitions for the judicial system.

CHAPTER 8 SUMMARY

This final chapter has critiqued current trends in jurisprudence and practice. Some of the areas covered include populism in the judiciary, independence, corruption, efficiency, inclusion, and diversification. The overall message from this concluding chapter is that there are challenges within the judicial system, but they are not insurmountable by any stretch of the imagination. The system has built systems and capacities that are resilient. That means that change is possible with the right investments and will. Analytical jurisprudence provides us with a prism for understanding the issues and possible solutions in the judiciary.

Concluding Remarks

This book has explored the topic of analytical jurisprudence from the perspective of trying to make the law more relevant to contemporary issues that are facing communities and the criminal justice systems across the globe. The book begins by introducing the analytical school of jurisprudence. This aspect involved philosophical development, new approaches, and the work of key figures such as Herbert Lionel Adolphus Hart and Jeremy Bentham. The book then distinguished analytical jurisprudence from legal formalism. This aspect explored the conceptualization of legal formalism, natural law, the work of David Hume, relating law with power, and relating law to morality.

The book then considered the use of language in law practice and development. Some of the key issues that were covered include the linguistic turn, British idealism, logical holism, ideal language, and ordinary language. We then provided an overview of general jurisprudence. The topics tackled under this heading include conceptual, normative, empirical, and legal generalizations as well as their implications for the delivery of justice. The idea behind these explorations is the notion that the law must always be turned into practice to make sense to the ordinary people who are most affected by it.

One of the arenas where theory is turned into practice is in the domain of geopolitics. This book therefore considered the intersection between human rights and religious law, cultural domains in the law, a case study of insolvency law as well as copyright law, and the limits or possibilities of commercial law. The book then moved to the categorization of analytical jurisprudence. Under this topic, the book considered ethics, sociological perspectives, traditional approaches, Hohfeld's analysis, and discourses on prison conditions. This background then provided a basis for the application of jurisprudence to contemporary problems, challenges, and gaps.

The application discussion focused on the contextualization of the law. For instance, the book suggested that contentious issues such as corruption are contextually bound. We considered the possibilities and limitations of diversities in legal education as well as inclusivity in practice. Two case studies illuminated these ideas by way of legal licensing in the USA and the reform agenda in UK law. The book also explored the impact of local customs when developing and implementing the law. Having set out an overview of analytical jurisprudence, the book then concluded by critiquing the status quo and proposing a better future.

Some of the areas of critical review and evaluation in this book include populism in legislation and policy. The book considered the desire and limitations of judicial independence as determined by the interdependence of this arm of government. The book tackled the sensitive issue of judicial corruption and inefficiency as well as the need to bring justice closer to people. Ultimately, the book called for diversification in the legal profession. I hope you have enjoyed reading the book and will follow the others in the series.

Bibliography

1. Abrams, P., (1996). Reservations about women: Population policy and reproductive rights. *Cornell International Law Journal*, *29*(1), 1–40. https://www.scopus.com/inward/record.uri?eid=2-s2.0–0030308291&partnerID=40&md5=a369e56d660764b6b5f88340b8591698 (accessed on 22 September 2023).
2. Agich, G. J., & Spielman, B. J., (1997). Ethics expert testimony: Against the skeptics. *Journal of Medicine and Philosophy*, *22*(4), 381–403. https://doi.org/10.1093/jmp/22.4.381 (accessed on 22 September 2023).
3. Allen, A. L., (1990). Surrogacy, slavery, and the ownership of life. *Harvard Journal of Law and Public Policy*, *13*(1), 139–149. https://www.scopus.com/inward/record.uri?eid=2-s2.0–0025574643&partnerID=40&md5=d00856640faba1b25c7af6f5c9f6c251 (accessed on 22 September 2023).
4. Allen, A. L., (1992). Autonomy's magic wand: abortion and constitutional interpretation. *Boston University Law Review*, *72*(4), 683–698. https://www.scopus.com/inward/record.uri?eid=2-s2.0–0026922848&partnerID=40&md5=e549541d589a0116b5639082d84c3dd2 (accessed on 22 September 2023).
5. Alward, P., (2002). Thomson, the right to life, and partial birth abortion or two MULES* for Sister Sarah. *Journal of Medical Ethics*, *28*(2), 99–101. https://doi.org/10.1136/jme.28.2.99 (accessed on 22 September 2023).

6. Amaraskekara, K., & Bagaric, M., (2004). Moving from voluntary euthanasia to non-voluntary euthanasia: Equality and compassion. *Ratio Juris*, *17*(3), 398–423. https://doi.org/10.1111/j.1467–9337.2004.00275.x (accessed on 22 September 2023).
7. Anderson, M. F., (1993). Encouraging bone marrow transplants from unrelated donors: Some proposed solutions to a pressing problem. *University of Pittsburgh Law Review*, *54*(2), 477–530. https://www.scopus.com/inward/record.uri?eid=2-s2.0–0027796562&partnerID=40&md5=47d6c5fedfb8d019615c89fc9767df0a (accessed on 22 September 2023).
8. Andrews, L. B., (1996). Prenatal screening and the culture of motherhood. *Hastings Law Journal*, *47*(4), 967. https://www.scopus.com/inward/record.uri?eid=2-s2.0–0030112032&partnerID=40&md5=26965348e7d1ba7c849cd524689b74af (accessed on 22 September 2023).
9. Arinta, P. R., Mendrofa, J. F., & Hadinata, F., (2021). Sociological jurisprudence: An alternative to seeking justice and certainty of law through roscoe pound's thinking. *Philosophy and the Everyday Lives*, 3–20. https://www.scopus.com/inward/record.uri?eid=2-s2.0–85109233526&partnerID=40&md5=8b0d9b441e2f5454b360733ead7e1c48 (accessed on 22 September 2023).
10. Ayres, I., Dooley, L. G., & Gaston, R. S., (1993). Unequal racial access to kidney transplantation. *Vanderbilt Law Review*, *46*(4), 805–863. https://www.scopus.com/inward/record.uri?eid=2-s2.0–0027596537&partnerID=40&md5=152fea3ceabee9f2ed22964e2a6613d2 (accessed on 22 September 2023).
11. Bekrycht, T., & Mańko, R., (2020). Polish jurisprudence in the 20th century: A general overview. *Review of Central and East European Law*, *45*(2), 181–199. https://doi.org/10.1163/15730352–04502001 (accessed on 22 September 2023).
12. Bianchi, A., (2017). International law theories: An inquiry into different ways of thinking. *International Law Theories: An Inquiry into Different Ways of Thinking*, 1–322. https://doi.org/10.1093/acprof:oso/9780198725114.001.0001 (accessed on 22 September 2023).
13. Blair, R. D., & Kaserman, D. L., (1991). The economics and ethics of alternative cadaveric organ procurement policies. *Yale Journal on Regulation*, *8*(2), 403–452. https://www.scopus.com/inward/record.uri?eid=2-s2.0–0026174593&partnerID=40&md5=9c1189f14aa5e7b

26e688ff4f5da0f7f (accessed on 22 September 2023).

14. Blustein, J. F., (1993). Doing what the patient orders: Maintaining integrity in the doctor-patient relationship. *Bioethics*, *7*(4), 289–314. https://doi.org/10.1111/j.1467–8519.1993.tb00220.x (accessed on 22 September 2023).
15. Bonnicksen, A. L., (1995). Ethical and policy issues in human embryo twinning. *Cambridge Quarterly of Healthcare Ethics*, *4*(3), 268–284. https://doi.org/10.1017/S0963180100006010 (accessed on 22 September 2023).
16. Bradley, G. V., (1993). Life's dominion: A review essay. *The Notre Dame Law Review*, *69*(2), 329–391. https://www.scopus.com/inward/record.uri?eid=2-s2.0–0027900101&partnerID=40&md5=c0a1d25c4299556f88fd71de70404594 (accessed on 22 September 2023).
17. Braithwaite, S. S., (1991). Anticruelty care: Commentary. *The Journal of Clinical Ethics*, *2*(2), 97–103. https://www.scopus.com/inward/record.uri?eid=2-s2.0–0026175467&partnerID=40&md5=c54d6ac20e2dc8905559a84d8b7b343a (accessed on 22 September 2023).
18. Brock, D. W., (1991). Decision-making competence and risk. *Bioethics*, *5*(2), 105–112. https://doi.org/10.1111/j.1467–8519.1991.tb00151.x (accessed on 22 September 2023).
19. Brock, D. W., (1995). The non-identity problem and genetic harms – the case of wrongful handicaps. *Bioethics*, *9*(3), 269–275. https://doi.org/10.1111/j.1467–8519.1995.tb00361.x (accessed on 22 September 2023).
20. Brock, D. W., (1999). A critique of three objections to physician-assisted suicide. *Ethics*, *109*(3), 519–547. https://doi.org/10.1086/233920 (accessed on 22 September 2023).
21. Brody, H., (1998). Physician-assisted suicide in the courts: Moral equivalence, double effect and clinical practice. *Minnesota Law Review*, *82*(4), 939. https://www.scopus.com/inward/record.uri?eid=2-s2.0–0032048697&partnerID=40&md5=f8b1512c0c75cb84652b75c5d82e9dad (accessed on 22 September 2023).
22. Cantor, N. L., (2005). The bane of surrogate decision-making: Defining the best interests of never-competent persons. *Journal of Legal Medicine*, *26*(2), 155–205. https://doi.org/10.1080/01947640590949922 (accessed on 22 September 2023).
23. Capron, A. M., (1990). The burden of decision. *Hastings Center*

Report, *20*(3), 36–41. https://doi.org/10.2307/3563160 (accessed on 22 September 2023).

24. Capron, A. M., (1999). What contributions have social science and the law made to the development of policy on bioethics? *Daedalus*, *128*(4), 295–325. https://www.scopus.com/inward/record.uri?eid=2-s2.0–0033185909&partnerID=40&md5=bcb30fc94d186db55b804c5032b660e0 (accessed on 22 September 2023).
25. Chandler, J., (1990). Killing and letting dieputting the debate in context. *Australasian Journal of Philosophy*, *68*(4), 420–431. https://doi.org/10.1080/00048409012344421 (accessed on 22 September 2023).
26. Chervenak, F. A., & McCullough, L. B., (1991). Inadequacies with the ACOG and AAP statements on managing ethical conflict during the intrapartum period. *The Journal of Clinical Ethics*, *2*(1), 23–24. https://www.scopus.com/inward/record.uri?eid=2-s2.0–0026129655&partnerID=40&md5=713f8b2a9ad11129602c8396c8d4e8aa (accessed on 22 September 2023).
27. Chesterman, S., (1998). Last rights: Euthanasia, the sanctity of life, and the law in the Netherlands and the Northern Territory of Australia. *The International and Comparative Law Quarterly*, *47*(2), 362–393. https://doi.org/10.1017/S0020589300061893 (accessed on 22 September 2023).
28. Clark, C. C., (2002). Trust in medicine. *Journal of Medicine and Philosophy*, *27*(1), 11–29. https://doi.org/10.1076/jmep.27.1.11.2975 (accessed on 22 September 2023).
29. Claviez, (2019). Neorealism, contingency, and the linguistic turn. *Humanities, 8*(4), 176.
30. Clerkin, C., (2021). Predicated predictions: How federal judges predict changes in state law? *Columbia Journal of Law and Social Problems*, *54*(2), 305–363. https://www.scopus.com/inward/record.uri?eid=2-s2.0–85129911725&partnerID=40&md5=d36935d41cda7933a6ace5e884518111 (accessed on 22 September 2023).
31. Coady, C. A. J., (2002). Religious meddling: A comment on Skene and Parker. *Journal of Medical Ethics*, *28*(4), 221–222. https://doi.org/10.1136/jme.28.4.221 (accessed on 22 September 2023).
32. Cohen, L. R., (1989). Increasing the supply of transplant organs: The virtues of a futures market. *George Washington Law Review*,

58(1), 1–51. https://www.scopus.com/inward/record.uri?eid=2-s2.0–0024766965&partnerID=40&md5=518b0b843de3f9693a2045bdaadd3f3f (accessed on 22 September 2023).

33. Coughlan, M. J., (1989). When did I begin? Conception of the human individual in history, philosophy and science by Norman M. Ford, Cambridge & New York, Cambridge University Press. *Bioethics*, *3*(4), 333–341. https://doi.org/10.1111/j.1467–8519.1989.tb00350.x (accessed on 22 September 2023).
34. Crigger, B. J., (1995). Negotiating the moral order: Paradoxes of ethics consultation. *Kennedy Institute of Ethics Journal*, *5*(2), 89–112. https://doi.org/10.1353/ken.0.0066 (accessed on 22 September 2023).
35. Crossley, M. A., (1993). Of diagnoses and discrimination: Discriminatory nontreatment of infants with HIV infection. *Columbia Law Review*, *93*(7), 1581–1667. https://doi.org/10.2307/1123057 (accessed on 22 September 2023).
36. Crouch, R. A., & Elliott, C., (1999). Moral agency and the 'family: The case of living related organ transplantation. *Cambridge Quarterly of Healthcare Ethics*, *8*(3), 275–287. https://doi.org/10.1017/S096318019980303X (accessed on 22 September 2023).
37. Daniels, N., & Sabin, J., (1997). Limits to health care: Fair procedures, democratic deliberation, and the legitimacy problem for insurers. *Philosophy and Public Affairs*, *26*(4), 303–350. https://doi.org/10.1111/j.1088–4963.1997.tb00082.x (accessed on 22 September 2023).
38. Den Hartogh, G., (1997). The values of life. *Bioethics*, *11*(1), 43–66. https://doi.org/10.1111/1467–8519.00043 (accessed on 22 September 2023).
39. Downie, R. S., & Randall, F., (1997). Parenting and the best interests of minors. *The Journal of Medicine and Philosophy*, *22*(3), 219–231. https://doi.org/10.1093/jmp/22.3.219 (accessed on 22 September 2023).
40. Downie, R., (1992). Health care ethics and casuistry. *Journal of Medical Ethics*, *18*(2), 61–62, 66. https://doi.org/10.1136/jme.18.2.61 (accessed on 22 September 2023).
41. Draper, E., (1993). Fetal exclusion policies and gendered constructions of suitable work. *Social Problems*, *40*(1), 90–107. https://doi.org/10.1525/sp.1993.40.1.03x0074v (accessed on 22 September 2023).
42. Dresser, R., (1995). Long-term contraceptives in the criminal

justice system. *Hastings Center Report*, *25*(1), S15–S18. https://doi.org/10.2307/3562506 (accessed on 22 September 2023).

43. Dresser, R., (2003). Precommitment: A misguided strategy for securing death with dignity. *Texas Law Review*, *81*(7), 1823–1847. https://www.scopus.com/inward/record.uri?eid=2-s2.0–0043246481&partnerID=40&md5=8929fa33fe951292bc8aa84879b21823 (accessed on 22 September 2023).
44. Dworkin, R., (1991). The right to death. *The New York Review of Books*, 14–17. https://www.scopus.com/inward/record.uri?eid=2-s2.0–0026434517&partnerID=40&md5=de420a683a9216be42f0a058ab523a49 (accessed on 22 September 2023).
45. Dworkin, R., (1992). Unenumerated rights: Whether and how Roe should be overruled. *The University of Chicago Law Review. University of Chicago. Law School*, *59*(1), 381–432. https://doi.org/10.2307/1599941 (accessed on 22 September 2023).
46. Dyck, A. J., (1992). Being a physician and being ethical. *The Linacre Quarterly*, *59*(3), 82–90. https://doi.org/10.1080/00243639.1992.11878172 (accessed on 22 September 2023).
47. Eisenstat, S., (1991). An analysis of the rationality of mandatory testing for the HIV antibody: Balancing the governmental public health interests with the individual's privacy interest. *University of Pittsburgh Law Review*, *52*(2), 327–382. https://www.scopus.com/inward/record.uri?eid=2-s2.0–0026411116&partnerID=40&md5=a009935c89aa3b0dc91eb7e2fe786693 (accessed on 22 September 2023).
48. Eldridge, L., (2021). Gone and forgotten: Vinogradoff's historical jurisprudence. *Legal Studies*, *41*(2), 194–213. https://doi.org/10.1017/lst.2020.41 (accessed on 22 September 2023).
49. Elhauge, E., (1994). Allocating health care morally. *California Law Review*, *82*(6), 1449–1544. https://doi.org/10.2307/3480858 (accessed on 22 September 2023).
50. Emanuel, E. J., (1999). What is the great benefit of legalizing euthanasia or physician-assisted suicide? *Ethics*, *109*(3), 629–642. https://doi.org/10.1086/233925 (accessed on 22 September 2023).
51. Feinberg, J., (1991). Overlooking the merits of the individual case: An unpromising approach to the right to die. *Ratio Juris*, *4*(2), 131–151. https://doi.org/10.1111/j.1467–9337.1991.tb00090.x (accessed on 22 September 2023).

52. Fentiman, L. C., (1989). Privacy and personhood revisited: A new framework for substitute decision-making for the incompetent, incurably ill adult. *George Washington Law Review*, *57*(4), 801–848. https://www.scopus.com/inward/record.uri?eid=2-s2.0–0024631446&partnerID=40&md5=b1ccb72f4ac36c5ffaa177efbdafe767 (accessed on 22 September 2023).

53. Field, M. A., (1990). The case against enforcement of surrogacy contracts. *Politics and the Life Sciences: The Journal of the Association for Politics and the Life Sciences*, *8*(2), 199–204. https://doi.org/10.1017/S0730938400009746 (accessed on 22 September 2023).

54. Field, M. A., (1991). Response of professor field. *Politics and the Life Sciences: The Journal of the Association for Politics and the Life Sciences*, *9*(2), 262–268. https://doi.org/10.1017/S0730938400010832 (accessed on 22 September 2023).

55. Figueira-McDonough, J., (1990). Abortion: Ambiguous criteria and confusing policies. *Affilia*, *5*(4), 27–54. https://doi.org/10.1177/088610999000500403 (accessed on 22 September 2023).

56. Finer, J. J., (1991). Toward guidelines for compelling cesarean surgery: Of rights, responsibility, and decisional authenticity. *Minnesota Law Review*, *76*(2), 239–294. https://www.scopus.com/inward/record.uri?eid=2-s2.0–0026363028&partnerID=40&md5=acbe515a9708fe8f6fe6583d6ba02d61 (accessed on 22 September 2023).

57. Fluss, S. S., & Zeegers, D., (1990). Reporting of AIDS and human immunodeficiency virus (HIV) infection: a worldwide review of legislative and regulatory patterns and issues. *AIDS and Public Policy Journal*, *5*(1), 32–36. https://www.scopus.com/inward/record.uri?eid=2-s2.0–0025646844&partnerID=40&md5=3c4847745d05f1d5b94d43684510ee67 (accessed on 22 September 2023).

58. Fortin, A. J., (1991). Ethics, culture, and medical power: AIDS research in the Third World. *AIDS and Public Policy Journal*, *6*(1), 15–24. https://www.scopus.com/inward/record.uri?eid=2-s2.0–0026092078&partnerID=40&md5=75c034243b64e265a470c2a76be12d00 (accessed on 22 September 2023).

59. Gelman, S., (1994). "Life" and "liberty": Their original meaning, historical antecedents, and current significance in the debate over abortion rights. *Minnesota Law Review*, *78*(3), 585–698. https://www.scopus.com/inward/record.uri?eid=2-s2.0–0028382379&partne

rID=40&md5=81e31277ef00dc0dad7ec0d983c1fc4c (accessed on 22 September 2023).

60. Glass, K. C., & Speyer-Ofenberg, M., (1996). Incompetent persons as research subjects and the ethics of minimal risk. *Cambridge Quarterly of Healthcare Ethics*, *5*(3), 362–372. https://doi.org/10.1017/s0963180100007179 (accessed on 22 September 2023).
61. Glick, H. R., (1992). Judicial innovation and policy re-invention: state supreme courts and the right to die. *Political Research Quarterly*, *45*(1), 71–92. https://doi.org/10.1177/106591299204500106 (accessed on 22 September 2023).
62. Gormally, L., (2002). Commentary on skene and parker: The role of the church in developing the law. *Journal of Medical Ethics*, *28*(4), 224–227. https://doi.org/10.1136/jme.28.4.224 (accessed on 22 September 2023).
63. Gostin, L. O., (1995). Health information privacy. *Cornell Law Review*, *80*(3), 451–528. https://www.scopus.com/inward/record.uri?eid=2-s2.0–0029259226&partnerID=40&md5=ea0e214c3d787e4ff4b8e08b11075eea (accessed on 22 September 2023).
64. Greenberg, W., & Kamin, D., (1993). Property rights and payment to patients for cell lines derived from human tissues: An economic analysis. *Social Science and Medicine*, *36*(8), 1071–1076. https://doi.org/10.1016/0277–9536(93)90125-N (accessed on 22 September 2023).
65. Grondelski, J. M., (1989). Removal of artificially supplied nutrition and hydration: A moral analysis. *Irish Theological Quarterly*, *55*(4), 291–302. https://doi.org/10.1177/002114008905500403 (accessed on 22 September 2023).
66. Hamblin, J., & Somerville, M. A., (1991). Surveillance and reporting of HIV infection and AIDS in Canada: ethics and law. *The University of Toronto Law Journal*, *41*(2), 224–246. https://doi.org/10.2307/825846 (accessed on 22 September 2023).
67. Hardwig, J., (1991). Treating the brain dead for the benefit of the family. *The Journal of Clinical Ethics*, *2*(1), 53–56. https://www.scopus.com/inward/record.uri?eid=2-s2.0–0026132245&partnerID=40&md5=a45310cff19f0c21070cea098dab1838 (accessed on 22 September 2023).
68. Harris, J., & Holm, S., (2002). Commentary on skene and parker: The role of a church (or other ideologically based interest group)

in developing the law – a plea for ethereal intervention. *Journal of Medical Ethics*, *28*(4), 219–220. https://doi.org/10.1136/jme.28.4.219.

69. Harris, J., (2003). Consent and end of life decisions. *Journal of Medical Ethics*, *29*(1), 10–15. https://doi.org/10.1136/jme.29.1.10 (accessed on 22 September 2023).
70. Harvey, I., & Chadwick, R., (1992). Compensation for harm: The implications for medical research. *Social Science and Medicine*, *34*(12), 1399–1404. https://doi.org/10.1016/0277–9536(92)90148-J (accessed on 22 September 2023).
71. Hasnas, J., (1995). From cannibalism to caesareans: Two conceptions of fundamental rights. *Northwestern University Law Review*, *89*(3), 900–941. https://www.scopus.com/inward/record.uri?eid=2-s2.0–0029259299&partnerID=40&md5=67b0d3f8568e2aad106c206ddab2756d (accessed on 22 September 2023).
72. Hill, J. L., (1990). The case for enforcement of the surrogate contract. *Politics and the Life Sciences: The Journal of the Association for Politics and the Life Sciences*, *8*(2), 147–160. https://doi.org/10.1017/S0730938400009692 (accessed on 22 September 2023).
73. Hill, J. L., (1991a). In defense of enforcement of the surrogate contract: A reply to Field. *Politics and the Life Sciences: The Journal of the Association for Politics and the Life Sciences*, *9*(2), 253–261. https://doi.org/10.1017/S0730938400010820 (accessed on 22 September 2023).
74. Hill, J. L., (1991b). What does it mean to be a "parent"? The claims of biology as the basis for parental rights. *New York University Law Review*, *66*(2), 353–420. https://www.scopus.com/inward/record.uri?eid=2-s2.0–0026159912&partnerID=40&md5=0206c5eed8a9212c9b383a87806ab52e (accessed on 22 September 2023).
75. Hope, T., & Fulford, K. W. M., (1994). Teaching medical ethics symposium. The Oxford practice skills project: Teaching ethics, law, and communication skills to clinical medical students. *Journal of Medical Ethics*, *20*(4), 229–234. https://doi.org/10.1136/jme.20.4.229 (accessed on 22 September 2023).
76. Hylton, K. N., (1990). The law and economics of organ procurement. *Law and Policy*, *12*(3), 197–224. https://doi.org/10.1111/j.1467–9930.1990.tb00047.x (accessed on 22 September 2023).
77. Kadish, S. H., (1992). Letting patients die: Legal and moral

reflections. *California Law Review*, *80*(4), 857–888. https://doi.org/10.2307/3480699 (accessed on 22 September 2023).

78. Kahn, J. P., (1991). Genetic harm: Bitten by the body that keeps you? *Bioethics*, *5*(4), 289–308. https://doi.org/10.1111/j.1467–8519.1991.tb00169.x (accessed on 22 September 2023).
79. Kalb, P. E., (1990). Controlling health care costs by controlling technology: A private contractual approach. *The Yale Law Journal*, *99*(5), 1109–1126. https://doi.org/10.2307/796598 (accessed on 22 September 2023).
80. Kamisar, Y., (1993). Are laws against assisted suicide unconstitutional? *Hastings Center Report*, *23*(3), 32–41. https://doi.org/10.2307/3563366 (accessed on 22 September 2023).
81. Kamm, F. M., (2001). Ronald Dworkin on abortion and assisted suicide. *Journal of Ethics*, *5*(3), 221–240. https://doi.org/10.1023/A:1012755208057 (accessed on 22 September 2023).
82. Kass, L. R., & Lund, N., (1996). Courting death: Assisted suicide, doctors, and the law. *Commentary (New York, N.Y.)*, *102*(6), 17–29. https://www.scopus.com/inward/record.uri?eid=2-s2.0–0030310135&partnerID=40&md5=5754c0fcc5245ed84d2efdba116b3e99 (accessed on 22 September 2023).
83. Kaveny, M. C., (1991). Toward a Thomistic perspective on abortion and the law in contemporary America. *The Thomist*, *55*(3), 343–396. https://doi.org/10.1353/tho.1991.0006 (accessed on 22 September 2023).
84. Kaveny, M. C., (2006). Diversity and deliberation: Bioethics commissions and moral reasoning. *Journal of Religious Ethics*, *34*(2), 311–337. https://doi.org/10.1111/j.1467–9795.2006.00270.x (accessed on 22 September 2023).
85. Khushf, G., (1994). Intolerant tolerance. *Journal of Medicine and Philosophy (United Kingdom)*, *19*(2), 161–181. https://doi.org/10.1093/jmp/19.2.161 (accessed on 22 September 2023).
86. Knoppers, B. M., & LeBris, S., (1991). Recent advances in medically assisted conception: Legal, ethical, and social issues. *American Journal of Law and Medicine*, *17*(4), 329–361. https://www.scopus.com/inward/record.uri?eid=2-s2.0–0026356159&partnerID=40&md5=dddb90138c9181d9efad17c5ec4ea64e (accessed on 22 September 2023).

87. Kozłowski, T., (2021). The concept of negative integrity: A call for philosophical re-emergence of the impeccable judiciary. *Krytyka Prawa, 13*(3), 47–63. https://doi.org/10.7206/KP.2080–1084.471 (accessed on 22 September 2023).

88. Lane, H., & Grodin, M., (1997). Ethical issues in cochlear implant surgery: An exploration into disease, disability, and the best interests of the child. *Kennedy Institute of Ethics Journal*, *7*(3), 231–251. https://www.scopus.com/inward/record.uri?eid=2-s2.0–0031236889&partnerID=40&md5=9f82598045d252a0102defacdc1abfb5 (accessed on 22 September 2023).

89. Mathieu, D., (1992). Crime and punishment: Abortion as murder? *Journal of Social Philosophy*, *23*(2), 5–22. https://doi.org/10.1111/j.1467–9833.1992.tb00290.x (accessed on 22 September 2023).

90. Matti, H., (2022). Scarcity, justice, and health crisis leadership. *Philosophies, 7*, 48.

91. May, T., (1999). Bioethics in a liberal society–political, not moral. *The International Journal of Applied Philosophy*, *13*(1), 1–19. https://doi.org/10.5840/ijap19991315 (accessed on 22 September 2023).

92. McConnell, M. W., (1991). The selective funding problem: Abortions and religious schools. *Harvard Law Review*, *104*(5), 989–1049. https://doi.org/10.2307/1341670 (accessed on 22 September 2023).

93. McCoy, T. J., (1992). Biomedical process patents: Should they be restricted by ethical limitations? *Journal of Legal Medicine*, *13*(4), 501–519. https://doi.org/10.1080/01947649209510894 (accessed on 22 September 2023).

94. Meisel, A., (1992). The legal consensus about foregoing life-sustaining treatment: Its status and its prospects. *Kennedy Institute of Ethics Journal*, *2*(4), 309–345. https://www.scopus.com/inward/record.uri?eid=2-s2.0–0027026601&partnerID=40&md5=4f65ccd396b37b3997acb2c1569244ef (accessed on 22 September 2023).

95. Meisel, A., (1996). The "right to die": A case study in American lawmaking. *European Journal of Health Law*, *3*(1), 49–74. https://doi.org/10.1007/bf02789867 (accessed on 22 September 2023).

96. Menzel, P. T., (1992). Just doctoring: Medical ethics in the liberal state, by Troyen Brennan. *American Journal of Law and Medicine*, *18*(1–2), 163–170. https://www.scopus.com/inward/record.uri?eid=2-

s2.0–0026676082&partnerID=40&md5=248e02dba976f7aeaacdacee167139cd (accessed on 22 September 2023).

97. Merrick, J. C., (1990). Selling reproductive rights: policy issues in surrogate motherhood. *Politics and the Life Sciences: The Journal of the Association for Politics and the Life Sciences*, *8*(2), 161–172. https://doi.org/10.1017/S0730938400009709 (accessed on 22 September 2023).
98. Morreim, E. H., (1991). Economic disclosure and economic advocacy: New duties in the medical standard of care. *Journal of Legal Medicine*, *12*(3), 275–329. https://doi.org/10.1080/01947649109510858 (accessed on 22 September 2023).
99. Munzer, S. R., (1994). An uneasy case against property rights in body parts. *Social Philosophy and Policy*, *11*(2), 259–286. https://doi.org/10.1017/S0265052500004519 (accessed on 22 September 2023).
100. Nelson, H. L., (1994). The architect and the bee: Some reflections on postmortem pregnancy. *Bioethics*, *8*(3), 247–267. https://doi.org/10.1111/j.1467–8519.1994.tb00257.x (accessed on 22 September 2023).
101. Nobles, R., (2012). A sociology of jurisprudence. *Law and Sociology*, 1–23. https://doi.org/10.1093/acprof:oso/9780199282548.003.0003 (accessed on 22 September 2023).
102. O'Donovan, K., & Gilbar, R., (2003). The loved ones: Families, intimates, and patient autonomy. *Legal Studies*, *23*(2), 332–358. https://doi.org/10.1111/j.1748–121X.2003.tb00217.x (accessed on 22 September 2023).
103. Oberman, M., (1992). Sex, drugs, pregnancy, and the law: Rethinking the problems of pregnant women who use drugs. *Hastings Law Journal*, *43*(3), 505–548. https://www.scopus.com/inward/record.uri?eid=2-s2.0–0026834212&partnerID=40&md5=f42202c1736b5ca0e0f7361cb24bb29a (accessed on 22 September 2023).
104. Okin, S. M., (1990). A critique of pregnancy contracts: comments on articles by Hill, Merrick, Shevory, and Woliver. *Politics and the Life Sciences: The Journal of the Association for Politics and the Life Sciences*, *8*(2), 205–210. https://doi.org/10.1017/S0730938400009758 (accessed on 22 September 2023).
105. Oster, J., (2021). Code is code and law is law – the law of digitalization and the digitalization of law. *International Journal of Law and*

Information Technology, *29*(2), 101–117. https://doi.org/10.1093/ijlit/eaab004 (accessed on 22 September 2023).

106. Paliwala, A., (2016). Rediscovering artificial intelligence and law: An inadequate jurisprudence? *International Review of Law, Computers, and Technology*, *30*(3), 107–114. https://doi.org/10.1080/13600869.2016.1229651 (accessed on 22 September 2023).
107. Paris, J. J., & Poorman, M., (1995). "Playing god" and the removal of life-prolonging therapy. *Journal of Medicine and Philosophy (United Kingdom)*, *20*(4), 403–418. https://doi.org/10.1093/jmp/20.4.403 (accessed on 22 September 2023).
108. Pellegrino, E. D., & Sharpe, V. A., (1989). Medical ethics in the courtroom: The need for scrutiny. *Perspectives in Biology and Medicine*, *32*(4), 547–564. https://doi.org/10.1353/pbm.1989.0015 (accessed on 22 September 2023).
109. Ploughman, P., (1995). Public policy versus private rights: The medical, social, ethical, and legal implications of the testing of newborns for HIV. *AIDS and Public Policy Journal*, *10*(4), 182–204. https://www.scopus.com/inward/record.uri?eid=2-s2.0–0029549535&partnerID=40&md5=e311e1ce882cbd4a602459c958512568 (accessed on 22 September 2023).
110. Pogge, T. W., (1991). The abortion battle and world hunger*. *Journal of Social Philosophy*, *22*(2), 12–13. https://doi.org/10.1111/j.1467–9833.1991.tb00033.x (accessed on 22 September 2023).
111. Purdy, L. M., (1990). Are pregnant women fetal containers? *Bioethics*, *4*(4), 273–291. https://doi.org/10.1111/j.1467–8519.1990.tb00092.x (accessed on 22 September 2023).
112. Quante, M., (1999). Precedent autonomy and personal identity. *Kennedy Institute of Ethics Journal*, *9*(4), 365–381. https://doi.org/10.1353/ken.1999.0028 (accessed on 22 September 2023).
113. Rae, S. B., & DeGiorgio, C. M., (1991). Ethical issues in fetal tissue transplants. *The Linacre Quarterly*, *58*(3), 12–32. https://doi.org/10.1080/00243639.1991.11878115 (accessed on 22 September 2023).
114. Ravven, H. M., (2016). Spinoza to Freud: The unraveling of a psychoanalytical perspective on moral responsibility and law. *International Journal of Law and Psychiatry*, *48*, 35–42. https://doi.org/10.1016/j.ijlp.2016.06.008 (accessed on 22 September 2023).

115. Raymond, D., (1999). "Fatal practices": A feminist analysis of physician-assisted suicide and euthanasia. *Hypatia*, *14*(2), 1–25. https://doi.org/10.2979/hyp.1999.14.2.1 (accessed on 22 September 2023).

116. Resnik, D. B., (1997). The morality of human gene patents. *Kennedy Institute of Ethics Journal*, *7*(1), 43–61. https://doi.org/10.1353/ken.1997.0008 (accessed on 22 September 2023).

117. Rich, B. A., (1997). A legacy of silence: Bioethics and the culture of pain. *Journal of Medical Humanities*, *18*(4), 233–259. https://doi.org/10.1023/A:1025697920944 (accessed on 22 September 2023).

118. Rivard, M. D., (1992). Toward a general theory of constitutional personhood: a theory of constitutional personhood for transgenic humanoid species. *UCLA Law Review*, *39*(5), 1425–1510. https://www.scopus.com/inward/record.uri?eid=2-s2.0–0026879891&partnerID=40&md5=e0284f47a71ec4c4c3c59dea3515a63f (accessed on 22 September 2023).

119. Robertson, J. A., (1996). Genetic selection of offspring characteristics. *Boston University Law Review*, *76*(3), 421–481. https://www.scopus.com/inward/record.uri?eid=2-s2.0–0030156354&partnerID=40&md5=ecce329e54ff8b72ddcaca269c1d0b08 (accessed on 22 September 2023).

120. Robertson, J. A., (1999). Ethics and policy in embryonic stem cell research. *Kennedy Institute of Ethics Journal*, *9*(2), 109–136. https://doi.org/10.1353/ken.1999.0013 (accessed on 22 September 2023).

121. Savulescu, J., (1994). Treatment limitation decisions under uncertainty: The value of subsequent euthanasia. *Bioethics*, *8*(1), 49–73. https://doi.org/10.1111/j.1467–8519.1994.tb00241.x (accessed on 22 September 2023).

122. Schneider, C. E., (1992). Cruzan and the constitutionalizing of American life. *Journal of Medicine and Philosophy (United Kingdom)*, *17*(6), 589–604. https://doi.org/10.1093/jmp/17.6.589 (accessed on 22 September 2023).

123. Schuck, P. H., (1994). Rethinking informed consent. *The Yale Law Journal*, *103*(4), 899–959. https://doi.org/10.2307/797066 (accessed on 22 September 2023).

124. Sevelin, E., (2019). What about the non-legal facts: Revising Allen and Pardo's analytical distinction between law and fact. *International*

Journal of Evidence and Proof, 23(4), 349–365. https://doi.org/10.1177/1365712719851043 (accessed on 22 September 2023).

125. Shanley, M. L., (1990). A case against pregnancy contracts: embodied selves, liberal theory and the law. *Politics and the Life Sciences: The Journal of the Association for Politics and the Life Sciences, 8*(2), 216–220. https://doi.org/10.1017/S0730938400009771 (accessed on 22 September 2023).
126. Sharpe, V. A., & Pellegrino, E. D., (1997). Medical ethics in the courtroom: A reappraisal. *Journal of Medicine and Philosophy, 22*(4), 373–379. https://doi.org/10.1093/jmp/22.4.373 (accessed on 22 September 2023).
127. Sheldon, S., & Wilkinson, S., (1997). Conjoined twins: The legality and ethics of sacrifice. *Medical Law Review, 5*(2), 149–171. https://doi.org/10.1093/medlaw/5.2.149 (accessed on 22 September 2023).
128. Sheldon, S., & Wilkinson, S., (1998). Female genital mutilation and cosmetic surgery: Regulating non-therapeutic body modification. *Bioethics, 12*(4), 263–285. https://doi.org/10.1111/1467–8519.00117 (accessed on 22 September 2023).
129. Shepherd, L., (1995). Protecting parents' freedom to have children with genetic differences. *University of Illinois Law Review, 4*, 761–812. https://www.scopus.com/inward/record.uri?eid=2-s2.0–0029414346&partnerID=40&md5=e0d06fc34b07d6facfe5bcb3db5b7565 (accessed on 22 September 2023).
130. Shevory, T. C., (1990). Rethinking public and private life via the surrogacy contract. *Politics and the Life Sciences: The Journal of the Association for Politics and the Life Sciences, 8*(2), 173–184. https://doi.org/10.1017/S0730938400009710 (accessed on 22 September 2023).
131. Shewmon, D. A., (1997). Recovery from "brain death": A neurologist's apologia. *The Linacre Quarterly, 64*(1), 30–96. https://doi.org/10.1080/20508549.1999.11878373 (accessed on 22 September 2023).
132. Shultz, M. M., (1990). Reproductive technology and intent-based parenthood: an opportunity for gender neutrality. *Wisconsin Law Review, 1990*(2), 297–398. https://www.scopus.com/inward/record.uri?eid=2-s2.0–0025577630&partnerID=40&md5=9c15e096e03b69dcf641744fdfc37880 (accessed on 22 September 2023).
133. Singleton Jr, R., (1989). Paradigms of science/society interaction: The

abortion controversy. *Perspectives in Biology and Medicine*, *32*(2), 174–193. https://doi.org/10.1353/pbm.1989.0004 (accessed on 22 September 2023).

134. Skene, L., & Parker, M., (2002). The role of the church in developing the law. *Journal of Medical Ethics*, *28*(4), 215–218. https://doi.org/10.1136/jme.28.4.215 (accessed on 22 September 2023).
135. Somerville, M. A., (1989). Justice across the generations. *Social Science and Medicine*, *29*(3), 385–394. https://doi.org/10.1016/0277-9536(89)90287-6 (accessed on 22 September 2023).
136. Spurr, S. J., (1993). The shortage of transplantable organs: An analysis and a proposal. *Law and Policy*, *15*(4), 355–395. https://doi.org/10.1111/j.1467–9930.1993.tb00113.x (accessed on 22 September 2023).
137. Stacy, T., (1994). Reconciling reason and religion: On Dworkin and religious freedom. *The George Washington Law Review*, *63*(1), 1–75. https://www.scopus.com/inward/record.uri?eid=2-s2.0–0028535740&partnerID=40&md5=37de67fe4c71247b40279e49b869b459 (accessed on 22 September 2023).
138. Stauch, M., (2000). Causal authorship and the equality principle: A defense of the acts/omissions distinction in euthanasia. *Journal of Medical Ethics*, *26*(4), 237–241. https://doi.org/10.1136/jme.26.4.237 (accessed on 22 September 2023).
139. Stein, E., (1998). Choosing the sexual orientation of children. *Bioethics*, *12*(1), 1–24. https://doi.org/10.1111/1467–8519.00089 (accessed on 22 September 2023).
140. Steinbock, B., & McClamrock, R., (1994). When is birth unfair to the child? *Hastings Center Report*, *24*(6), 15–21. https://doi.org/10.2307/3563460 (accessed on 22 September 2023).
141. Strauss, D. A., (1992). Abortion, toleration, and moral uncertainty. *The Supreme Court Review*, 1–28. https://doi.org/10.1086/scr.1992.3109666 (accessed on 22 September 2023).
142. Stroud, S., (1996). Dworkin and Casey on abortion. *Philosophy and Public Affairs*, *25*(2), 140–170. https://doi.org/10.1111/j.1088–4963.1996.tb00037.x (accessed on 22 September 2023).
143. Sullivan, P. A., & Goldzwig, S. R., (1995). A relational approach to moral decision-making: The majority opinion in planned parenthood vs. Casey. *Quarterly Journal of Speech*, *81*(2), 167–190. https://doi.

org/10.1080/00335639509384107 (accessed on 22 September 2023).

144. Sulmasy, D. P., (1989). By whose authority? Emerging issues in medical ethics. *Theological Studies*, *50*, 95–119. https://doi.org/10.1177/004056398905000105 (accessed on 22 September 2023).

145. TÄNnsjÖ, T., (1992). Who are the beneficiaries? *Bioethics*, *6*(4), 288–296. https://doi.org/10.1111/j.1467–8519.1992.tb00207.x (accessed on 22 September 2023).

146. Thomson, J. J., (1999). Physician-assisted suicide: Two moral arguments. *Ethics*, *109*(3), 497–518. https://doi.org/10.1086/233919 (accessed on 22 September 2023).

147. Truog, R. D., Arnold, J. H., & Rockoff, M. A., (1991). Sedation before ventilator withdrawal: Medical and ethical considerations. *The Journal of Clinical Ethics*, *2*(2), 127–129. https://www.scopus.com/inward/record.uri?eid=2-s2.0–0026175249&partnerID=40&md5=1476e41a6d2dc7c1abfb6d46845add3c (accessed on 22 September 2023).

148. Turrina, S., Bortoletto, E., Giannini, G., & De Leo, D., (2021). Monozygotic twins: Identical or distinguishable for science and law? *Medicine, Science, and the Law*, *61*(1), 62–66. https://doi.org/10.1177/0025802420922335 (accessed on 22 September 2023).

149. van Delden, J. J. M., & Laurie, G., (2004). The unfeasibility of requests for euthanasia in advance directives. *Journal of Medical Ethics*, *30*(5), 447–452. https://doi.org/10.1136/jme.2002.002857 (accessed on 22 September 2023).

150. Van der Burg, W., & Brom, F., (2000). Legislation on ethical issues: Towards an interactive paradigm. *Ethical Theory and Moral Practice: An International Forum*, *3*(1), 57–75. https://doi.org/10.1023/A:1009987819400 (accessed on 22 September 2023).

151. Van Der Burg, W., (1997). Bioethics and law: A developmental perspective. *Bioethics*, *11*(2), 91–114. https://doi.org/10.1111/1467–8519.00048 (accessed on 22 September 2023).

152. van Schooten, H., (2014). Towards a new analytical framework for legal communication. *International Journal for the Semiotics of Law*, *27*(3), 425–461. https://doi.org/10.1007/s11196–014–9356-y (accessed on 22 September 2023).

153. Viljoen, F., (2012). International human rights law in Africa. *International Human Rights Law in Africa*, 1–720. https://doi.org/10.1093/acprof:oso/9780199218585.001.0001 (accessed on 22

September 2023).

154. Walters, J. W., (1991). Anencephalic infants as organ sources: Report from North America. *Bioethics*, *5*(4), 326–341. https://doi.org/10.1111/j.1467–8519.1991.tb00173.x (accessed on 22 September 2023).
155. Walters, M. D., (2012). Dicey on writing the law of the constitution. *Oxford Journal of Legal Studies*, *32*(1), 21–49. https://doi.org/10.1093/ojls/gqr031 (accessed on 22 September 2023).
156. Waymack, M. H., (1991). AIDS, ethics, and health insurance. *Business and Professional Ethics Journal*, *10*(3), 73–84. https://doi.org/10.5840/bpej199110317 (accessed on 22 September 2023).
157. Weithman, P. J., (1999). Of assisted suicide and "the philosophers' brief." *Ethics*, *109*(3), 548–578. https://doi.org/10.1086/233921 (accessed on 22 September 2023).
158. Whitaker, R. E. D., & Edwards, R. K., (1990). An ethical analysis of the US immigration policy of screening foreigners for the human immunodeficiency virus. *AIDS and Public Policy Journal*, *5*(4), 145–156. https://www.scopus.com/inward/record.uri?eid=2-s2.0–0025547537&partnerID=40&md5=0ff239331fe8b6e57a7cde0e6738906a (accessed on 22 September 2023).
159. White, R. F., (1990). The enforcement of moral obligations to potential fetuses: Johnson Controls vs. the United Auto Workers. *Business and Professional Ethics Journal*, *9*(3–4), 55–68. https://doi.org/10.5840/bpej199093/419 (accessed on 22 September 2023).
160. Wicclair, M. R., (1991a). Patient decision-making capacity and risk. *Bioethics*, *5*(2), 91–104. https://doi.org/10.1111/j.1467–8519.1991.tb00150.x (accessed on 22 September 2023).
161. Wicclair, M. R., (1991b). A response to brock and skene. *Bioethics*, *5*(2), 118–122. https://doi.org/10.1111/j.1467–8519.1991.tb00153.x (accessed on 22 September 2023).
162. Wildes, K. W., (1997). Healthy skepticism: The emperor has very few clothes. *Journal of Medicine and Philosophy*, *22*(4), 365–371. https://doi.org/10.1093/jmp/22.4.365 (accessed on 22 September 2023).
163. Wilson, J. Q., (1994). On abortion. *Commentary*, *97*(1), 21–29. https://www.scopus.com/inward/record.uri?eid=2-s2.0–0028327986&partnerID=40&md5=227cb52e816cbf530830ff2906613551 (accessed on 22 September 2023).

164. Woliver, L. R., (1990). Reproductive technologies and surrogacy: Policy concerns for women. *Politics and the Life Sciences: The Journal of the Association for Politics and the Life Sciences*, *8*(2), 185–193. https://doi.org/10.1017/s0730938400009722 (accessed on 22 September 2023).

165. Wyld, D. C., & Cappel, S. D., (1990). The big easy? Legal and managerial perspectives on AIDS and health care delivery in the 1990s. *AIDS and Public Policy Journal*, *5*(3), 99–106. https://www.scopus.com/inward/record.uri?eid=2-s2.0–0025687812&partnerID=40&md5=2abe80ff3779fab5cbfd211fe878ae5d (accessed on 22 September 2023).

166. Yamada, D. C., (2019). On anger, shock, fear, and trauma: Therapeutic jurisprudence as a response to dignity denials in public policy. *International Journal of Law and Psychiatry*, *63*, 35–44. https://doi.org/10.1016/j.ijlp.2018.06.009 (accessed on 22 September 2023).

167. Zohar, N. J., (1991). Prospects for "genetic therapy" – can a person benefit from being altered? Prenatal genetic intervention: A dubious duty? *Bioethics*, *5*(4), 275–288. https://doi.org/10.1111/j.1467–8519.1991.tb00168.x (accessed on 22 September 2023).

168. Zomerski, W., (2020). Stanisław Ehrlich's critique of legal dogmatics: Then and now. *Review of Central and East European Law*, *45*(2), 314–333. https://doi.org/10.1163/15730352-bja10005 (accessed on 22 September 2023).

INDEX

L

M

N

O

P

R